Harvesting the Chesapeake
Tools and Traditions

Revised and Expanded 2nd Edition

LARRY S. CHOWNING

Schiffer Publishing Ltd

4880 Lower Valley Road • Atglen, PA 19310

Designed by Molly Shields
Type set in Baskerville Old Face/Garamond

ISBN: 978-0-87033-634-8
Printed in The United States of America

Published by Schiffer Publishing, Ltd.
4880 Lower Valley Road
Atglen, PA 19310
Phone: (610) 593-1777; Fax: (610) 593-2002
E-mail: Info@schifferbooks.com

For our complete selection of fine books on this and related subjects, please visit our website at www.schifferbooks.com. You may also write for a free catalog.

This book may be purchased from the publisher. Please try your bookstore first.

We are always looking for people to write books on new and related subjects. If you have an idea for a book, please contact us at proposals@schifferbooks.com

Schiffer Publishing's titles are available at special discounts for bulk purchases for sales promotions or premiums. Special editions, including personalized covers, corporate imprints, and excerpts can be created in large quantities for special needs. For more information, contact the publisher.

CONTENTS

PREFACE

Throughout the 20th century, there were dramatic changes in the lifestyles of people living along the shores of Chesapeake Bay. Electricity, atomic energy, computers, internet, automobiles, televisions, and telephones all came into their own in that century and have changed the way people live. But what has fascinated me is that with all these changes, Chesapeake Bay watermen are still harvesting the water with many of the same types of gear that were being used in the 1600s, 1700s, and 1800s. Hand tongs, dredges, patent tongs, pound nets, gill nets, and haul seines were all used by watermen before the 20th century. In fact, the crab, peeler, and fish pots and hydraulic clam dredge are probably the only types of gear developed in the 20th century that have had a major impact on any of the fisheries.

There have, however, been many other changes for watermen. In the 1950s, most rural waterfront communities like Urbanna, Virginia, where I grew up, still had more folks around who depended on the water and land for their livelihood than those who did not. Back then, I spent many summer days down on the fish docks with my Chesapeake Bay retriever, Blitz, and my crab net catching jimmies (male hard crabs) off pilings. There were usually more workboats moored on the creek than recreational boats and there were many older watermen around the docks who would give me more advice than I wanted about the best time to catch a mess of soft crabs or the best bait to use to catch trout. Those were gentle, easygoing years that passed so quickly I hardly noticed.

Every Sunday after church, Mom and Dad would take my sister and me to Grandma and Granddaddy's farm at Harmony Village, Virginia, for dinner. Grandma would fix fried chicken using chickens she had raised on the farm, ham granddaddy had cured with salt and brown sugar, canned and fresh vegetables grown in their garden, and, during the oyster season, oysters Granddaddy had brought home during the week. My grandfather hand tonged for oysters in the winter and farmed the rest of the year—the same as his father had done and his father before him.

My maternal grandparents had eight children and, although my father was an only child, the Chownings had lived in or near Urbanna since the 1650s, so everywhere I turned there were young, middle-aged, and very old relatives—first, second and third cousins, aunts and uncles, and great- aunts and great-uncles. Down the street was a great-uncle, whom I saw daily, who would never let me forget the family stories that had been passed down to him. I heard them over and over again until I could tell them better than he could. His father had fought in the Civil War, so, in his mind, that war was something that had happened just yesterday and his stories mostly came from that era.

The men in my family had been captains of steamboats, worked aboard sail-driven log canoes, run lumber in sailing schooners, and worked in tomato factories, shucking houses, and striker houses. The highlight of family gatherings on Thanksgiving and Christmas was always the leisurely sit-around story-telling session.

Into the sixties and seventies, however, I watched the changes within my own family and along the waterfront. Many of my favorite people died. There were fewer and fewer wooden workboats around, and attitudes toward watermen and their boats were changing. Often the lifestyles of working watermen and those of the new urban, upwardly mobile, recreational summer folk clashed. Accepted as part of everyday life in the fifties, the ways of the water suddenly were fine as long as they were practiced somewhere else. Some summer residents didn't want an old workboat moored in front of their cottage or a peeler trap or pound net put off their shoreline. The traditional deadrise workboats, which just a few years before had been moored to the docks in town, had been replaced with high-powered pleasure boats. Empty fish boxes, once used as seats for watermen, were no longer scattered along these docks—replaced by deck chairs and beer coolers of weekenders trying to escape the pressure of city life.

Also, the traditional farmer/fisherman lifestyle was passing. My grandfather's generation was the last on the Chesapeake to be able to provide a livelihood for a family by working a pair of oyster tongs and a pair of horses on a few acres of land. Many of these changes have to do with the high cost of farming and the decline in the Bay's fisheries—you've got to work a lot of land to pay for a combine today, and the price of a sail on the old canoes was considerable less than the cost of the engines used in today's workboats.

By the early 1980s, the changes in my family and on the Bay were dramatic. Although watermen were still harvesting fish in pound nets and haul seines, and oysters with hand tongs and dredges from sail-driven skipjacks, there were fewer of them around and even fewer watermen were getting into the fisheries. By then, I was already thinking about recording some of the history and lore of the waterways, but I was becoming more and more aware that time was of the essence. Not only were the people around me, who had insight into the past, passing away, but the Bay's fisheries were changing even more rapidly than in the sixties and seventies. There were moratoriums, for example, on shad and rockfish, and there was a dramatic decline in the oyster fishery. Also, recreational fishermen had grown in numbers and clout, and they were targeting certain gear styles, such as purse nets, pound nets, and gill nets, as the main culprits in the decline of the finfish fisheries. It was a good bet then, and it still is, that several gear forms that were in use when this nation was first formed will be gone by the twenty-first century.

Even though I realized how important time was to this project, I had to move slowly because I had to make a living. Year after year, I chipped away at it. Sometimes I would be on assignment for the Southside Sentinel or National Fisherman and just happen upon someone I would eventually go back to see. Other people I had known all my life like my grandfather Raymond Blake and my great-aunt Oleathia Heath Carlton.

The people I've interviewed have made this project worthwhile for me. Years from now, when I think back on all this, I'm sure my fondest memories won't be only of the things written in the following pages. I'll also remember the oysterman Roosevelt Wingfield who broke down in tears as he spoke of his young son who had slipped overboard and drowned while culling oysters. I'll remember the loving expression on the wife's face as she said the best years of her life were when her children were small and underfoot. I'll remember catching a fair wind in a Chesapeake Bay log canoe with Damon my 12 year-old son at the helm.

Undertaking this work has been an opportunity of a lifetime, and I want to thank each person who allowed me to go out on his boat, fed me at mealtime, or gave me a place to lay my head at night. Many wonderful people can be found between the covers of this book.

I am grateful, too, to the editors of the several publications in which earlier versions of some of these chapters appeared; I appreciate the confidence in me that their support represents.

Also, I want to thank Diane Walker, of the Virginia Institute of Marine Science library, for her help with the research involved in this project and Mike Oesterling, retired commercial fisheries specialist at VIMS, for always steering me in the right direction whenever I had a question. A special thanks goes to Paula Johnson and others at the Calvert Marine Museum in Solomons, Maryland, for their help with the chapter on patent tongs and general information concerning Maryland's oyster fishery, and to the late John Frye and the Mariner's Museum in Newport News, for information provided on the patent dip trotline. I am grateful, too, to the scores of writers such as George Brown Goode, James Wharton, John Frye, and others, who took the time to record for posterity the ways of the water.

I want especially to thank Ray V. Rodgers III for the illustrations he has created for the book. Ray and I grew up together in Urbanna, and he knew from the start why I was doing this work. He has spent hours and hours on drawings without any other reward than a thank you.

Finally, I want to thank my wife, Dee, for her efforts on some of the drawings, but more importantly, of having the patience to allow this work to be completed. Although it has taken time away from our family, she has always understood the importance of the project to me.

CHAPTER ONE

HARVESTING STURGEON
AND SHEEPSHEAD

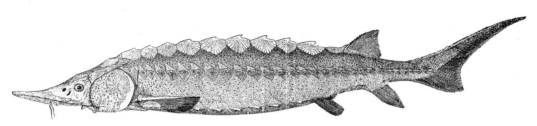

THE COMMON STURGEON.
Acipenser sturio L. (=A. oxyrhynchus). (p. 660.)
Drawing by H. L. Todd, from No. 22495, U. S. National Museum, collected in Potomac River by William Woltz.

The common sturgeon. (From George Brown Goode's The Fisheries and
Fishery Industries of the United States, *section 1, published in 1887)*

I first met Henion Brown in May 1981 at the Dragon Run Folk Lore Festival in Glenns, Virginia. A crowd had gathered around Capt. Henion as the old experienced fisherman demonstrated the use of a pound net with a miniature version. Shortly after that, I saw Henion at his home in Guinea Neck, in Gloucester County—the first of many visits.

In 1987, after my interest in the once-flourishing sheepshead fishery had been piqued by a talk with another elderly fisherman, I was on my way to Gloucester and met Henion at the local clam house where he was getting a mess of clams. As we sat on the pier, and talked, his wonderful memory took us both back to the days before the turn of the century when sheepshead and sturgeon were harvested along the shores of the Bay. Capt. Henion, 99, died February 9, 1991, and is buried in Gloucester Point Cemetery in Gloucester County, Virginia. He lived long enough to read and enjoy this chapter on him in Harvesting, *first published in 1990.*

Years ago, sturgeon and sheepshead were found in abundance in the waters of the Chesapeake. For three centuries, these fish played a major role in the economy of the Bay's fisheries, but since both species declined so substantially before the turn of this century, there are only a few people around who can even recall that they were here, much less how they were harvested.

James Wharton, in his book *The Bounty of the Chesapeake—Fishing in Colonial Virginia,* wrote that, before tobacco became the money crop for Virginia colonists, there was an

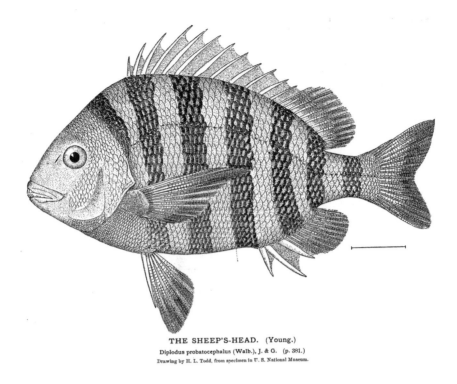

THE SHEEP'S-HEAD. (Young.)
Diplodus probatocephalus (Walb.), J. & G. (p. 381.)
Drawing by H. L. Todd, from specimen in U. S. National Museum.

The sheepshead. (From Goode's The Fisheries and Fishery
Industry of the United States, *second 1 published in 1887)*

attempt to export the meat and roe of sturgeon to England. The growing of tobacco on a commercial basis by John Rolfe in 1612, however, led the colonists to pursue this more profitable commodity.

Sturgeon and sheepshead were harvested commercially from the Bay until the early part of the twentieth century, and both were highly sought after for their tasty flavor. The roe of sturgeon was often transformed into caviar, a delicacy even to this day. In an 1880 U. S. fish report, Marshall McDonald estimated that 108,000 sturgeon were caught on the James River that year, 288,000 were harvested on the Potomac, and 17,700 on the Rappahannock River.

The York River and its tributaries were also excellent for sturgeon, reported McDonald, who wrote that the fish were harvested there in float seines (gill nets that floated with the tide) and were shipped to market by railroad through West Point, Sweet Hall, Lester Manor, Cohoke, and White House, all stations on the York River Railroad. Seafood was sent chiefly to Richmond, and some to Baltimore and Philadelphia, but sturgeon went to Richmond almost exclusively and were known there as Charles City bacon."

Although sturgeon were harvested in Maryland in the late 1800s, sheepshead were also highly sought after by Marylanders. In a fish report written during that period, entitled "Maryland: Saltwater Fisheries," R. Edward Earll recounts that a number of

Maryland fishermen were employed in the capture of sheepshead with hook and line, while others used seines.

Earll documented an unusual method of harvesting sheepshead employed then by fishermen in both Maryland and Virginia. As he described it, they used small trees or "hurdles," consisting of a dozen to twenty piles that were driven into the mud, and around which the sheepshead gathered in considerable numbers. Fishermen harvested the fish while they were around the hurdles. The sheepshead taken were very large, averaging fully seven to eight pounds each, while some weighing fourteen to fifteen pounds were seen in the Crisfield market. They found a ready sale at seven to twelve cents a pound; the fishermen often made good wages in the business. Several instances were reported where men made as much as eighteen to twenty dollars in a single day.

• • •

What Earll briefly alluded to is a method of harvesting sheepshead that was used extensively on the Bay until the decline of the fishery. In Virginia, the line of piles was called a "sheepshead bunch." To find anyone who might remember this, I had to look for someone in his late nineties or older, which led me to Henion Brown. Born in 1892, Henion would be the right age to have some recollection of this method of fishing.

Sure enough, he knew exactly what a sheepshead bunch was and had watched them being fished as a boy on the York River. "Now I'm glad you asked me that," he said. "I'll bet you a dollar gold piece there's not ten men alive on the whole Chesapeake Bay that's seen a sheepshead bunch being fished. Now I'll tell ya the way they were made. The old boys would go out into the woods in the winter and cut 100 to 125 pine saplings between ten and twelve feet long. They were about an inch to an inch and a half in diameter.

Then they would take them out in a good spot for sheepshead and put them down in sort of a circle with about twenty-five feet inside the ring. It was called a sheepshead bunch. You could tell when the fish were there because they would feed on the growth that grew on the poles and the poles would wiggle back and forth. They had a seine with large mesh because sheepshead have big heads and they would circle the bunch with the net and haul the fish on up.

I can remember sitting up beside my daddy at the helm of his sailboat coming in from fishing pound nets and seeing old Simon Green of Gloucester County working his bunch. I was just a little fellow. Now, there weren't many around fishing sheepsheads when I was a boy, but my daddy knew a lot about them. He told me one time that way back so many sheepshead were caught that some of the old people had dammed up a small creek and put the fish in it trying to keep them alive and fresh for market.

They did about the same thing with sturgeon. Now I've seen this. They would tie them to stakes in creeks, and I've seen creeks filled up with poles wiggling

*Henion Brown recalls harvesting sturgeon and sheepshead on the
Chesapeake at the turn of the twentieth century.*

and bending from the fish trying to get away. There was a fish camp on the York River where the fishermen would stay, and they would tie the sturgeon to stakes and then carry them to Gloucester Point to be shipped on a steamboat. I've been to Gloucester Point when I was a little boy and sturgeon would be laying up on the dock with a card tacked in the head of each fish.

Now I fished pound nets most all my life and I only caught one sturgeon worth talking about and one sheepshead. I caught the sturgeon in April of 1915 in a net three miles below Yorktown in twenty-four feet of water. I remember the year because I'd been married to my little wife for just one year to the month. The sturgeon was a big old cow and was about ten feet long. I don't remember what she weighed, but I shipped her to Richmond to Evans and Sharp Fish House, and I got a check and letter back from them that said she was a nice one. She had roe in her but the roe was overripe, and I didn't get anything for it.

Henion doesn't recall anyone producing caviar with the roe locally. Most of the roe was shipped elsewhere where caviar was considered a real delicacy. George Brown Goode wrote in an 1800s fish report that, as an article of food:

Sturgeon are generally popular, but few people in the cities knew the modes of cooking them that make their meat a palatable dish... With a good, hearty, outdoor appetite this is very palatable food, but too rich in the flavor of the oil of the fish for ordinary use. The flavor of the sturgeon meat has very little of the taste of fish, and the bouillon, when carefully prepared by skimming off the oil, is very much like chicken soup. A very good pickled meat is made of it by boiling it and preserving it in vinegar.

But the best form of preparing sturgeon is by smoking it. A method employed . . . is the following: Sturgeons are skinned and the viscera taken away. The thick meat is cut into strips, and after a slight pickling in brine it is smoked. The thin portions and offal are boiled down for oil, the spawn is made into caviar, and from the bladders isinglass is manufactured.

The caviar is made by pressing the ova through sieves, leaving the membranes of the ovaries remaining in the sieve and the eggs falling through into a tub. This is continued until the eggs are entirely free from particles of membrane, when they are put into salt pickle and allowed to remain for some time.

For making caviar, the best roe are those not entirely matured for spawning, but when they are "hard roes." The quantity of eggs varies with the size and condition of a female and may range between five and 15 gallons or from three to five pailfuls in bulk, and from about 800,000 to 2,400,000 in numbers (eggs). The color of the fully ripe eggs is generally almost black, but varies from "light roe" to "dark roe." Care is taken by the fishermen not to mix the two colors, as a "salt and pepper" appearance is not considered desirable by dealers.

Henion recalls his father talking about sturgeon.

They were plentiful when Daddy was young. He told me a man came down from up north and was paying eight to ten dollars for a peck bucket of eggs. They didn't go by the pound back then. Those big old sturgeon were something to get out of a pound net. I remember him catching some big ones. My brother and I would go with him on Saturdays when school was out. He caught some big ones.

"Daddy was a great fisherman. He died in 1905 when I was thirteen years old. He's been laying up there in that cemetery for eighty-four years," Henion said with a sigh. "He was a little man but he had a big heart."

The sheepshead and the sturgeon are all gone now, and I'll tell you something, there aren't many fish at all compared to when I was young. You want to know why? All you've got to do is read Joshua, the fourth chapter in the Bible. It says for lying, stealing, and fighting, the fish will be taken from the sea. You check it and see if I'm not right. There's a terrible scarcity of fish now and if people don't change their ways, it's going to get a lot worse.

Atlantic sturgeon were commercially harvested on Chesapeake Bay from the 1600s until 1998 when the Atlantic States Marine Fisheries Commission instituted a coast-wide moratorium on the harvesting of sturgeon. In 2009, National Oceanic and Atmospheric Administration Fisheries Service made the decision to list Chesapeake Bay Atlantic sturgeon as endangered and today the ancient fish is protected under the Federal Endangered Species Act. Sheepshead are making a comeback and can be harvested commercially and recreationally on Chesapeake Bay in accordance with Virginia and Maryland size and catch quota regulations.

CHAPTER TWO

HAUL SEINING

It was September 1988 when I happened upon Willis Wilson. My editor at the Southside Sentinel *had sent me to cover a meeting of the Deltaville (Virginia) Improvement Association, featuring a group of "pioneer watermen." Willis was one of several speakers at the affair, where he literally stole the show with his humorous and vivid recollections of his younger days as a fisherman working a haul seine.*

After hearing him reminisce, I made several trips to his boat yard on Broad Creek in Deltaville, where, on each occasion, he would stop whatever he was doing to share with me some of his colorful experiences of the days when there were enough fish to support a viable haul seine fishery on the Chesapeake Bay.

Many Chesapeake Bay watermen remember when the croakers and spot in the rivers of Virginia and Maryland were so abundant that one old-timer described those days by saying, "Let me tell ya there, young fellow, those fish were here so thick you could near 'bout walk across the Bay on the backs of hardheads."

Perhaps the fish weren't quite that thick, but small fortunes were made during the post-World War II era by fishermen using haul seines. Stories abound from those times as retired haul seiners recall making enough in one night to buy a brand-new Cadillac and enough in a week to build a new two-story home. Although some may think these stories are exaggerated, to this day, the fine homes of many of those fishermen stand as proof that there was good money made during those days.

• • •

Willis Wilson fished during the heyday of the croakers and spot, but he also has fond memories of the water and haul seining long before the "money years." Willis was born and reared near Kilmarnock, Virginia, on the Northern Neck. His earliest recollections start around 1927, when he was but a boy of six. It was then that, on Saturdays, his father began taking Willis with him on his boat, the *Paul Jones.*

Daddy would haul fish scales for a plant in Reedville. They bought herring scales from striker houses (where salt herring was processed and the roe packaged) and pound net fishermen. They used some kind of process where they would use ammonia to get the glitter off the scales and then after that

Willis Wilson started working a haul seine as a boy in the 1920s and continued until fishing became so bad he had to quit in 1957.

they were shipped somewhere to be used to make fake pearls for cuff links and tie clasps.

The *Paul Jones* was a thirty-six-foot round-stern bateau with a twelve-horsepower Bridgeport engine. During the herring run [from the first of April to the middle of May], Daddy would take his boat around and pick up scales in baskets that were woven from willow branches and haul them back to Reedville. He was probably getting ten to twenty-five cents a basket for making the run. At first, he was buying all his scales from striker houses where they processed herring. Later, though, he started buying from pound net boys who rigged up a real fine mesh net that was placed under the main net. This way when the scales would fall off the herring that were trapped in the pound, the bottom net would catch 'em.

On his run, Daddy would go to Gwynn Island and pick up scales from Newton Foster, who had a striker house there, and from some of the pound netters. Then, he would go to Little Bay, Dymer Creek, Indian Creek, and Ditchley [all on the Northern Neck]. All of these places had striker houses back then. That was one of the first things I remember about being on the water.

The next thing was the haul seine nets that everybody had around home on Dymer Creek. They were little nets about a hundred yards long. They would tie one end to the shore and run the other end out from the stern of a skiff. Most everyone had one, you know, to catch fish to feed themselves.

That was in the twenties, but later Daddy got into it in a bigger way. He rented a 250-fathom cotton net from two men who lived on Locklies Creek on the south side of the Rappahannock River. With that net, we'd go out and catch five hundred to a thousand pounds of fish a night in two sets. We were getting a big price—two, three cents a pound. The rent for using another man's net back then was one-fifth of the catch. Then the rest was split up so the boat would get a third, the captain got a third, and the crew got a third.

For our main boat, Daddy had a thirty-foot log canoe with a five-horsepower, two-cycle, Victor engine. He also had a twenty-two-foot seine skiff that we used to pay out the net and a real small skiff that we would use to go back and forth to the big boat from shore.

In those days, we always fished with the tide and there were five of us in a crew. Three would get out on shore and tie a line, which was attached to one end of the net, to a tree stump. Most of the time after that, the boys on shore would lie down in the sand and take a quick snooze, while Daddy would take the big boat out with the twenty-two-foot skiff tied to its stern. The seine skiff was full of net and a man was in it keeping the seine straight as it went over the stern.

Daddy would pretty much take the boat straight out from shore and when he had the right amount of net out, he would signal to us by waving a lantern. We had a lantern, too, and we'd wave it back and forth to let him know we were ready. Then, we boys on land would untie the line from the stump, loop it around our waists and start pulling the net down the beach as Daddy began to sweep the end off from shore in the same direction that we were walking on the beach.

When Daddy finished the sweep and was inshore as close as he could get, we would go out in the little skiff to fetch the end of the rope. This rope was tied to the net in the seine skiff. Then, we would pull on the line and haul some of the

A typical way that fishermen along the East Coast and on Chesapeake Bay set a haul seine in the eighteenth and nineteenth centuries. (From sketch by Capt. B. F. Conklin in Goode's The History of the American Menhaden)

net up on shore. Sometimes, we'd have to jump overboard to get it to the beach. Back then, we didn't have any of those waist-high waders to keep us dry, I'll tell ya that. All we had were those little boots about up to our ankles with holes cut in the toes and heels so the water could run out on the ground. Believe me, there were times in the early spring when my feet were some kinda cold!

Once we got Daddy's end of the net tied to a stump on shore, we went back down to the other end, untied the line and started pulling the net by the cork line and bottom line up on the beach. Ya see, as we pulled, the fish that were trapped between the shore and net would swim farther down towards a pocket that was near Daddy's end of the net. When all the net, except the pocket, was hauled, we had a small hand dip net and we'd dip the fish up into a sixteen-foot skiff. We fished like this for three or four years until the net rotted out and then Daddy went big time.

Willis haul seined from about 1929 until the business went into a major slump in the late 1950s. Over those years, he saw many changes, but his early method of hauling a seine, described above, was not much different from generations of haul seiners that had come before him. The haul seine was used in colonial days up and down the East Coast to harvest fish.

The use of the haul seine on the Chesapeake was enhanced greatly in the late eighteenth century when Virginia-cured herring became a preferred dish for many plantation owners and the formerly esteemed sturgeon was not as accepted as it had once been.

Perhaps the most notable haul seiner was the first president of the United States, George Washington. Washington owned and operated several nets along the shores of Mount Vernon, his plantation on the Potomac River. During those days, the sale of herring and shad added a financial boost to the pocketbooks of many plantation owners. The fish also provided a means for them to feed their slaves. Throughout the year, salt

Fish were harvested by pulling the seine to shore as fishermen hauled the catch up on the beach in baskets. (From sketch by Capt. B. F. Conklin in Goode's The History of the American Menhaden)

fish was a staple food for many slaves living on shoreline plantations. Washington, like many plantation owners, had a fish house at Mount Vernon where herring and shad were gutted, salted down, and then sold to domestic buyers in the colonies and also shipped on consignment to the West Indies, principally Jamaica.

Washington's diary entries of 1760 tell us something of haul seine fishing during that time:

> April 4 ... Apprehending the Herring were come, Hauled the Sein, but catches only a few of them, tho a good many of other sorts.
>
> April 5... Hauled the Sein again, catchd 2 or 3 White Fish (Shad), more Herring then Yesterday, and a great Number of Cats.
>
> April 10... I therefore employed the hands in making two or three hauls of the Sein, and found that the Herrings were come.
>
> April 11... Abt. 11 o'clock set the people to Hauling the Sein and by Night and in the Night catched and dressed—Barrels of Herring and 60 White Fish.
>
> April 12... Haul'd the Sein but without Success; some said it was owing to the wind setting on the Shore, which seems in some Measure confirmed by the quantity we catchd yesterday when the wind blew upon it.
>
> April 13... My Negroes asked the lent of the Sein today, but caught little or no Fish. Note the Wind blew upon the Shore today.

Throughout his life, Washington was involved in fishing enterprises at Mount Vernon. In 1770, he recorded an interesting business contract involving his herring catch:

> Agreed with Mr. Robt. Adam for the Fish catches at the Fish Landing I bought of Posey, on the following terms to wit:
>
> He is obliged to take all I catch at the place, provided the quantity does not exceed 500 Barls; and will take more than this qty. if he can get cask to put them in. He is to take them as fast as they are catchd, without giving any interruption to my people; and is to have the use of the Fish House for his Salt, fish &ca., taking care to have the House clear at least before the next Fishing Season.
>
> In consideration of which he is to pay me Ten pounds for the use of the House; give 3/ a thousd. for the Herrings (Virg. Money) and 8/4 a hundred (Maryland curry) for the white fish. *(Washington's Diary)*

Before the American Revolution, Washington ordered haul seine supplies from Robert Cary and Co., of London, England. In 1771, he ordered one seine, seventy-five fathoms long when rigged for hauling; to be ten feet deep in the middle and eight at the ends with meshes fit for the herring fishery. The corks were to be spaced at every two and a half feet and the leads five feet apart. It was to be made of the best three-strand (small) twine and tanned.

Fishing rights along the shoreline of Virginia were often for sale or rent in colonial times. William Byrd, who was advertising the sale of some lots near Richmond to be distributed by a lottery in 1767, stated that one fishing beach on the south shore of the James River was valued at £600 and rented for £30 a year while another fish landing was valued at £2000 and rented for £100 a year.

There were also public fishing grounds, some of which were established in 1770, when a group of private haul seine fishermen tried to patent land near Cape Henry at the mouth of the Chesapeake for their own fishing use. This met with such opposition from the people of Princess Anne that the petitioners were denied and the land was officially set aside for public use.

Haul seines and their uses in Maryland and Virginia were mentioned in fish reports and personal diaries of fishermen over the next 150 years, but the real transformation of the fishery came in the twentieth century with the introduction of the combustion engine, better refrigeration, and the purse pocket, which was a rig similar to today's pockets in purse nets used in the menhaden fishery.

Willis Wilson saw these changes come and many others that would affect his life:

> When I was eight years old, my Mama died. She got sick but nobody knew exactly what she got. Not long after Mama went, Daddy's brother passed away. His widow had one child and Daddy was a widower with three children, so they got married and moved us all across the Rappahannock River near Broad Creek. My Daddy had been born and raised in a one-room log cabin there. He had moved to the Northern Neck when he married Mama and started out working as a dry boatman [striker—see Chapter 7] for a menhaden company. About the time Daddy remarried, motors and haul seine nets began to get bigger and this changed fishing forever. We didn't catch many fish when we first started because we didn't have the rig. The only man I knew that caught a lot of fish way back was Lee Simmons on Carters Creek, and he had such a big net that it took ten or twelve black men to haul it ashore. It was in the late 1930s that Daddy rigged up big and we started making big bucks—for then. We were catching a hundred to two hundred boxes (a hundred pounds to a box) of fish a night. We were big chips then.
>
> We had three main places to sell our fish. Elwood Callis at Callis Wharf on Gwynn Island, Raymond Morgan on Carters Creek, and W. F. Morgan & Son on Little Bay were all big fish buyers.

When the fish were running, Willis's life centered around the catch and the weather. Elizabeth, his wife of fifty years, recalls that they were to be married in 1938 during the peak of the fishing season. "It was October 1938 and we were ready to get married, but I couldn't get him to tell me the exact day of the wedding because he was fishing night and day," she said. "So, on October 28, I checked the weather and it was a blowing a northeaster. So, I figured it would drive him in. Sure enough, the wind drove him home and we were married that day by Reverend Duncan. It's a good bet we wouldn't have been married then if that storm hadn't come up."

In 1948, Willis and two partners, Lennie Callis and Charles Montgomery, built a fifty-foot deck (buy) boat for haul seining and crab dredging that was named the *Dolphin*. By that time, haul seining was big business. "We'd leave home on Sunday at midnight and wouldn't come home before Saturday. We always fished at night with the tide and would sleep during the day. Some of those hot days the flies would get to me, but we would try to sleep anyway. I've still got fish scales in my arms left from the 1940s." Holding up both arms, Willis pointed out images of scales that had become embedded in his skin. "I reckon if I had washed at the time they would have come right off, but now they'd have to cut a lot of skin away to get that out of me," he said.

There were two things we hated to see in a haul seine net and that was stinging nettles and those (cownose) stingrays. Once the stinging nettles came in the late spring and early summer that meant the end of fishing until the fall. So, we hated to see them coming. Also, sometimes we'd catch a boatload of stingrays and have to turn the whole business loose. Now how that worked was, if we caught just a few rays, one man would reach down into the pocket, hook his finger in the ray's nose and yank him out. If there were a dozen of so, I had a pole with a hook that we'd use to reach down and hook them by their noses. For years, we pulled them out by hand, but the time Albert Games got stung by one got us all to being more careful. When Albert got stung, he and Hervey Norton were fishing off Jackson Creek not far from Stingray Point where Captain John Smith first got tangled up with a stingray. [This point of land near Deltaville was named for an incident in which Smith, on a early expedition up the Bay, used a sword to spear a ray. The ray stung him and he nearly died. After that, the point of land near where this happened was forever called Stingray Point.]

When we got to the 1940s and 1950s, we were all big time. We used bigger boats and bigger motors. We had a 6-71 Detroit Diesel engine in the big boat and that was a far cry from the little Victor Daddy had in that log canoe. We weren't having to tie lines to tree stumps anymore either. Ya see, the nets changed. Around 1938, Earl Hudgins of Mathews County [Virginia] invented the purse pocket so the fish couldn't escape. It's a lot like the purse net that is used in menhaden fishing today. What this meant was that we no longer had to bail fish in close to shore. With this new net, we were able to set a net in three foot of water—up close to shore—make our set, close the pocket, and then take the net and pocket full of fish into deeper water where we would empty it at sunrise, all without getting on the shore.

When we were fishing in the twenties and thirties, we couldn't work just any shoreline because we had to haul the net by hand to the beach. So, it had to be a long beach without a bunch of trees and things that would keep us from being able to work the net up to the shore. The new net gave us a wider range to work in. We could also lose a lot of fish back then with the old nets because when we'd make a big, big catch, many of the fish would smother in the shallow water before we could get them out of the pocket. This new net changed things a lot.

The technique, however, of setting and harvesting the modern haul seine, was similar to the way the old style nets were worked. Willis continued:

When we used the big bateau with the 6-71. A line tied to one end of the net was hooked to the mast of the bateau. I ran the bateau and would pull the net and tow a thirty-foot dory (seine) skiff that was full of net. By then, we were using nets five hundred fathoms long by twelve feet deep, but some of the boys were using even longer ones. It was against the law to go over five hundred, but we seldom saw any marine police so whatever we wanted to do, we did.

We would fish by the moon. Ya see, we would fish on flood tide or when the tide was rising so we watched the moon. That would tell us what time to start. The first of the month, say, if we started at sundown, then flood tide would start three-quarters of an hour later every night during the moon's cycle. After it had gone through the cycle, then we'd go back and start over. Ya know, the moon controls the tide.

We would anchor one end of the net with a hundred-pound anchor in about three feet of water while the other end was being towed in the dory skiff. I would tow that skiff, while a man standing on the stern would pay out the net. We always fished with a tide, so I would make a sweep down the shoreline going with the tide, just like we did years back when we used the old nets. In later years, we also used what we called a back net. It was separate from the haul seine and was just a straight line of net starting from the anchored end running down the shoreline in front of the pocket. It was about fifty fathoms long and it was to help guide the fish into the pocket. This, too, was first used by Earl Hudgins.

We also had a twenty-seven-foot boat that had a five-horsepower donkey engine in the stern. It used to be that we would stand in the water and haul it all ashore by hand, but with the donkey boat, as we called it, the engine would web the net in the boat as it moved closer to the pocket. The donkey engine was water-cooled so we had to pour water in her every so often because when she'd get hot the water would all boil out of her.

There were two other skiffs, both about sixteen feet long. One stayed with the big boat and was used when we fished the net, while the other was a spare that we would anchor at a particular spot we thought would be a good place to fish. Ya see, fishermen had a code where if a haul seine skiff was anchored out from shore then that meant the spot was taken. Sometimes when we went home for a while, we would leave both skiffs to let everyone know that we were planning on coming back soon. Everybody did it, and we all understood what it meant so no one would ever taken another man's spot.

We even had some special names for places that had done good over the years and everybody knew them by those names. There was Ol' Maid and Streetcar Annie. Ol' Maid was named after a bunch of old maids from Richmond [Virginia] that had a cottage near a good fishing spot on the Rappahannock, and Streetcar Annie was named after a lady named Annie that moved a streetcar down here and lived in it. We would fish off from the streetcar. Then, there were good places that had always had a name. Stove Point, Boss's Bar, Sturgeon Bar, and Mosquito Point were all good places to haul seine. I spent two-thirds of my time at Sturgeon Bar near Sturgeon Creek on the Rappahannock and I caught a many a fish there.

Once we got the net set, I would get in one of the little skiffs because it was my job to put sticks in the net as the donkey boat hauled the net in. Now, these sticks were to keep the net spread so it could be easily hauled. One end of the stick would go in a becket on the cork-line, while the other end was put in a becket on the bottom line. I would paddle out in front of the donkey boat and every fifty fathoms or so put in a stick. The donkey boat took up all but the last hundred fathoms of the net before getting to the pocket and then we would all have to get in the water and haul the last bit into the boat. We had waders by this time and it was much better than those little boots with holes cut in the heels and toes.

Once all the net was up, then the pocket was closed and we'd haul everything out into deep water so the fish wouldn't drown. By then, it was about 2:00 to 3:00 A.M. and we'd all go back to the big bateau and get some sleep before sunrise. Around 5 A.M., we'd get up and fish the net. If it was a small haul, we'd use the sixteen-foot skiff to get the fish out of the net. If it was bigger, we might use the dory skiff. We used a hand scoop net that would hold a bushel to get the fish out of the pocket.

A lot of money was made during those days. Ya know, for the time. One Halloween night, Guy Armistead of Mathews County caught enough bluefish at Wolf Trap Lighthouse to buy a brand-new Palmer engine. They cost about seven hundred dollars then and, let me tell ya, that was big money.

But even bigger bucks were made at times. Willis continued:

One night just above Windmill Point on the Bay side, we hit a mess of spot. In one set, we landed twenty-two thousand pounds. Spot were bringing twenty-two cents a pound so we grossed $4,840 in one night. I had more money than I knew what to do with. That was something, but I'll tell you something else, I never got into the croakers like some of those boys upriver. They made some money. I'll tell you that.

It wasn't always good though. The least I ever caught was a peck. I'd bring them home to eat. We never knew what we were going to do because we made blind sets. It wasn't like the menhaden boys who have airplanes to tell them where the fish are. It was all potluck with us. They were either there or they weren't, and when they were things were good, but when they weren't, it was a lot of work for nothing.

I quit in 1957. Some of the boys kept going into the sixties, but it just went on down until it wasn't worth going out there. I don't know what happened to all the fish. Maybe we caught them all up.

The decline of the fish population, particularly croakers on the Bay, and more cost-effective forms of gear hastened the decline of the haul seine fishery, so that today there are very few haul seines being fished on the Chesapeake.

At the age of 91, Willis Wilson died June 12, 2006. Elizabeth ask me to speak at his funeral that was held at Philippi Christian Church in Deltaville. I graciously agreed and told their story of how she got him to the altar. Unlike most funerals, there were few tears or regrets, mostly laughter and joy celebrating the life of a fisherman and wonderful man—the way Willis would have wanted it. Today, there are still a few haul seines being worked on the Chesapeake.

CHAPTER THREE

HAUL SEINE TALES

The idea for this chapter on haul seine tales goes back to my childhood days in the 1950s growing up in Urbanna. Back then, families who lived in the biggest houses and drove the finest cars in town did not come from homes where the breadwinners were professional people or real estate agents, as so often is the case today. In those days, families with the best of everything were those whose fathers worked a haul seine.

In the late 1940s and early 1950s, Chesapeake Bay watermen made more money working haul seines than in any other fishery, before or since. I love to tell the story of the fisherman who attended my church, Urbanna Baptist Church, when I was a child. He would drive his family to Sunday school each week in a shiny 1948 two-tone Cadillac. Legend had it, he paid for it with the earnings from one set of croakers caught off Hoghouse Bar on the Rappahannock River. In 1972, when I arrived home from four years of college at the University of Richmond, that waterman was driving to church that same, not-so-shiny, Cadillac.

The boom years of fishing with haul seines on the Bay were extremely lucrative for many fishermen and their families. Many of these fishermen had lived through the Great Depression with little hope of ever having much of anything. For those who hit the big catches, there was more money than many of them knew what to do with. It was one of those things that comes perhaps only once in a lifetime and is never forgotten. Many stories are left from those years and here are just a few.

In the spring of 1929, Willis Cannon was fishing with Captain Wilber Evans on Morattico Bar on the Rappahannock River, near the mouth of Farnham Creek on Virginia's Northern Neck. There they hit on a "solid" boatload of spot. Willis recalls that the night started with great delight but in the end there was great disappointment.

We'd been working all over the Bay, Pocomoke Sound, Silver Beach, and around, but Captain decided we'd best go back close to home because we weren't doing much. On one of the first nights back on the Rappahannock, we hit a solid mess of spot. It was an early spring run, so the price was right much high. Spot were bringing twelve cents a pound. Before the night was over, we had landed twenty-two tons and there was great excitement as we headed to Urbanna to sell our catch to J.W. Hurley & Son Seafood. We figured we had over five thousand dollars worth of fish and that was big, big money in those days. But when we got to the dock, Boyd Hurley told us fish prices had gone down two cents and spot were now bringing ten cents a pound.

Well, this didn't set well with Captain Evans and he told Boyd, "Thanks but no thanks, we'll ship our fish to Norfolk where we'll get our big price." You got to figure two cents was $880. It would cost us about a cent a pound to ice 'em down and ship them down to Norfolk on a buy boat so we would make $440 more and that wasn't nothing to sneeze at.

Things didn't work out that way though. We got the fish all ready and shipped them down to Norfolk, but when they got there the price had dropped to two cents. By then, everybody was catching fish and the bottom had dropped out of the market. That five thousand dollars shrunk to $440 mighty quick—plus it cost us $220 to ship them down there. I believe that was one day you could have seen five grown men crying if you had walked up on us. There was a season's work and we gave it away. That's fishing for ya!

One of the largest hauls ever made on the Chesapeake Bay came in 1952, when Captain Albert Games and his crew landed two thousand boxes (200,000 pounds) of croakers in one haul. Although everyone who worked that haul has since passed away, Tim Haley of Hartfield, Virginia, recalls the event because his grandfather Hervey Norton was a member of the crew.

I remember it well because, right after my grandfather collected his share, he and my grandmother went out and bought a brand-new 1952 blue DeSoto that cost $1,850. It all came from that one haul.

It was on Boss's Bar near Stingray Point that they made the set. They were in Captain Games's boat, the *Peggy G.*, which would only carry two hundred boxes. So, they had to load the dory boat and then get several buy boats from Deltaville to come out and help carry the load to Gwynn Island. Just figuring what my grandfather got for his share (two thousand dollars), they must have gotten about six cents a pound for them, which was a good price. Normally, croakers brought four to six cents a pound at the dock.

It was a twelve-thousand-dollar haul, which was a pile of money in those days. They were the days when the average man was making two to three thousand dollars a year. An unskilled worker would bring him forty dollars a week. So, when my grandfather made two thousand dollars in one night, he had made some bucks. He got the money one day and went out and bought that brand-new blue Desoto the next.

She had four doors and a three-speed automatic shift. My grandmother was so proud of that car. She kept it until the late 1960s when Chrysler came out with the push-button shift.

That was one of the last years that any big money was made on the river with a haul seine because right after that the croakers left the Bay. Croakers and spot

Tim Haley

were the best money fish back then. They would even bring more money than trout because they stayed firm longer. None of the boats had any refrigeration and croakers could stand the heat much better than trout.

My grandfather had to quit about 1958 when it just got so there weren't any fish. He went to work on a buy boat, crab dredging in the winter and hauling crabs to Crisfield, Maryland, in the summer.

I'll tell ya this though, he never made the money again that he made when he was haul seining. That was a once-in-a-lifetime thing, that probably won't ever happen on the Bay again.

My grandfather died in 1974 at the age of seventy-seven.

Frank Jessie, of Jamaica, Virginia, was a teenager in the 1950s when haul seining was big, but he'll never forget the late nights when school was not in session that he spent working a haul. The names of the people involved in his story have been left out to protect the families.

Well, it happened like this. We'd been fishing over on one of the bars across the river when we got into a good mess of croakers. I guess we landed three hundred

Frank Jessie

boxes (thirty thousand pounds). Now, we had caught more fish than that from time to time, but something happened with this catch that I'll always remember.

Captain knew the price was still high on croakers, but he also knew that the price might drop at the dock if he brought in three hundred boxes. He'd asked the price before we left to fish, but he knew that didn't always mean nothing. The price would sometimes, all of a sudden like, just drop when a big load came in. So, we boxed up about forty boxes of those fish and put them in the seine skiff and took them ashore. Captain figured the price wouldn't drop on those forty boxes.

Sure enough, the price was still up when we unloaded the small load. "Oh boss, I got me a few more boxes of fish out on the big boat that I could not get in the skiff. I'll bring them to ya in my big boat," said Captain to the buyer.

You should have seen their faces when we pulled up with 260 more boxes.

Well, they didn't pay us the day we caught the fish. Pay day was always on a Friday. When Friday came along, Captain went to get the check for the week so he could pay off the men. Well, they shorted us, saying the price had dropped right before we brought that big load in.

Lordy, Captain was mad! He said, "Take me home!"

Captain went home and got his rifle, loaded her, and we all went back down to the dock. He broke in the main office with his gun aimed. You should have seen them scrambling around that place.

"I'll tell you one thing, he had the right amount of money in his hand when he left there."

Dorothy and Woodrow Abbott recall with great fondness the years when haul seining was big business and there were plenty of fish to be caught. Dorothy, Woodrow's wife of fifty-seven years, remembers best a catch in 1946 when Woodrow, who was called by some the "Croaker King of Chesapeake," got into a mess of croaker. She said:

I'll tell ya the catch I remember best. Woodrow caught 666 boxes of croakers one night and I'll never forget that.

Ya see, times had been tight and Woodrow hadn't been catching many fish at all. So, one day, just joking, I said, "Woodrow, you catch over five hundred boxes tonight—I want me a brand-new electric refrigerator."

All I had ever had was an icebox that we would put block ice in. An electric icebox was uptown back then.

Before Woodrow started fishing, he worked at a sawmill for eight and a half cents an hour, eighty-five cents a day. So, I guess I was lucky to have an icebox.

He promised me, with a grin on his face, when he left the house, that if he caught five hundred boxes or more, I would get my new refrigerator.

Sure enough, I got it. I'll never forget that.

Dorothy Abbott

The largest single catch that Woodrow Abbott was ever involved in was a fifteen-hundred-box (150,000-pound) landing of croaker near Nomini Creek on the Potomac River, but he also recalls a back-to-back thousand-box catch near Corbin Hall on the Rappahannock. He graciously agreed to share these stories.

This was in 1946, when fishing dropped off on the Rappahannock and several of us decided we would try our luck on the Potomac. The first night there we made a set near Stratford Hall and landed three hundred boxes. This would have been all right, but those Potomac fishermen didn't want us Rappahannock boys on the Potomac and the commonwealth's attorney from Westmoreland County came down with the sheriff and claimed we had caught the fish wrong—ya know, according to the law. I hated to do it but they made us turn the whole bunch loose.

We decided after that we would go home. On the way, we ran into a haul seiner who had landed a solid load of fish. There were so many croakers in the net that mud was boiling up from the bottom just like when a tugboat is too close into shore.

Woodrow Abbott

I was a great one for guessing the amount of fish in a net. So when the boys aboard asked me how many there were, I guessed a thousand boxes. I was wrong, but I was right about one thing. That man wasn't going to get all those fish unloaded without some help. He was an old man with just two boys helping him. I offered to help and told him that he'd end up smothering half of them if he didn't let us help, but he didn't want any.

We went into Nomini Creek to spend the night and were planning on leaving for the Rappahannock the next morning. The next day, when we were coming out there were dead croakers everywhere. "Lord man, what have you done? You've smothered those fish," I said.

He had driven a bunch of them into the bunt and didn't have the manpower to get them out in time. I know there were five hundred boxes (fifty thousand pounds) of croakers floating down that creek.

Well, he wanted some help then and we took our rig with seven men and got what was left out of her.

This is hard to believe, but there were still fifteen hundred boxes of croakers in that net.

He paid us five thousand dollars for helping him. I didn't catch many fish on the Potomac, but we made some money anyway and that was one Potomac River fisherman who was glad to see us around.

Woodrow Abbott resumes his recollections:

Toward the end of the good fishing years, I had two good hauls back to back. It was 1956, two years before I quit, when we landed two thousand boxes of croakers in two hauls off Corbin Hall Farm. The price had dropped to three cents a pound and we all knew it. After making the first set, we started talking amongst us and we all decided we weren't going to sell for three dollars a box. So, we stacked the net and held the fish for nine days. We had somebody stay with them all the time. There were so many croakers in that net that they sounded like thunder from the sky when they were all croaking.

On the ninth day, we heard the price had jumped to six cents and we had fifty tons ready for market. That was one of the few times it ever paid off to hold fish. But what was even more unbelievable is that we went right back out the next night and caught another thousand boxes with the price still at six cents a pound.

Lord, boy, I've caught some fish. That was some pretty stuff back then—a net full of hardheads.

It was no easy job handling all those fish. We worked seven to a crew. Usually, it was six men and a boy. The boy pulled out gill fish (fish that have gilled in the mesh of the haul seine). We paid the boy as high as thirteen hundred dollars a week just to pick out the gill fish. That was a job, too. I bet there were fifteen boxes of them on that night we caught a thousand boxes.

It was money in it. I've been to Hampton to pick up our money for a week and brought home as high as twenty-two thousand dollars. If we had gotten anything for the fish, like they do now, it would have taken a truck to haul the money home.

That night we caught a thousand boxes, I told my brother, just by looking, that there were a thousand boxes in her. I was good at that and it wa'n't easy either. I remember old Mr. Shackelford guessing what was in his net. One night, he said there were a thousand boxes in a net and all there was was thirty-eight. It wa'n't always easy to tell.

I've done it all on the water—fished, crabbed, and oystered, but I never made the money like I did in the haul seine years.

The only thing that bothers me about it all now is I bet we caught them all up, because there aren't any fish compared to those days.

Sherman Holmes was a youngster when he first started working a haul seine. He recalls this particular story with great fondness.

Sherman Holmes

This happened during the depression years. I'd say around 1928, when I was fourteen or fifteen years old. Me and several other boys would go haul seine fishing with Jimmy and Leroy Key on the Piankatank River. Jimmy was cap'n [captain] and Leroy was mate and they had an old cotton net which we would fish in the spring and fall.

We'd go real far up in brackish water near Freeport [on the Piankatank] and fish for carp. Also, sometimes in the spring we'd get into a mess of bluefish, but they didn't do us younger boys much good because Cap', and Leroy always got the best fish. Ya see, we were paid off with fish. At the end of the catch, all the fish were piled up on shore, in one big pile. Then, Cap'n and Leroy would sort the fish out according to shares. The biggest pile went to Cap'n, the second biggest to Leroy, and the rest were split up evenly among the crew. Naturally, our piles were always small and the best fish never came our way.

Cap'n was a hard man. He had worked the water all his life and had seen some tough times. I've seen the time when a net would break, he would jump right down in that cold water to keep one fish from getting away.

He was a hard-working, God-fearing man, but he did do something that I used to think was a little strange. He always had a little ritual before dividing up the fish. After the fish were sorted and placed in piles on the beach, he would call us all over to where they were. Then, he would stand in front of the biggest pile with his back turned, hands behind his back, and head bent down. Suddenly, he would say a little chant in a language none of us could understand. It may have been something left over from slave days, because it wasn't English. After the chant, he would ask in a very loud voice. "Whose pile is this?"

The mate would say "seine," which meant it was Captain's and then he would go to the next pile and do the same thing, "Whose pile is this?" Cap'n would ask again.

Leroy would say "mate," which meant it was his own pile. They would do that right on down to the last pile of fish.

Then, Cap'n and Leroy would take their fish and ship them on a steamboat to a fish house in Baltimore, while us boys had to go around and sell ours door to door. It wasn't that hard to sell carp because most everybody liked them and what we didn't sell we'd salt down for our own use. The best eaten' carp was a two-pounder. The real big ones tasted coarse. Us boys never made much money because we got the least amount of fish and they always gave us the poorest ones, but two of us one night decided we were going to do something about that.

On this night, we had gotten into a good mess of carp and bluefish. When Cap'n and Leroy had divided up the fish and had gone over to the boat, we took four nice bluefish from Captain's pile and buried them underneath the fish in our own little piles, two in mine and two in my buddy's. They would never let us have a bluefish because they brought better money than carp. I'll never forget it. We would normally get about twenty-five cents for a dozen carp, but I was able to

John Morey

sell those two bluefish for twenty-five cents. That was good money.

Years later, I told Cap'n about what I had done and he laughed and laughed, but I wouldn't have told him when it happened because he would have knocked the devil out of me.

John Morey has fished the York River vfor over forty years and has seen some big schools of fish, but none as big as the one in the 1950s when a school of striped bass came stampeding upriver.

This was in the late fifties when my partner and I were oystering over on Purtan Bay near Allmonds Wharf on York River. We were catching' a few oysters when we saw the biggest school of rock (striped bass) coming down the river that I had ever seen.

We had a small haul seine in the bottom of the boat and we hauled it out and set it as quickly as we could. I carried my end to shore, got out of the boat, and we pursed her up. Lordy, was she loaded down with rockfish.

When we had finished harvesting the net, there wasn't a rock smaller then fifty pounds, and they all had pieces of net mesh hung to their heads and gills.

I didn't know it then, but I found out later Jake Green had set twenty-five stake (gill) nets the night before, and the fish were so big and strong that they went right through them. The only thing he had left were the lines.

We didn't get but a small corner of the school, but we ended up with 279 boxes (27,900) of rockfish. It was the worst time I ever had getting a box of a hundred [pounds] because we didn't have any small fish. We just didn't catch any in the fifteen-to thirty-pound range. A lot of boxes had only the one [hundred-pound] fish, but that was a small problem. We were excited about catchin' all those fish because we got fifteen cents a pound for them and that was right good money.

Once we had them all ashore in piles, old man Jessie Stublefield, who was in his late eighties then and had fished the river since the turn of the century, said he'd never seen so many rockfish in his life.

We were happy but I felt kinda sorry for Jake. Those rockfish set him back for the rest of the season. Lordy, I never seen so many rockfish!

Tim Haley owns and operates H & H Distributing Co. out of Saluda, Va. and runs a wooden deadrise in the area charter boat business. Frank Jessie, Dorothy and Woodrow Abbott, Sherman Holmes and John Morey are deceased.

CHAPTER FOUR

STAKE GILL NETS

There is no finer fare served in this world than at a Chesapeake Bay oyster roast, crab pickin', or shad planking, and it was at a shad planking in Deltaville, Virginia, that I first learned of Allie Walton. After indulging myself with some of the most tasty shad that I had ever eaten, I asked who had harvested the fish. I was given the name of Allie Walton and told that he had caught the shad in stake gill nets on York River.

The next day I was on the telephone to Allie, and, although he did not know me, he graciously agreed to show me how he works his nets. Several days later, we went out on the York River; this chapter is the result of his kindness in taking me along.

Each spring on Chesapeake Bay, American shad (*Alosa sapidissima*) ascend the coastal rivers and streams to spawn in fresh water. Before the English arrived on the scene

Gill nets were introduced on the Chesapeake around 1838 and one of the variations used was the stake gill net. (Courtesy of the Virginia Institute of Marine Science)

here, American Indians harvest shad in bush nets (made of vines), and later shad were harvested extensively by the colonists with haul seines.

The haul seine was the main form of gear used in the spring shad fishery until around 1838, when gill nets from the north were introduced on the Potomac River. Their use quickly spread to other rivers on the Bay and as the years passed, two styles of gill nets evolved for spring fishing. One is a drift (floating) gill net, which is fished as the tide is changing, and the other is a stake gill net.

Federal fish reports from the 1880s document well the shad fishery on the Bay to that point. On the Rappahannock River from Bowlers Wharf to Layton, stake nets were then the main form of gear used to harvest shad. Each staker fished from twenty-five to fifty nets, each nine yards long, with a stretched mesh of 4½ to 5 inches, the depth of the net varying with the depth of the water.

"Before obstructions existed in the Rappahannock, the shad ascended its main tributaries almost to the base of the Blue Ridge," the report said. "The obstructions of the streams by dams began in colonial times, and petitions for arresting the encroachment of mill owners and manufacturers upon the general right was filed in the House of Burgesses. As is usual, however, the march of progress triumphed, and the 'annually recurring bounty of Providence,' i.e., the fish, was entirely cut off them the upper waters of the rivers."

The obstruction of spawning grounds has been the plight of all the anadromous fish (those that live in the ocean but ascend the rivers once a year to spawn in fresh water). Before the dams, fish would travel to the headwaters almost as far as the streams would allow them to go. Archaeologists have collected Indian "net-sinkers" used to harvest shad and pottery that show unmistakable markings of the vertebrae of the shad on the Susquehanna River, near Wyoming, Pennsylvania, about fifty miles from the New York State line. There are also reports by early settlers that once shad were harvested in streams that feed the Susquehanna all the way up into New York State.

Shortly after the gill net was introduced on the Chesapeake, it very quickly became the main form of gear used in harvesting finfish. It took over as the haul seine began to see a decline. This widespread acceptance, however, was short lived—the pound net, introduced in the 1870s, soon became the most popular gear and remained so well into the twentieth century.

• • •

Allie Walton, of Mathews County, has fished the Chesapeake most of his life. For the past fifteen years, in late winter and early spring, he has driven the twenty-some miles to Poropotank River, a winding, marshy body of water that empties into the upper York River, to harvest shad with stake nets. Allie keeps his shad skiff, an eighteen-foot Privateer, and his classic wooden forty-two-foot deadrise workboat, named *Sputnik II*, a short distance from Poropotank public landing.

Allie Walton holds an American shad caught in his stake gill net on the York River.

Generally, Allie and his mate leave the dock in the *Privateer*, but on this morning he planned to take *Sputnik II* back around to the Piankatank River to get her ready for gill net fishing in the Bay, come warmer weather. During the summer months, he runs a thousand fathoms of anchored gill net up and down the Chesapeake.

A misty fog lay over the water as the chilling air touched the surface of the warmer water. "You take these cold nights," says Allie. "It don't help the fishing. We've had frost three nights in a row and it might slow things up somewhat. Now that I've said that, watch us catch a boatload today."

"Watch the step there, there's a skim of ice on the deck," he said as he and the mate made the *Sputnik II* ready. The Privateer would be pulled behind the big boat, because it would be used to fish the nets later.

John Morey, a fisherman friend of Allie's, passed by in his wooden seine skiff (see picture of John in Chapter 3). "Don't catch' em all John," yelled Allie. The fisherman, clad in oilskins, threw up his hand and quickly disappeared into the mist. The traditional wooden shad skiffs for working stake nets, like Morey's, are seldom seen these days, but are a curiosity to anyone who's a student of Chesapeake Bay fisheries. Most of these skiffs are outboard-powered and have a small house enclosed on three sides or, like Morey's, a wooden frame shelter with a windshield but no sides that keeps the water off the helmsman in choppy seas. Since nets are fished by the tide, a fisherman must go when the time is right, night or day, good weather or bad.

Another feature on the traditional shad skiff, which gives its use away, is a bow pin. Made of wood or sometimes pipe, the pin extends from the bow deck about a foot and is used to help guide and hold the boat as it is being fished. Since most shad nets are fished in protected waters, the skiffs are all that are needed for fishing.

"Now there's a man who can tell ya about shad," said Allie. "John has been out there for forty years.

"A shad is some fish," continued Allie. "They're a deepwater ocean fish but every three years the females come back to where they were born to spawn. They live in real deep water in the ocean. That's why they have so many bones because of the pressure of the deep ocean floor."

The large amount of bones has made many people consider shad unfit to eat. The English, for instance, were so unimpressed with the fish that for nearly one hundred years they rejected shad as a food fish. In the 1700s, however, the demand surfaced and literally thousands of barrels of shad were salted down for Baltimore and New York market.

The roe of shad, on the other hand, has been considered a real delicacy. Many times the market for roe has so outweighed the market for the fish that the roe was extracted and the shad thrown away or used for crab bait.

On this particular day, the market for roe shad was forty cents a pound. "It's not a very good price," says Allie. "Shad started out at a dollar a pound, dropped to eighty cents and then to sixty cents a pound all in one week. The next week it hit forty-five cents and now it's forty cents. I guess it will stay there since the run is just about over."

At the helm, Allie directed *Sputnik II* along the winding Poropotank. A great blue heron lifting off from the marshy shoreline through the mist, gave the impression of some prehistoric time long since past. "Plenty of good duck hunting around here," said Allie as the boat passed several duck blinds covered with marsh grass. A small line of stakes came into view. "There's a net," says Allie. "She ain't been fished recently. Look at the dead maul heads [catfish] floating." Several fish could be seen floating in the net.

The *Sputnik II* is a traditional Bay forty-two-foot, deadrise workboat that Allie has used over the spring to set and clean his poles. The spruce pine poles used to stake the nets must be cleaned of barnacles from time to time and this is done with the use of a standard patent tong rig, which is set up on the *Sputnik II*. Many watermen who fish for shad in the spring also oyster or clam in the winter, so a patent tong rig already set up for these fisheries can easily be adapted to clean the poles once the tong head is removed. A heavy chain, with links bigger than the poles, is hooked to a line from the hoisting rig and one link is slipped over a pole. When it is raised up and down the pole, the chain knocks barnacles loose from top to bottom.

The last turn on the Poropotank brought *Sputnik II* and its crew into the York, not far from the mouths of the two rivers that make up its headwaters, the Pamunkey and Mattaponi. The smoke from Chesapeake Corporation, a pulp mill in the town of West Point, could be seen off in the distance boiling into the air. West Point is at the tip of the peninsula where the Pamunkey and Mattaponi converge to form the York.

Sputnik II was anchored and the captain and mate headed off into the fog to fish their fish net in the Privateer. After a short ways, a line of stakes with cormorants and gulls perched on each stake came into clear view. "There she is," yelled Allie above the outboard engine.

The spruce pine stakes are set every twenty-some feet apart, as each section of net is twenty feet long and made of $4^7/_8$-inch mesh (the size of the open spaces of the net). Allie's stakes are set in a relatively straight line perpendicular to the river bank. "We used to use a lot of 4 ¾-inch mesh nets but they caught so many buck shad that we went to the larger mesh size," says Allie.

Each section of net is called a net so when a fisherman says he's got sixty nets, it means he is fishing sixty, twenty-foot nets. The nets reach the bottom and extend upward nearly to the surface of the water. One end of a nylon line is tied to the top of the net, while the other end is tied to each stake to hold the top taut. The bottom of the net is held down by the weight of heavy metal rings that are looped over each stake. The rings are tied to lines that are attached to the bottom of the net. Two rings are looped over each stake. (Early stake net fishermen made rings from muscadine vines. There are still a few watermen on the Bay who use vine rings.) The nets are actually fished from the bottom. The end with the rigs is pulled up the pole and, once the net is fished, the rings carry the bottom of the net back down as they slide down the stake.

Allie and his mate pulled up to their first net and began fishing. It was empty, but on the second they landed several large roe shad. "Ya see that shad," says Allie, holding up a large white fish. "Isn't she the prettiest thing you've ever seen? But after she spawns

Allie's nets are attached to a line of spruce pine stakes set in a relatively straight line perpendicular to the river bank. The captain and mate fish the stake gill nets at flood tide.

she's the ugliest thing in the world. When she goes back out to sea to die, she ain't half as wide as she is now."

The next net also had some shad. "The best day we've had so far this year is 650 pounds. Now, I'd like to do even better than that. Back in the seventies, we'd average twelve hundred pounds a day. Not any more."

Toward the end of the first line of nets, Allie pulled in about an eight-pound striped bass (rockfish). "Damn, I hate catching' these things. He's dead. Most of them are dead when we pull them in." [The harvesting of striped bass was not permitted on the Chesapeake then. With improvements in striped bass stocks on Chesapeake, a commercial and recreational rockfish season has been reinstated in Maryland and Virginia].

Allie threw the fish overboard and watched it sink toward the bottom. "It seems like they should at least let us give them to the nursing home or something," he says. "I don't want to sell them. But if they're dead, why waste them? I threw a dozen of them back to the bottom yesterday. It's a damn shame."

The last net in this line of stakes yielded a duck with a blue bill. "Ruddy duck," says Allie holding up the dead bird. "They dive down to get the fish and their heads get hung up in the mesh."

A lively eight-pound American shad is caught in the net. Before the day was out, Allie harvested seven hundred pounds of shad - his best day of the year.

"I ain't never seen a ruddy duck with a blue bill," says his mate. "As old as you are, I reckon you've seen everything."

Right at the end of the net was a lively eight-pound shad. "That shad just got in there," says Allie. "I bet he hasn't been in there five minutes."

As the mate dropped the bottom of the net back over and the metal rings slid down the pole into the water, Allie noticed the sun making its way through the fog. "Boy, we can enjoy a day like today," he says. "We came down here the other day with the bow just dipping under. You can get good and wet out here."

The next line of nets was very profitable and the captain and mate predicted the best day of the season if things continued. "These are the biggest shad we've caught this year," says Allie. "It could be the best day yet, but for as many nets as I've got we should be catching twelve to fifteen hundred pounds of American shad a day. Three years ago, we were doing it."

Allie has 120 nets, four lines of stakes, in the York and he says each line of stakes must by law be nine hundred feet apart.

By the time the fishermen finished working their last net, the sun was high in the sky and the boat was loaded with about seven hundred pounds of American shad and one trout. Several catfish were caught but thrown back. Allie says that the domestic growing of catfish has killed the market for James River and York River cats. "That's why they're so plentiful now, I've been told," he says.

Heading back to the deadrise Allie pondered the future of stake nets on the Chesapeake. "I don't know how stake netting got started, but I bet the guy who put the first one down isn't around anymore," he says. "If things don't change though, there might not be anybody around who remembers how to put one down."

The morning sun was high now as the rays cast a sparkle over the water that looked like millions of little diamonds. "Well, you brought us good luck," Allie says speaking to me. "Anytime you want to go again, just let us know."

Allie left in *Sputnik II* for a three-hour run over to the Piankatank, while his mate headed back to the public landing to load the truck with their best catch of the season.

Allie Walton no longer fishes for shad in the York River as Virginia Marine Resources Commission established a moratorium on the taking of American shad in Virginia's portion of the Bay and its tributaries on January 1, 1994. Allie, however, still works the Sputnick II *in the oyster and blue crab fisheries.*

 # SHAD FISHING

The American Indian has played a significant role in the development of the Chesapeake Bay fisheries. I felt from the start that a book of this nature had to include something about those early Americans who were harvesting the waters of the Bay long before the first white men set foot on the marshy shores of Jamestown.

Since I live just a few miles from the Pamunkey and Mattaponi Indian tribes and knew of their use of floating gill nets, I began to ask around about who would be a good person to take me out for a day of fishing. Pamunkey Chief William Miles was suggested. On the day we went out together, the weather wasn't the best and the fishing didn't turn out to be so great either, but my desire to capture a wonderful and beautiful bit of Americana was fulfilled.

Drift nets were once widely used to harvest shad up and down the Bay. The ideal time to work a drift net is at ebb tide and to catch the tide just right that means fishing night and day. Kerosene lanterns were used to locate the nets at night. Lanterns were set on small floats which were fastened to the ends of the net. (From Goode's 1887 The Fisheries and Fishery of the United States.*)*

When Captain John Smith and others first ventured to explore the region of the Chesapeake Bay, they marveled at the abundance of seafood found in the waters of the Bay.

William Strachey, secretary of state of the early Virginia Colony and author of *The Historie of Travaile into Virginia Britannia*, wrote that the Indians used nets for fishing that were braided to form a mesh. The nets were made of bark from certain trees, deer sinews, and a kind of grass they call pemmenaw, which their women would spin between their hands and thighs to make a very even mesh.

The Indians also used long fishing rods, reported Strachey, with crude hooks made of bone. They also used long arrows tied to a line with which they would shoot fish as they swam by in the rivers and streams. The Accowmack (Accomac) Indians of the Eastern Shore used staves, like javelins, with bones as points. The Accowmacks would spear fish as they swam through the water, Strachey wrote.

When the first settlers arrived in the new world, one of the largest tribes in Virginia was the Pamunkey Tribe. The Pamunkeys live on the neck of land in King William County formed by the confluence of the Pamunkey and the Mattaponi rivers. One of the principal villages there was Clinquoateck, located near where the present town of West Point, Virginia, now stands. Ben C. McCary wrote in his book, *Indians in Seventeenth Century Virginia* that the Pamunkey were a part of a much larger group known as the Algonquian Tribes, which the famous chief Powhatan ruled in 1607, when Jamestown was first founded. The Algonquian Tribes occupied land in Virginia south of Washington D.C., through Fredericksburg, Richmond, Petersburg, and then turning along the Blackwater River and extending into coastal North Carolina as far as the Neuse River.

The Pamunkey Indians were very proficient fishermen and, from colonial times to this day, fishing has played a vital role in the lives of the people within the tribe.

William H. Miles, chief of the Pamunkey Indian Tribe, lives on the 1,250-acre Indian reservation in King William County. The oldest reservation in America, the Pamunkey homestead was first established in a treaty with the British back in 1646 and re-established with the newly formed American revolutionary government in 1777.

Many things have changed for the Pamunkeys since that first treaty some 320 years ago, but there are some things that never seem to change. The Pamunkey River, named after them, still meanders along their shoreline and, from March to May each year, it shares with them its bounty of American (white) shad. The Pamunkeys, like their forefathers, harvest the shad and extract the delicious roe. Long before the English arrived on the scene, the Pamunkeys were harvesting shad with crude weir traps made from rocks and brush. They'd build a dam of rocks across the river leaving gaps. In the gaps, they would secure woven funnel-shaped baskets that snagged the shad as they swam upriver to spawn.

• • •

"That was many moons ago," said Chief Miles, as he waited on the banks of the river for his son to arrive. "Naturally, we don't fish like that anymore."

As his ancestors did before him, Pamunkey Indian Chief William Miles lowers his net into the Pamunkey River to harvest shad.

45

Chief Miles and his son Billy wait for the gill nets to drift down the reach.

Chief Miles and several other Indians have shanties built right on the Pamunkey River, and from there they fish each spring for shad. The chief is now seventy-one years old and was born on the reservation. He lived there until he was in the second grade, when his father pulled up roots and moved to Colts Neck, New Jersey.

"My father was a farmer and fisherman, but he couldn't make a living on the reservation doing either, so we moved to New Jersey where we all did fantastic," he said.

The chief worked for the postal service in New Jersey until his retirement in 1978, when he and his wife moved home to the reservation. "I always wanted to move back someday, but I really didn't know whether my wife would come back," he said.

Miles's father was a full-blooded Pamunkey, but his mother was white, and his wife is white. The treaty of 1646 spells out that only full-, half-, and quarter-blooded Pamunkeys can live on the reservation. Mile's son, Billy, opted to move to the reservation, but he's the last generation of the Miles family that will be allowed to live there.

"I bet Billy has overslept," the chief said as a light mist of rain began to fall in the darkness. "I'm going to get him because we've got to catch the tide just right." Catching the ebb tide is of paramount importance if Miles is to harvest shad. Ebb tide was to begin just after dawn.

Before he left in his pickup truck to fetch Billy, the chief glanced at the river. "Yeah, the tide's still coming in," he said. "I hope this storm hasn't driven all the fish away." The tide was exceptionally high; the docks along the shoreline were half-covered with water.

In about five minutes, Miles returned and shortly thereafter Billy arrived with sleep still in his eyes. The chief went inside his shanty and brought out two plastic laundry baskets filled with nets.

During the week, Billy, forty-three, works in Richmond and commutes back and forth. On weekends he helps his father fish. He moved from New Jersey to the reservation with his wife in 1982. "I was just tired of being a corporate gypsy so we decided to move here," said Billy. "Oh, I love it here on the reservation. You come down here when the sun is coming up; it's some kind of beautiful."

The drizzle had picked up. "Well, Dad, I guess we'll get wet today. Where are you going to fish?" Billy asked.

Chief Miles motioned to the water in front of the shanties. "Let's try it right here. Henry picked up twenty-five or thirty here last Saturday," he said.

The Pamunkey River is a winding stream with many turns and short straightaways. The straightaways are referred to by fishermen as "reaches." The Indians use drift (floating) nets that are set inside the reach, preferably at the upstream end and, as the tide ebbs, the net floats downriver. It is generally fished at the other end of the reach.

Chief Miles cranked up the fifteen-horsepower Evinrude that was on the stern of his fourteen-foot aluminum jon boat, and off into the overcast weather they went. After arriving at the far end of the reach, Miles cut the engine and Billy picked up the oars. Since the tide had not ebbed, Billy rowed into the incoming tide, as the chief began to slip the first net over the stern into the muddy waters of the Pamunkey.

"Well, at least the water is good and muddy," said Billy. "If it's muddy it's better because the fish can't see the net and swim away from it. The nets do the most fishing when the tide is still [right before it begins to ebb] because the nets are deepest then," he explained.

The shad nets are about five hundred feet long with 5½" mesh, and are forty-five to fifty meshes deep. During the shad run, the nets are fished whenever the tide ebbs, day or night. Generally four nets are worked by the chief at an ebb tide. At night a kerosene lantern is attached to a board, which is tied to one end of each net so its location is visible in the darkness. Often several fishermen work the same reach; this has forced the Indians to work out a system so their nets will not tangle. The first boat to arrive on a reach gets to float two nets, the next boat follows with two, and so on until all are finished.

As Chief Miles continued to slide the net over the stern, a great blue heron meandered across the reach. "My ancestors have been doing this for a long time," said the chief. "I've been told we taught the English how to catch and prepare shad and shad roe. The first ones to come over were mostly gentry, and they didn't know how to look after themselves. Pocahontas was a Pamunkey and she helped the English. We helped them until they got greedy," emphasized the chief.

As the end of the net zinged over the stern, the chief motioned to Billy to pull in his oars and off they went a little farther downstream to set the second net. By this time, the tide had begun to ebb some and Billy didn't have to row as hard because the flow was moving the boat downstream. When the second net was set, Billy and the chief went ashore and stationed themselves at a dock to watch the nets float down the reach.

As they watched, the Indians talked about life on the reservation. "We have certain rights that go along with our treaty that most people don't have," said Billy. "We don't need a license to hunt or fish anywhere in the state, and we don't have to pay property taxes the way most people do."

Once a year, usually during Thanksgiving week in November, Chief Miles delivers a slain deer to the governor of Virginia at the Capitol building in Richmond. "That's for our taxes," said Billy.

The Indians actually do not own any land on the reservation, but do own the improvements on the land, They are allowed to sell a house or a shanty to another Indian.

The treaty also states that Indian women have very few rights. For instance, an Indian women cannot live on the reservation if she is married to a white man, an Indian widow can stay on the reservation as long as she does not marry a white, and a single or divorced daughter can only live on the reservation in her father's house.

As the nets floated to the end of the reach, the chief motioned to his son to get ready to fish. Miles, putting on a pair of rubber gloves, said with a grin on his face, "In the old days, they didn't have this luxury."

Dawn had passed and the sun, although unable to peek through the overcast, had made our surroundings much more visible. With great expectation, the fishermen moved toward the first net. Chief Miles diligently worked the net and harvested only two roe shad. There were also some "trash fish," small herring and menhaden.

Miles explained that in May he would stop fishing because of the trash fish. "When we start getting German carp, garfish, and other stuff, I generally stop because it is more trouble than it's worth.

The second net yielded a little better catch as the chief landed three more roe shad but, for the most part, the catch was disappointing. The best day the chief had had this season was when he landed over fifty roe shad in a haul.

Chief Miles sells most of his roe to New Jersey buyers. A set of roe brings $3.50 and the fish sell for about $1 to $1.50.

"It would be tough if this was all I had to pay the bills with," said the chief. "Thank goodness, it's not."

Arriving at shore, the fishermen were greeted by Tecumseh Deerfoot Cook, a former chief of the Pamunkeys who had served in that capacity for forty-some years.

Chief Cook, eighty-seven, talked about the harvest that morning and asked Chief Miles if he had ever caught a walloon (American coot) in his nets. Miles said he had not, and Cook explained how the feathers of a walloon made a fine headdress. "I had a headdress made from the feathers of a walloon, but my wife threw it away," he said. "She thought it was just an old piece of junk." Miles assured the old chief that he would save the feathers of a walloon, if one ever ended up in his net.

A

B

Cook, a spry man for his many years, said, "People say I don't look to be eighty-seven years old and one day a man asked me how I stayed so young looking. I said, 'Eat plenty of shad, catfish, opossum, deer, and beaver, and drink all the Pamunkey water you can get.' That fellow said he guessed he'd die young," mused the old chief.

The chatter continued as the two chiefs stood on the bank of the Pamunkey, laughing and talking about next year's harvest just as their forefathers had done for centuries.

"Well, the shad will be gone soon," said old Chief Cook. "There won't be anything but trash fish to be had."

"Yep," said Chief Miles. "But, they'll be back next spring."

After the talk, Chief Miles began to cut the roe from the "cows" (female fish). He put the cow shad on a cutting stand that is attached to the porch of his shanty. Using a special knife designed to cut the shad's belly without damaging the thin membrane that covers the sack of eggs, he made a short horizontal cut on the fish's belly just under the pectoral fins (photo A). A second horizontal cut was made just in front of the anal fin and then from the first cut, a long vertical slice back to the second cut which opened the belly (photo B). The chief then reached inside the fish and gently pulled the set of roe out and place it in a pan (photos C and D).

After all the roe was extracted, the nets were cleaned with a water hose. "Those old garfish, hickory shad, and herring make a mess in these nets," says the chief. "When

C

you start catching them, it's about time to be giving up."

With the roe extracted and gear ready for another ebb tide the chief and his son, tired from a day's work that started almost before sunup, jumped in their trucks and headed for home.

Chief Williams Miles (Swift Eagle) died in August of 1990 and Billy went on to become chief. Former Virginia governor Gerald L. Baliles spoke at chief Miles funeral and chiefs of the other Virginia tribes laid wild turkey feathers on his casket. Although there are less than one hundred Pamunkey's living on the reservation today, they are allowed through an ancient treaty to harvest shad for sustenance—but not to sell.

D

CHAPTER SIX

POUND NETTING

While researching the history of the pound net on the Bay, I discovered that one of the first places the gear was used was on Mobjack Bay in Mathews County. From that bit of information, I decided to go to Mathews and see if I could find an old-time pound netter. I began my search at the home of Mr. and Mrs. Charles Edwards on Gwynn Island. They had befriended me shortly after my first book Barcat Skipper *was published in 1983. After making a call to make sure he was home, the Edwardses sent me to the doorstep of Wilson Rowe.*

It didn't take but one look at his classic Chesapeake Bay deadrise pound boat for me to realize that he was my man, and I made arrangements on the spot to go fishing with him. Once out on the boat, it didn't take long for me to realize that not only was Wilson's boat a classic, but so was he.

Gwynn Island lies in the Chesapeake Bay near the mouth of the Piankatank River. Its history goes back to the very beginning of this country; legend has it that the island was once a gift from Pocahontas, the daughter of the great Indian chief Powhatan,

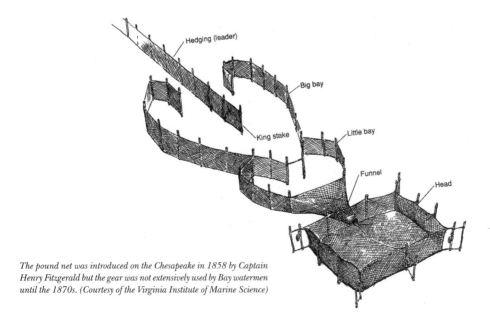

The pound net was introduced on the Chesapeake in 1858 by Captain Henry Fitzgerald but the gear was not extensively used by Bay watermen until the 1870s. (Courtesy of the Virginia Institute of Marine Science)

to an "individual" who saved her from drowning while she was attempting to swim the Piankatank.

Mathews County's history also has deep roots in this country's heritage, as it was once a center for shipbuilding. From the 1770s to the 1840s, ship construction was the most important industry in the county. In some years as many as twelve twenty-ton vessels were turned out by local yards.

The county also has another distinction that few people know about. Mathews was where some of the earliest pound nets were successfully employed on the Chesapeake Bay, and Gwynn Island was a center for this new fishery before and after the turn of the twentieth century.

The history of the pound net is well documented in an 1880s report on the Spanish mackerel fishery in the United States by R. Edward Earll. That year, out of the 1,887,423 pounds of Spanish mackerel harvested across the nation, 1,609,000 pounds were caught in the Chesapeake Bay. The primary reason for this successful harvest was the pound net.

The origin of the pound net has been lost to time, but the first recorded use of one was in 1849 when the nets were being employed in New England waters near Old Saybrook, Connecticut. The first pound net used on the Chesapeake was constructed in 1858 by Captain Henry Fitzgerald, but his net was not properly made and was so unsuccessful that it was soon taken up. About 1870, George Snediker, of Gravesend, Long Island, New York, and Charles Doughty, of Fairhaven, New Jersey, came to the region and located on the banks of the James River a few miles from its mouth. Snediker is considered by some to be the "father" of the pound net fishery, because it was through his efforts that the nets were introduced into New Jersey, Delaware Bay, and Chesapeake Bay.

While on the James River, Snediker and Doughty fished mainly for shad and menhaden, but after about three years, they disposed of their property and went back up north. Snediker, however, returned to the Bay in 1875 and placed a net in Mobjack Bay near New Point in Mathews County. Earll's report includes a colorful story surrounding the early pound net in Mathews.

> Mr. Sendiker went to New Point, Va., and built a large pound in the waters of Mobjack Bay for the capture of shad and other species. The fishermen of the neighborhood, being wholly unacquainted with the pound net, were very jealous of the stranger that came among them with such destructive apparatus.
>
> They watched Mr. Snediker's movement closely for several weeks, and, after seeing the enormous quantities of fish taken by him, at once informed him that he must take his "traps" and leave the country. Refusing to comply with their demands, a number of them sawed off the stakes of the pound even with the water and carried the netting to shore, assuring Mr. Snediker that if he attempted to put it down again they would destroy it.
>
> Seeing it was useless to continue the fishery there, Snediker decided to seek a more favorable locality. Before leaving he sold the stakes that remained in

the water to a resident fisherman, who obtained from them a pattern of the pound, and in a short time had one properly arranged for fishing. This was also destroyed by the fishermen, but not until enough had been learned to convince them that pound nets could be used for great profit.

Within a year from that time, 12 pounds were fished in Mobjack Bay and by 1879 the number had more than doubled. On our visit to the region in 1880 we found that every available site was taken up, and often three, or even four, nets were placed in a line. The leader of one was attached to the outer end of another, for the purpose both of economizing space and of securing the fish that chanced to be passing at a distance from the shore.

Snediker, on leaving New Point, went across the bay to the Eastern Shore of Virginia and associated himself with one of the most popular fisherman of the region, hoping in this way to prevent any organized opposition on the part of the resident fishermen against the use of the pound. By this means he was successful in avoiding any open hostilities, and it was not long before others became interested in the use of the pound.

Though the pound net was introduced into the Chesapeake against the prejudice of the fishermen, it has entirely revolutionized the bay's fisheries. Prior to 1870, the fisheries of the region were of little importance, the business being largely in the hands of farmers, who fished with hand-lines and drag-seines for a few weeks in the spring and fall. Their chief object being to secure a supply of fish for themselves and their neighbors; while today the Chesapeake is the center of one of the most important shore fisheries in the United States. The pound net has not only more than doubled the catch of ordinary fishes, but it has brought to the notice of the fishermen many valuable species that were previously almost unknown to them. The most important of these being the Spanish mackerel. In 1880, 162 pound nets were fished in Virginia waters, with two others located at Crisfield, Md., just above the Virginia line.

• • •

One of those first fishermen to try out the pound net in Mathews County, after Snediker left, was Isaac W. Diggs, of Gwynn Island. His grandson, Wilson Rowe, is a third-generation pound netter and he's still working his net near where his father and grandfather once fished.

At 5:00 A.M. on a July morning, Captain Rowe and his crew of two headed out Edwards Creek into Milford Haven and under the draw bridge that connects the island to the mainland. "We used to have a pull (cable) ferry right there that they'd pull by hand to get to and from the island and later they got a small boat to push the ferry across," said Wilson as he passed beneath the bridge in his 1936-built pound boat.

Constructed in Susan, Virginia, the *Linda R.* is a classic-style pound boat, which evolved shortly after combustion engines began to be installed in boats. These boats

*Wilson Rowe has worked pound nets on the Chesapeake most of his
life. Gwynn Island born and bred, Wilson started working nets when
he was eight years old.*

Built in Susan, Virginia, in 1936, The Linda R. *is a classic-style deadrise pound boat. Few are seen on the Bay these days.*

were built exclusively for the pound net fishery and just a few years ago many could be found up and down the Chesapeake. Today, they've become harder and harder to find as the fishery has declined.

The large pound boat is close in style to the Chesapeake Bay buy boat, which was the first large freight boat to evolve after engines replaced sail as the main source of marine power. The deadrise hull shape of buy boats was taken directly from smaller sailing craft that had plied the waters of the Bay for years. As on the old sailing schooners, the main house was aft and a large mast forward. The pound boat came along about the same time as the buy boat and it too has similar hull characteristics of early sailing craft. It also has the house aft and generally there is a mast forward. It has a similar deadrise hull but is smaller in size than buy boats. The *Linda R.* is forty-two feet in length with a twelve-foot beam and had a mast, but Wilson had it taken off about five years ago.

As the two crew members slept—one on the stern and the other up by the bow—Wilson was bent over an old compass. The *Linda R.* moved out of Milford Haven into Hills Bay and passed out the mouth of the Piankatank into the Chesapeake. In the early morning darkness, a dim light helped Wilson see the compass. Over the sound of the engine, he talked about his life as a pound netter. "Over sixty years I've been doing this," he said. "I'll be seventy-six come November 4 and I started working nets when

I was a boy not much older than eight or nine. My granddaddy and my daddy did it ahead of me. My granddaddy was one of the first around here to get into it. When I was a boy I guess there were fifty-five pound netters living on Gwynn Island and now there are only two, my brother and me. I used to work as high as five nets. I had nets at Back River near Poquoson, Lynnhaven, and Buckroe. Now I only fish one and it's all I can handle. Sometimes I have to fish it by myself."

Watching his course, Wilson went back in the small house and again bent down close to see the reading on the compass. "I'm blind in one eye and deaf in one ear. A ball hit me up beside my head and knocked my eyesight out of one eye and the hearing out of one ear. So you know I'm half crazy to be out here in the dark," he said with a chuckle. "This ol' compass was my daddy's. She was made by David A. Hay & Co. out of Wilmington, Delaware. He got it when I was just a boy. I fished with Daddy as long as he lived, but he died young. He had an old Navy boat named the *Jersey* that came off a battleship. We fished up and down the Bay. That compass is one of the few things I got left of my daddy's. I'm going to try and hold on to her."

With his hand on the wheel and himself half in and half out the door of the small house, Wilson stuck his head back in to check the compass and then popped back out. "I was born in 1912 in my grandfather's house right on Gwynn Island. I went to school some, but you can't keep a waterman off the water. Mama always wanted me to go to school. She had thirteen children but the first two died. They would have been in their eighties now. Mama was ninety-four when she died," he said. After a pause he continued, "I just always wanted to be on the water. Anyway, I was to mean to stay in school and learn anything," he said with a smile.

People talk about the croakers when they came into the Bay in the 1940s and 50s, but the best fishin' I ever had was in the sixties. I had a net over on Deep Rock and when we went to her there was thirty-five thousand pounds of black drum in her. By golly, she was loaded down, Captain. We couldn't get her up to fish her so I went to Cape Charles and hired on five extra men to help. We couldn't bail them with a dip net. They weighted between seventy-five and ninety pounds each so we would pull the net as tight as we could, reach over and catch 'em by the gills with our hands and pull 'em in the boat. They were bringing about five cents a pound and I was selling them there at Cape Charles, but they weren't buying every day so we'd carry about five thousand pounds in and I would call each night to see when they were buying. It took us a while to empty the net from that one catch. We just tied off the funnel so no more fish could get in or out and we went back every day they were buying until she was empty.

They talk about rockfish. Well, I've landed more rock than all the boys on the island put together. In the sixties, I caught eleven tons of rockfish in one day. My granddaddy and daddy were never ahead of me when it came to rockfish. There were 230 boxes on that dock and they weighted one hundred pounds a piece. There were some of the prettiest rock you've ever seen in your life.

Lord, Captain, I've seen some fish in my lifetime—drum, shad, spot, trout, croaker, blues, mackerel, rock. You name it, if it's been here I've caught it. I bet you've never heard of Labrador herring? The ol' heads on the island used to call 'em "downeasters." They're giant ol' hearing and I used to catch a ton of them in cold weather—like in February.

Suddenly, he pointed off into the hazy morning. "There she be, Captain! Get up boys," he yelled. The pound net, located off of Stingray Point in Chesapeake Bay, could just barely be seen through the darkness. Even with the full moon, the haze made it hard to see.

Wilson's crew was made up of Buddy Mitchell and Wilson's son Eddie, both of Gwynn Island. When Wilson came alongside the net, Buddy tied the *Linda R.* to one of the pound stakes and tossed three side fenders over the side. The braided rope fenders were given to Wilson by a friend, who had made them while working on a menhaden steamer.

Eddie pulled the seine skiff that was being towed behind the pound boat up alongside the *Linda R.* Inside the little skiff were a dip net, a white oak sculling paddle, and two large gaffs with pine wood handles that had knots here and there. With the exception of not having any bark, the gaff handles appeared to have come right out of the woods. The gaffs are used to catch the poles on the net to keep the skiff in the desired position while fishing inside the net. Years back, when there were plenty of fish, Wilson used the mast on the *Linda R.* and a hoister, which runs off the main engine, to haul fish from the pound head. A large dip net was tied to the mast, and the fish were dipped right into the big boat. Now, a skiff goes inside the pound head and fish are harvested into the skiff with a small hand dip net.

The pound net consists of a rectangular or squared bowl, or "head," which is where the fish are caught. One or two heart-shaped "bays," often called big bay and little bay or big heart and little heart, lead the fish into the head. Wilson says the use of just one bay is something new to the Chesapeake. It saves him about twelve stakes and thirty extra fathoms of net. "Those old-timers would never do it this way," he says of his one-bay net. "I always used to use the two-bay nets and they do catch some fish better. Spanish mackerel catch better in the two-bay, but we don't catch many of them anymore."

The hedging or leader is a straight line of poles and net that runs from the mouth of the big bay toward shore. This directs the fish into the bay. From the bay or bays, fish are directed into a funnel that leads them into the head. On the *Linda R.,* the hoister, just forward of the Perkins engine, is used to hoist the poles out of the mud when Wilson takes up his net for the winter. When the *Linda R.* had a mast and pile driver, these, along with the hoister, were used to drive the poles into the bottom. Since Wilson now has only one net, he sets his poles in mud bottom where they can be worked in by hand.

Wilson sculled the skiff over to the pound head and Eddie began to slack off the "downhauls" or lines. After the lines were loosened, Wilson paddled inside the net and positioned the skiff lengthwise across the opening from the bay. The

This dip net is used to harvest the fish from the net and just to the right
is a hand-made braided fender that was given to Wilson by a friend
who mends menhaden purse nets for a living.

Eddie Rowe strains to haul the pocket of the net, full of fish, to the surface.

funnel was then drawn up, which blocked the escape of the fish inside the head. Then Eddie, Wilson and Buddy pulled the net onto the gunwales of the skiff.

"All right, Eddie boy, let's pull her up," said Buddy. "What's the matter, Wilson?"

"These old bones don't move like they use to," Wilson said, pulling on his oilskins.

"Oh, this net is heavy," said Eddie.

"You know the old saying 'Come hard, pull hard!'" said Wilson.

"When you need a little sea, ya ain't got it," said Buddy referring to the roll of the sea which would have helped them haul the net to the surface.

As the floor of the net began to rise, Eddie pointed to menhaden captured in the pound. "Looks like you've got a little bait today, Daddy," said Eddie.

"Hold up boy, we've got a little hole," said Wilson.

"Sounds good to me," said Buddy who was sweating from working hard to get the net up.

"Now isn't that something, a brand-new net, and I've got a hole in her," said Wilson as he pulled out a seine needle and mended the hole. As the men complained about how hard it was to haul, Wilson determined that the new net was made from heavier stuff than some of his older nets. This concerned him because he often had to fish alone—a feat few men would try. Wilson is able to do it by pulling up the net and penning his haul to his skiff with small stakes, giving himself time to rest.

"There aren't many left around that can pull a net by themselves, but that man can," said Buddy as he pointed to Wilson.

With the hole mended, the captain and crew continued to pull. "Are we going to get her?" asked Eddie as they struggled to raise the net.

"I'm going to get her up if I live," said Wilson.

"Looks like we've got some Spanish mackerel in there, but I don't see any of those jumbo croakers like we caught last week," said Buddy.

"Yeah, they were the same kind we caught years back all the time," said Wilson. "Good fish are scarce now."

As they continued to raise the floor of the net, the movement on the skiff toward the other side combined to form a pocket in the head on the side opposite the funnel. In this pocket the fish are trapped and hauled out with either a dip net or a scoop. The bailing is generally done with either a hand net or a winch-lifted net. The winch system generally requires that fish be moved from the pound head into the big boat. Wilson uses a hand dip net now because there aren't the large quantities of fish that there used to be.

"She's full of bait fish," said Eddie.

"Come on, gal! Come on, gal!" Wilson said to the net as they pulled.

"Last year, we had a good year," said Wilson between pulls. "Some days I'd catch as high as 150 to 175 baskets of croakers and we caught some star butters (butterfish), too. This year it's been average."

"Well, the first part of the year, the wind stayed to the northward," said Eddie as a reason for the poor start.

"Yes sir, yes sir, we got some mackerel down there. Look-a-there!" Buddy said.

"You catch 'em, you catch 'em. You don't, you don't, and no two years are ever alike," said Wilson. "Lord, she's (net) got some slime on her, Captain, and we just coppered her too."

Wilson uses thinned copper paint on his nets in the summer. In the spring he applies tar. Once a net is treated, it can be fished four to six weeks. After this, Wilson takes the net out of the water, allows it to dry, and gives it another application of copper. When Wilson first started in the pound net business, all he used was tar. In the spring, tar still holds up well because of the cool water. Wilson uses the very same cast-iron pot to melt the tar down that his father used. "It takes two barrels of tar and I sit the pot over the very brick firebox that my daddy made when he started, and I got the same pot, too."

When the net was raised and the pocket full of fish ready for the taking, Wilson reached over and picked up his dip net. A center portion of the skiff was sectioned off for the catch to be emptied into. Buddy and Eddie took a break, while Wilson dipped the fish out of the head. There was a good mess of Spanish mackerel, some blue, trout, star butters, a horseshoe crab that was tossed back, and a mess of Chesapeake Bay blue crabs.

Wilson bails the fish from the pocket with a hand dip net.

"You've got some peelers in there," said Eddie.

"Yeah, we done caught more crabs then fish," said Wilson.

"Here comes someone looking for bait," said Buddy as a crab potter pulled up close and then motioned that he would be back later when the net was fished.

"We'll have some bunkers [menhaden] for him," said Eddie.

In about twenty minutes, Wilson had emptied the net and had it all prepared for another day of fishing. The crab potter had returned and Wilson dropped Eddie and me off at the *Linda R.* while Buddy and he sold the crabbers a couple of bushels of fresh menhaden, at $5 a basket.

By now, dawn had come and gone, and the full light of the day guided us home to Gwynn Island. Sea gulls sat on the gunwales of the skiff as Wilson towed it to Milford Haven Fish House on the island.

Homeward bound, Wilson continued to talk about fishing. "Now I fish from February to Thanksgiving and I've put nets out in January during mild years, but old ice will pull your stakes up if it's out there. In the winter, I go out into the wood and cut down pine trees for my stakes. I saw down sixty-five to seventy poles between

With their catch safely aboard the skiff, the crew of the Linda R. *take a break as Wilson guides his boat to Milford Haven Fish House on Gwynn Island.*

twenty-five and thirty-eight feet long. We punch the poles down in places where there's slick mud, but on hard bottom I used to use my pile driver." [A model of the *Linda R.* with the mast and pile driver on it is proudly displayed on Wilson' livingroom mantel.]

I've been pound netting all my life. The only time I quit was to try working at Newport News Shipyard and I about starved to death. They were paying twenty dollars a week and it was costing thirteen dollars in expenses, so I wasn't making but seven dollars a week then. I figured I could do better fishing, so I went back to it and never quit again.

The worse time I ever had fishing was during the August storm of 1933. I lost everything—stakes, nets, funnels. It was all gone. I finally found some of my stuff two weeks later five miles down the Bay. Another time Daddy and I had a net that a storm took away so we put her back and the next day another storm come through and she was gone again.

"Another thing that will break a net down are stinging nettles," he said. "I've had them in a net so thick that they broke the stakes right off. They haven't been too bad this year. But it looks like the more of them you catch sometimes, the more fish you catch. I had plenty of nettles last year, Captain, and I had a good year. Fishing has been worse this year."

When I first started on the water I ran fish with my Uncle Jim to Norfolk on the buy boat, *Harold*. Uncle Jim was Captain Jim Rowe, of Gwynn Island. Now let me tell ya, Captain, he knew the water. He would be over a hundred years old now. Those old fellows didn't have any education but they had an instinct about things.

My grandfather had a thirty-five foot log canoe that he fished nets from and he was a fine waterman. My daddy used to catch sturgeon. He told me about the times when he would catch three a day. I never caught many because they were just about gone when I started.

Another thing that's changed is that the nets are all machine-made now. The women on the island used to knit all the nets by hand. They could do it prettier than a machine. There were some that could do it just as square as a button. That was a long time ago, Captain.

"There she be, Captain," said Wilson pointing to the shore. The fish house was just off in the distance. As Wilson slid the *Linda R.* up to the dock, Eddie pulled the skiff up to the other side and began to shovel the catch into a bucket that was hooked to a block and tackle on the dock. Wilson and Buddy helped the crew on the dock sort the fish. The catch was sorted according to species, weighed, and put in bushel baskets. "We didn't do much today," said Wilson as the last basket was filled, and he received a receipt for his catch.

*Eddie shovels the fish into a bucket that Wilson and crew hoist up to
a set of scales.*

Wilson stands before a model of his beloved Linda R., *fully rigged with a pile driver for setting pound stakes and having a mast/boom for hoisting the fish from the pocket.*

Back aboard the *Linda R.*, Wilson headed on into Edwards Creek where he tied to a stake off from the island's public landing. It was about 10:00 A.M. when the *Linda R.* got back home, and Wilson and his crew boarded the narrow seine skiff bound for the public dock. All told, the trip had taken about five hours. Wilson picked up an old white oak sculling paddle and proceeded to scull the skiff into the shore.

"I'll bet you can't find anybody on the Bay that can scull a skiff as fast as Wilson," said Buddy. "He used to win every sculling race that we had around here." Sculling races were common place within the Chesapeake Bay water culture, until small outboard engines replaced the sculling paddle. One of the last venue of sculling was with the small skiffs used in the Bay's pound net fishery.

"Shoot, Captain, you'd have a hard time finding too many around that can scull anymore, much less very fast," said Wilson. "Yeah, boy, a lot's changed around there. Pretty soon, there won't be anybody working nets on Gwynn Island. It just isn't what it used to be on the Bay, but maybe all the cleanup stuff will help. Lord, I hope so, Captain."

With the day done, Wilson got in his 1972 pickup truck and headed for home where his wife, Hilda, had breakfast all ready for him. "Well, Captain, you've seen how it's done. The pound net has been around a long time, but its time is short. They cost so much to put out, and there just aren't the fish there used to be, but I guess I'll keep on as long as the Good Lord lets me. It's my life. What else would I want to do?

Wilson Rowe is deceased and no one today from Gwynn Island works pounds nets. A few pound nets, however, can still be found in Virginia and Maryland waters. Last seen, the Linda R. *had the tide rising and falling inside her up close to shore on an upper branch of Stutts Creek in Mathews County.*

CHAPTER SEVEN

A STRIKER FOR MENHADEN

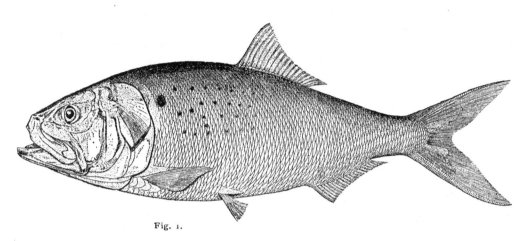

Fig. 1.

Since the beginning of this country, menhaden have been utilized in some manner. Indians used them for fertilizer, Colonial Americans found them good to eat, and, today, fish meal, made from menhaden, is used in animal feed as a protein additive. Also, fish oil is extracted to create Omega-3 fatty acids an essential nutrient additive in human foods.

My first of several interviews with Melvin Dize goes back to the mid-1970s, and I have known him all my life. The Dizes are one of several families who moved to town from Tangier Island, Virginia, and I was in the Boy Scouts with one of Melvin's grandsons.

I had learned from earlier talks with him that he had worked aboard several menhaden vessels during the days of sail, and although I had interviewed several other watermen of that era who had worked in the fishery, his clear memory and love of the past made Melvin my first choice for this chapter.

Menhaden, bunker, alewife, moss bunker, pogo, bony-fish, greentail, bug-fish, and fatbacks are just some of the more popular names given to the fish *Brevoortia tyrannus*. Although seldom considered fit to eat today, menhaden, as they're more commonly known, have been a valuable commodity to the fishing industry on the Chesapeake and elsewhere.

Indians first used the fish to fertilize their crops, and the names menhaden and poghaden (pogy) came from Indian words meaning fertilizer and manure. Thomas Morton wrote in 1632 that in some Indian townships in Virginia, Indians would use a thousand fish to fertilize one acre of land and this one acre would yield as much corn as three acres that were not fertilized.

Surprisingly, in colonial days, the fish were often found to be good to eat. William Bryd of Virginia attested to this in his 1737 writings: "Fat back. This is a small but very good fish, as fat as butter and is splendid fish when it is baked." George Brown Goode wrote in his 1877 volume, *History of the American Menhaden,* that menhaden were in good demand on the shores of the Chesapeake and that in 1874 he frequently saw twenty to thirty strings of fish on tables in the Washington fish market. According to Goode, they seemed to meet with a ready sale at forty cents a string, a price nearly as high as that of striped bass, the favorite fish in Washington.

Sometime in the nineteenth century, people discovered that the fish oil from menhaden had many applications. For years, the country and much of the world had depended on whale oil to light lamps, for tanning, currying leather, soap and rope making, and as an ingredient in paints. Since whales were the primary source of oil, American ships roamed the high seas stalking the monsters of the deep. Fortunes were made and lost on a single trip. The business of hunting whales was so unpredictable and expensive that many businessmen began looking for other ways of supplying the growing country with oil. The discovery of petroleum at Titusville, Pennsylvania, was still some years off, and menhaden were in abundance up and down the East Coast and in the Gulf of Mexico—and much easier to harvest than whales.

Early records show that around 1811, Christopher Barker and John Tallman of Rhode Island extracted fish oil from menhaden by boiling the fish in a pot. When the oil rose to the top it was skimmed off and placed into barrels. One of the more colorful stories of how the industry developed was recorded by Goode in his 1877 writings. He wrote, then, that about 1850 an elderly lady named Mrs. John Bartlett of Blue Hill, near Mount Desert, Maine, was boiling a kettle of fish for her chickens when she noticed oil on the water. She skimmed the oil off, bottled it, and carried it to a Boston oil merchant. Merchant E. B. Phillips promised her eleven dollars for every barrel she could produce and furnished gill nets and kettles for the harvesting and cooking of the fish.

Once the industry got on its feet, it did not take long for it to move into Chesapeake Bay. The first of the Yankee skippers to test the waters of the Chesapeake probably arrived in the 1860s, but the so-called "father of the industry on the Chesapeake" was Captain Elijah Warren Reed, of Brooklin, Maine. John Frye in his book, *The Men All Singing—A Story of the Menhaden Fishery*, wrote that Reed was forty years old in the summer of 1867, already retired after twenty years at sea as a captain, when he sailed two schooners toward the Chesapeake with the notion of harvesting menhaden. Captain Reed set up a plant near Old Point Comfort and began to harvest menhaden by the thousands. Later, he moved his kettle plant to the Northern Neck of Virginia. The town of Reedville, Virginia, on the Northern Neck is named after him.

After this, the industry began to grow and, by the 1870s, there were as many as fifteen plants along the shores of the Chesapeake, with at least two on Tangier Island. The men of Tangier have long been noted for their ability to harvest the bounty of the

Melvin Dize was born on Tangier Island in 1897. There he worked in the menhaden industry aboard both sail- and steam-driven vessels until the 1930s. Melvin retired from working the water in 1974 and started carving models of some of the vessels he recalled from his youth. His models of the schooners, bugeyes, and skipjacks are considered to be some of the finest folk art around.

Bay. Isolated on that tiny stretch of marsh and sand, the men and women of Tangier have worked the water for centuries to support their families.

• • •

Melvin Dize was born in 1897 on Tangier and like his ancestors he knew at an early age that he would spend his days as a Chesapeake Bay waterman. Melvin was fourteen years old when he took a job culling oysters on a little skipjack for ten cents out of every dollar made. At sixteen he went to work on a sail-driven pungy that was being used to harvest menhaden. Before the turn of the century, steam-powered vessels, fueled with coal, were already being used extensively in the menhaden industry. There are few men left, now, who can remember firsthand that sail power was once used in the harvesting of bunkers. Melvin remembers clearly what it was like, because he was there. His first job, on the two-masted pungy *Twilight*, was the start of a career in the menhaden business that was to last until 1931 when he decided it was time to make a living closer to home. He recalls:

It was around 1913 when I first went to work aboard the *Twilight*. She was the sister ship to the *Amanda F. Lewis* and was one of four sailing vessels that were being used to purse net for bunkers then on the Bay. There were plenty of steamers, but sail was about done by then. The *Wagner, Twilight,* and *Amanda F. Lewis* were all pungies and being used to fish bunkers. The only other sail-powered snapper rig (as they were called) was the *Clyde*. She was a round-stern bugeye.

A snapper rig is a boat used for fishing menhaden that's not owned by a fish plant. We sold to a menhaden plant on Dividing Creek on the Northern Neck, but the *Twilight* was owned and operated independent of the company. A lot of the plants had their own boats, but they were not called snappers.

When I was a boy, there were snappers being worked by men from Tangier, so it was easy to get a job on one. The *Twilight* was captained by Shad Crockett. He hired me for that summer and everybody on board was from the island. We always fished close to the *Amanda F. Lewis,* because she had a Tangier crew on her, too.

The *Twilight* was about fifty feet or so long and had two tall raking masts and a thin main topmast that was bowed slightly forward. A crow's nest was built into one of the masts. I would spend a lot of my time up there spotting fish because I was the striker. The captain, first mate, and the striker would stay up top a lot looking for "whips." [Whips describes the color of the water above a school of menhaden.] On the *Twilight* there was canvas around the crow's nest to keep the cold wind off of us, but on some there wasn't anything to protect the spotters from the weather. On many North Carolina steamers they had a wood-framed crow's nest. There wa'n't no airplanes buzzing around like they have today to spot fish.

The striker (or driver as he was also called) was one of the most important men in the crew. You had to have good eyes, and I had one old captain tell me I was the only man who could see more fish than he could. I was good at it. When the captain would scream, "Fish! In your boats! In your boats!" it was a scrambling time around there. The men rushed to get in the two purse boats, while I was sliding down the ratlines to get in the drive boat. The first mate was in charge of one purse boat and the captain manned the other. One man, usually an older fellow, stayed on the big boat to move it into place to load up. He was the cook, too.

I had to be fast, because I was the first one in my boat. The drive boat was only for one man and sometimes we'd throw it overboard if it wasn't already in the water. It was my job to row towards the school. You see, I would guide the two purse boats towards the fish and would signal to them with my oar which direction the school was headed. I would have to stand up and row and I could do it just as good standing as I could sitting down. I couldn't sit down because I had to always be able to see where the fish were. Once I got to the fish I would try to get to the far side of them and then I'd direct the purse boats as to where to go. I'd use my oar to tell them what to do. If the fish weren't moving very fast I'd hold it up and down [vertically].

I would also tell them when to close the purse nets by raising my hands straight over my head. Sometimes the captain would tell them when to close it. It would depend on who was in the better spot to tell them what to do.

Over the years, menhaden were harvested with weirs, gill nets, haul seines, and purse nets. The purse net seems to have been, and is today, the method used most extensively on the Chesapeake to harvest the fish. One of the best accounts of working a purse seine during those glorious days of sail comes from G.B. Goode's writings of how it was done in Maine.

The sailing vessel has a cook who manages the vessel while the crew are working the seine. Each boat carries a "seine setter" and two men to row. The captain of the gang is in charge of one purse-boat, the first mate of the other, and in addition to these most gangs have a "fish driver," who keeps close to the school in a small boat and guides the gang in setting the seine. Four men to row, two to set the seines and one (cook) to manage the vessel, seven in all, are all that are really necessary for steamer or sail-vessel, the other functionaries being added as may be convenient.

Before the days of steam and combustion engines, sailing vessels were used in the harvesting of menhaden up and down the East Coast. (Drawing from Goode's The History of the American Menhaden)

On some of the larger sail vessels, more men were utilized, as on the *Amanda F. Lewis*, which had a crew of thirty-two men working a set in some capacity. According to Melvin, "She was one of the largest doing that kind of stuff."

Goode recounts:

> The seines are 280 fathoms long and 100 feet deep. One-half of the seine is put in each boat. The vessel cruises with men at mast-head looking for fish. When they raise a school they put what are called a striker boat on them. He rows close to the school of fish, observes its course, and they by signs directs the purse crew how to set their seine to catch them. If fish get scared, the striker drives them back with white sea-pebbles which they carry in their boats. If the fish turn to run out of the seine, they throw pebbles before them, and as the pebbles hit the water, they turn and swim back into the direction of the net. After the fish are surrounded the purse-crew and striker all work together to get the seine around them.

White pebbles were never used by Melvin, but he did strike the water with his oar in an effort to drive the fish into the seine.

> I guess that's how the name striker came about because we would strike the water to keep the fish going in the right direction.
>
> After I would start out after the fish, the two purse boats, side by side, were cast off. The captain's boat had three oars on its starboard side and two on port, while the mate's boat had three on port and two on starboard. This was so they could turn easily as they made the set around the fish.
>
> When I raised my hands to let them know it was time to open, they would circle the school and as they made the circle the seine setters let the nets out. When the net was completely around the school, the tom man would drop the tom overboard to close the purse. [The tom is an anchor that when thrown overboard anchors the end of the purse line and holds the net on the bottom. In those days, the tom could weigh as much as four hundred pounds so it would take a strong man to heave it over.] The tom man was the strongest in the crew and was on the captain's boat.
>
> Once the fish were in the net, I'd stay on the other side holding the corks out so the net stayed in a circle. I've seen them so thick in the net, they would push it out of the water. One time in the fall, the fish hit so hard I had them jumping over the net into the drive boat. I had to bail fish out to keep it from sinking. I have seen it though when we'd make a lot of sets and come up with nothing, but usually you'd get a few. They don't even use strikers now. Everything is run off hydraulics and is real modern.
>
> The *Twilight* had a big box built on deck that would hold the fish. We lived in the hold so they didn't put fish down there. We had bunks and there was a table

we ate on. The food was good. We had bacon and eggs, cod fish and potatoes, beans, pies, and hot rolls. A lot of times, we wouldn't get any breakfast if the fish were there. We'd eat after the set was made.

I remember one thing though. When we'd sleep below sometimes the fish juice from the menhaden would come through the deck and drop down on my face at night and wake me up. It didn't bother me much. We were just a bunch of youngsters. Nothing bothered us much.

Everything was done by hand back then. We'd pull the net up tight so the fish were in the bunt [the central bulging part of the net] and we had a big dip net with a long handle, hooked to the mast of the *Twilight*, that we'd drop down in the fish and hoist them up into the box. Captain Shad was real particular about the *Twilight* and the gear on board and we had to work hard to keep things nice when we weren't fishing. Sometimes, I'd go to Reedville on Sunday just for something to do. Later on, when I got to working on the big steamers I went home every other weekend, but when we were up in Delaware Bay it was once a month.

When I was on some of the boats with Negro crews, they would sing all kinds of old hymns as they pulled up the net. There were old chanteys, too, that I don't remember. Most of those boys are all right, but some I've met were just as contrary.

The problem with sail was we couldn't go where we wanted to very fast when the wind wa'n't blowing. But I'll tell you something, there's one thing I did miss about working on a sailboat. I didn't have to worry about hauling coal on board. On those old coal-fired steamers it was a job shoveling that stuff on deck. We didn't have to do that when I was working on the *Twilight*. It was backbreaking work. The coal steamers had tall stacks. Early on, there were only one or two steamers with oil furnaces.

In later years, I worked on several boats as cook and engineer. Some of the steamers' names were the *Joseph F. Bellows, Louise,* and *Chesapeake*. I would get paid about fifty to sixty dollars a month on them and a bonus of two and a half cents on every thousand fish caught. It was good money for them days. I stopped working the fleet around 1930. It was dangerous work. My grandfather drowned on a fish boat and not long after I left the *Twilight,* the *Amanda F. Lewis* capsized near Wolftrap Lighthouse and a nineteen-year-old boy was drowned.

Also, my wife and I got tired of me being off all the time. I'd go off on a boat and not see her and the children for a solid month or more. It just got to be too much.

Melvin continued to work the water after retiring from menhaden fishing. "After I stopped fishing on the boats, I worked a patent dip trotline and pound nets, and tonged oysters until I retired from it all."

Around 1974, Melvin began to carve and sell wooden models of sailing craft and coal-fired steamers that he had known on the Bay. His work is considered to be some of the finest Chesapeake Bay folk art being produced today.

This is just something I took up in the past years to give me something to do in the wintertime. All the models of the boats that I build I knew firsthand. I used to sail and work on the things, and I've got memories of what they looked like and how they were built. I could tell which boat it was way off in the distance just by the way she moved on the water.

Yep, those days are gone for me but my models are just one way of recalling some good old times.

Charles "Melvin" Dize died October 13, 1992, at the ripe old age of 94. He was building boat models right on up until his death.

CHAPTER EIGHT

FISHING FOR EEL WITH
BOBS AND GIGS

Over the years, Chesapeake Bay watermen have found a variety of markets for the sale of eels and have used different types of tools to harvest them. (From Goode's The Fisheries of Fishery Industries of the United States, *section 1, published in 1887)*

It was in the early 1980s that Billy LeCompte, a longtime friend and retired waterman, told me about an eel bob. We were sitting around on the dock at old Payne's Crab House in Urbanna, just chatting about the way life used to be for him, when he brought up the subject. Even back then, I knew that one day I was going to do this project and was counting on Billy to be around to be in my book. But by the time I got around to it, Billy had died.

I made numerous phone calls trying to find someone who might be willing to demonstrate how a bob was made. After months of casual searching, I'd just about given up because almost everyone knew about the eel gig, but no one seemed to know about the bob. Then, I happened to mention my dilemma to Willis Cannon one Sunday morning in church. A slight grin came over his face, as he told me that he knew plenty about ell bobs and gigs.

Years back, many watermen on the Chesapeake harvested eels to provide bait for the summer and fall, hard-crab trotline fishery. As a youngster growing up on the Rappahannock River, Willis Cannon fished for eels using bobs and eel gigs or spears.

The eel bob is a simple form of gear, but most effective in catching eels during certain times of the year. Willis recalls:

Willis Cannon fished for eels with this nine-prong eel gig and with eel bobs. Willis is one of just a few old-time watermen who can still recall how to make a bob that can catch a solid mess of eels.

The best time to catch eels with a bob is in early spring, March or April, when the water has warmed up enough for ol' eel to come out of his hole, but is still cool enough for him not to be moving around a lot. You see, an eel bob is made from night crawlers (worms) that are threaded onto a fine silk thread. The eel bites the worms and gets its teeth hung in the thread. Silk thread is the best type because cotton or other types won't catch in its teeth just right. Eels have fine, hacksaw teeth and silk catches them the best. As soon as you feel an eel bite, you yank the line into the boat. Once it's in the boat, shake the line and old eel will drop right down into the bottom of the skiff. In the early spring, they are still moving slow from the cold water of winter and they can't wiggle loose like they do later in the spring and summer.

Eel bobbing was done primarily at night in certain locations where large numbers of eels congregated.

We had several spots that were great for bobbing but our best one was under the pier at Lord Mott oyster shucking house [on the Rappahannock River near Urbanna]. There was one place there where they'd dump the leftover water from an oyster skimmer, and the eels would go there to eat

Willis starts his eel bob by threading worms, with a broom straw as a needle, onto No. 74 silk thread.

the real fine oyster cuttings that had been left in the bottom of the skimmer. We'd catch a boatload there in a half an hour. By golly, they were big eels. I know some of them weighed three pounds.

I was about sixteen or seventeen years old when I started and Ed Evans, who was a schoolmate of mine, taught me to bob. That would have been about 1927. His father was a good waterman and he taught Ed how to make one [a bob]. I don't know where his father got it from, but there were others around that would do it. You see, eels were bringing thirty-five cents a pound. That was good money back then. We'd sell them to watermen for catching hard crabs. They used them for bait on trotlines.

Many times we'd come home with a solid skiff full of eels and throw them down in a big barrel full of water that we had loaded up with salt. They'd drink the water and get all that salt in them and when they floated to the top dead the next day, we'd dry salt them in a smaller barrel. We made good money for a while until the crabbers started using tripe [the belly of a cow] because they could get it for ten cents a pound. It was decent bait—if you could stand the smell. That stuff stank.

Another good place to bob was under the draw of a bridge. We'd make our bobs during the day and go out around dusk to get the spot ready. We'd save

Once enough worms have been threaded onto the silk, the worms are tied in a ball with a piece of cotton twine.

enough worms to throw overboard near where we were going to eel. It was sort of like baiting ducks with corn. The worms would draw in the eels and then we'd catch them with the bob. It was a lot of fun and wasn't like fishing. If you hook a fish and lose him he most likely won't come back because he has a sore mouth, but when we'd hook an eel and he would drop off, we figured he'd be back soon. He would most of the time too.

Now, the first thing you do to make an eel bob is to go out and fetch yourself some worms. If you have a woodpile, they like to live under the pieces of wood on the ground. You can lift the wood up and find a lot of worms. Worms can also be found in a garden spot that has been cultivated regularly. In the early spring, we could always get worms around when someone was having their garden plowed. To make a good bob, it takes a good yard or so of worms. But if you want a small one, you can make it with less. The bigger the bob, the longer it'll last. I've made them as big as a tennis ball.

The next thing you do is find a broom and pull out a very fine broom straw to use as a needle to thread the worms on the silk thread. You need a fine straw, especially if you've got small worms because they must be pushed through the straw onto the thread. I use No. 74 silk thread and I tie the thread

The eel bob and gig were used extensively by watermen at the turn of this century.

to the bottom straw with two half hitches. Then, I start threading the worms onto the thread. Once I've got the number of worms threaded that I want, I take a piece of cotton string and lay it down on a table. I take the string of worms and zig-zag it over the cotton string. Finally, I pull the two ends of the cotton string together, catching the worms and then I tie them into a ball with two half hitches.

You can see, it's not hard to make, but there aren't many people left who would know how to make an eel bob. Some things just get lost with time. People just don't do it anymore.

Willis also fished for eels with a gig, which is a method much more well known than bobbing. Eel gigs, or spears as they were often called, were used in colonial times to harvest eels. The gig (see photo of a nine-pronged eel gig) is designed so that the eel is caught between the prongs and cannot escape.

C. G. Atkins in an 1880s fisheries report, "The River Fisheries of Maine," described the gig or spear as the implement most widely known and used for the capture of eels. Atkins wrote:

The spear consisted of spatula-formed center piece with three teeth on either side, each tooth having a single barb on the inner side. The teeth are of steel, about 8 inches long, slender, elastic, spreading at the tips about 8 inches. With this implement at the head of a long wooden pole the fisherman industriously prods the soft muddy bottom through a hole in the ice, or sometimes from a boat. Each thrust is made entirely at random, but experience guides the fisherman to a choice of the proper kind of bottom and the topographical location and extent of the beds.

Gigs, as they're commonly referred to on the Chesapeake, came in many styles. Some had three prongs, others five, seven and even nine. When Willis was eeling with a gig in the 1920s, many communities, like Urbanna where he grew up, still had the local blacksmith shop just down the street. Horses and the need for horseshoes were on their way out, but for the blacksmith the needs of working watermen provided a livelihood long after the automobile made his occupation a thing of the past. Many shops specialized in hand-forged oyster tongs, clam and oyster shucking knives, clam rakes, and eel gigs.

We always got our gigs from Joe Pierce, who was the local blacksmith. They were hand-forged, and his style would catch better than others I had tried. Most of his were seven-prong, but he made other styles too.

We gigged for eels in the winter when they would bury in the mud. Perkins Creek is a little creek where we'd catch a lot of them. There was a foot bridge going across the creek. You don't see them much anymore, but foot bridges were common across marshes or small coves in those days. On one side of the bridge was hard bottom and on the other side was mud. It was on the mud side where we'd work the gig. You see, when an eel buries in the mud, he leaves holes in the bottom to come in and out of. So, we'd look for those holes and when we spotted two holes about a yard apart we would drive the gig down right in the middle of them. Yep, nine times out of ten, we'd have us a big old eel.

We gigged and bobbed for eels as much for the fun of it as for making a little money," says Willis. "There wasn't much a boy could do back then for fun. There wa'n't no movie theaters yet or much else around for entertainment, so fooling around on the water took the place of that. I treasure those boyhood days. Whether I had an eel bob or a crab net in my hand, it was good wholesome fun for me."

Willis S. Cannon died August 8, 1994, at the age of 82. Occasionally, a gig can be found in an antique store and, as often as not, the store owner does not know what it was used for.

CHAPTER NINE

HARVESTING EELS
WITH POTS

When I first met George Meade, I was on assignment at Mt. Holly, Virginia, to do a magazine story on George Robberecht, the Dutch entrepreneur who gave the Bay eel fishery a real shot in the arm when he and his family started exporting Chesapeake Bay eels to Europe in the early 1960s.

I was waiting around for Robberecht to get back from a doctor's appointment so we could hold the interview, when George Meade drove up in his truck filled with eels. As he unloaded his catch at the eel plant, we talked for quite a while about his work and I knew then that he was the right person for this chapter on eel pots.

The American eel has been sought by Chesapeake Bay watermen for years. One of the earliest methods of harvesting eels utilized pots. Indians and early colonists first made eel pots of willow branches. Later, watermen began making pots of baskets woven from white oak splints. These were cylindrically shaped by fishermen who would weave the splints over a wooden mold.

Another early eel pot used on the Chesapeake was the barrel pot. A 1800s U.S. fish report describes the barrel eel pot:

> Pots and baskets of various forms are much used in some districts. The most approved form, of late, is made from a barrel by substituting funnel-formed screens for the heads. Baited with fresh fish, free from taint, these are sunk to the bottom in favorable positions often alongside fish weirs. The eel, probably scenting the bait, push their way in by the tunnel-formed entrance, but are unable to escape. This is a very old method of fishing.

• • •

George and Calvin Meade, of Morattico on Virginia's Northern Neck, are professional eelers today. George remembers, as a boy in the 1940s, going out in the early morning with his grandfather, Robert "Woody" Meade, and fishing barrel pots on the Rappahannock and Potomac rivers. "My granddaddy was an eeler and he used wooden barrels for pots. Granddaddy would take a burlap grass sack, cut funnels the size he wanted, and tie them inside the barrel, just right for catching eels.

Pots have long been used by watermen as a tool to harvest eels. George Meade, left, and his son, Calvin, of Morattico, Virginia, utilize both round and square pots to catch eels. Their eels are sold to a distributor at Mt. Holly, Virginia that ships them to Europe for human consumption.

"Granddaddy had a little skiff with an eight-horsepower engine, and he would eel in the spring and fall. Those barrel pots would catch a lot of eels, but later on he went to square pots made of wire, sort of like what we have now. He was selling his eels to Gordon's Seafood, in Baltimore, Maryland, for twelve cents a pound. I guess they were being sold to trotline fishermen for crab bait, but I know some were going to New York City, where some of those Europeans living there like to eat eel.

Eels have never been considered much of a delicacy in the United States, but in Europe and Asia people have been eating eels for centuries and consider them quite tasty.

Years back, some fishermen on the Bay even considered eels to be a nuisance. This was revealed in a letter, written by Harrison Wright on May 27, 1881, about drift-netting for shad on the Susquehanna River.

> The most important fishing industry on the Susquehanna is the gill-net fishing, though twenty large haul-seines are operated at various points, in what is termed the "head of the bay," the Northeast River, and in the Susquehanna itself, a short distance above Havre De Grace.
>
> The gill nets are set to drift with the tide to catch shad. The necessity for not leaving the nets too long is the presence of great quantities of eels, which soon spoil the shad for the market or for the table. Sitting in my boat while the oarsman was quietly rowing behind a "giller" we were attracted by a continual splashing in a net nearby. We thought it to be a sturgeon rolling and entangling himself in the twine as they sometimes do. Heading the boat in the direction of the sound and coming near, it seemed at first to be a number of herring meshed in a singularly close huddle, and in their struggles flashing their white sides in the dim starlight.
>
> As we came nearer I turned the light of the lantern full upon them and discovered a swarm of eels tearing and stripping the flesh from the bones of a shad which had gilled itself near the cork line. Gathered in a writhing mass, with their heads centered upon the fragment of the fish, we had before us the living model of a drowning Medusa. There was at least a bushel of them, greedily crowding each other, fastening their teeth in the flesh of the shad, and by a quick, muscular torsion snatching pieces from the dying fish.
>
> It is not uncommon to see a dozen heads of shad, each with a long, slender backbone attached, taken one after the other out of the nets, when a fisherman has delayed a little too long. Six good eels have been thrown into the boat by a dexterous jerk of the net where a mutilated shad was hanging. I have seen four eels fall out of the abdominal cavity of a shad, when no eels were visible, when the fish came over the gunnel. They had devoured the viscera, which always seems to be the first portion sought by them.
>
> The habit is to run the net and as soon as it is all out, take the fish out immediately, before they can be injured by the eels. The eels never mesh; they

are too slippery to get entangled. In the shoal fishing, when the weather becomes warm, the "eel cuts" as these are called, often out number the marketable shad. The fishermen salt down the better ones for their winter food.

In the 1800s, the main market for eels was New York City. The same letter stated:

> Eels taken in summer with pots and traps are for the most part packed whole "round" with ice in barrels and shipped to New York. The demand is very lively during the first part of the season, and shippers receive about 6 cents a pound, free of freights and commissions. The product of the spear (or gig) fisheries, on the other hand, is dressed before marketing, and bring about seven cents per pound in New York. [She chapter on eel gigs and bobs.] As the shipper has to pay freight and charges, and as 200 pounds of live weight will not dress more than 140 pounds, it will be seen that the round eels, the product of pots and traps, give the best profits.

It's certainly fair to say, though, that these early eel markets in the cities were relatively small compared to the demand for eels today. This demand skyrocketed, in the 1960s, when Dutchman George Robberecht came to Mt. Holly, on the Potomac River's Nomini Creek, and started buying eels to sell to the European markets. Robberecht buys about two million pounds of eels a year, which has contributed greatly to the growth of the fishery on the Chesapeake.

Before dawn, at 5:00 A.M., on an overcast June day, the Meades cast off from Sharps Landing. Sharps was once a busy steamboat landing and riverfront town where there was steady traffic of two- and three-masted schooners coming and going. Today, it is a quaint little village, with a small gut of a harbor where George and Calvin Meade moor their boat. The steamboat landing that once extended far out into the Rappahannock River has long-since gone. A few pilings are all that's left of those golden years when Sharps was a regular stop for steamboats out of Baltimore and Norfolk.

For years, George and Calvin used a traditional, forty-foot, wooden deadrise workboat to eel. In the winter months, they also used the forty-footer to tong for oysters. But with the 1987 bust in the oyster fishery, Calvin was forced to the land, working heavy equipment. As a result, father and son reassessed their needs as working watermen and bought a new, KenCraft, fiberglass boat with a three-hundred-horsepower engine. "We gave it a lot of thought before making the investment," said George. "We needed a boat to go into shallow water. This boat has tunnel drive which allows us to go in sixteen inches of water. Sometimes we fish in the headwaters of creeks where it's so shallow the pots are half out of the water."

The Meades also needed a boat with plenty of power. "You see, eeling is not like crab potting. A man will put a string of crab pots out and leave them all season. Eels, on the other hand, don't stay in one place, so we've got to move pots every three or four days. We need a boat fast enough and big enough that we can go all over the river," said George, as Calvin headed the boat out into the Rappahannock.

A rarity on the Bay, George and Calvin eel all through the spring, summer, and fall. Most Bay watermen eel during early spring and late fall and crab the rest of the time.

"We work real hard at it," George says. "It's been the worst year that I've ever seen for eels though. But we're still catching 250 to 300 pounds a day. A few years ago, we were averaging five hundred pounds a day, but we were only getting seventy cents a pound. Now, we are getting a dollar-and-a-half to two dollars depending on the size. Money-wise, we're still doing as good."

The decline in the eel population still has George concerned. "Most everyone else has already quit eeling until the fall because it's been so bad. We've had a better season here than the boys on the Potomac. Part of the problem is there are so many people into it now," he says. "There were twelve eelers working the Rappahannock in March, all with two hundred to three hundred pots each. You can catch them all up in a hurry. I remember on August 25, 1979, when it was just me and a couple of other eelers working the river, I caught nine hundred pounds in sixty pots. I'll never forget that as long as I live. Yesterday, we caught 273 pounds in 280 pots. Another problem is that they tell me it takes a long time for an eel to grow to adult size."

The life cycle of the American eel was not understood until the late 1800s when it was discovered that, like European eels, the American eel travels to the Sargasso Sea, off the coast of Bermuda, to spawn. There, adult eels lay their eggs and die. In the spring, the elvers (small eels) start their long journey to European waters or to the East Coast of the United States and Canada. For many, it can be as much as a two-thousand-mile swim. Eels will take anywhere from seven to twelve years to reach the adult breeding age.

George points to five bushel baskets loaded with maninose (small soft-shell clams) in the bottom of the boat. "That's what has been catching eels for us for the last few days," he says. "Eels are funny, sometimes they'll catch on peelers, sometimes on horseshoe crab, sometimes menhaden and now, on maninose. We try them all from one time to another, and when we find out which bait is the best, we go with it. I bet we're the only ones on the Rappahannock using maninose. It takes 4½ bushels a day, and a bushel costs $19.75." The maninose are caught by watermen in Maryland's hydraulic clam fishery.

Eels are used in the Maryland trotline hard crab fishery. (See Chapter 21.) Eels about a half inch in diameter are the preferred size in that fishery, for which they are cleaned, gutted, and salted. Some Maryland hard crabbers prefer salted bait because they believe it catches better than fresh. Calvin and George, though, sell their eels live to George Robberecht, who ships them live by air freight to Europe for human consumption.

The fishermen no longer use the old barrel pots of their forefathers. "We use mostly square pots now with inch-by-inch mesh," says George. "We have round pots, but they don't catch as good as square in tidal waters. The round ones have a tendency to roll with the tide." Calvin and George have a hundred or so round pots that they use in the upper reaches of creeks and inlets where the water is very calm.

Square or rectangular pots vary in size and are generally made from either galvanized or vinyl-coated, sixteen- or fourteen-gauge wire. These pots range in size from eighteen inches by eighteen inches by eighteen inches (square) to twenty-four inches by sixteen

The Meades primarily use square pots in tidal rivers.

inches by sixteen inches. Some eelers place concrete in the corners of the square pot to help hold it to the bottom, but most use metal frames. Round pots are about twelve inches long with two cloth funnels inside and a cloth lid for emptying and putting bait inside. These pots are made from the same gauge and mesh size as the square pots, and concrete is also used to hold them on the bottom. In some very shallow areas, round pots are staked to the bottom.

With the overcast sky shielding the dawn, Calvin slows the engine and George jumps up from the cooler he was sitting on. "We baited a couple of pots with bunkers (menhaden) and put them in deep water just to see what they'd do," says George.

The pots were full of small crabs, but no eels. "I can see right now they're not potting on fish," he says.

Since eels must be kept alive, a large wooden live box is situated just in front of the engine/console configuration. The console is built over the engine box, allowing enough space for the live box.

An electric pump circulates salt water into the box to keep the eels alive, and a culling screen sits over a portion of the top of the tank. When George dumps a pot over the screen, eels slip through the small holes cut in the screen, while mud toads, small fish, etc. accumulate on the top of the screen. Every so often, George dumps the contents of the screen overboard.

The first line of pots yields a good catch of eels and a large number of mud toads. George dumps the culling screen full of toads overboard after the first string of pots is fished. "This isn't many toads," says George. "We catch a lot more of them on horseshoe crab."

The second line of pots is not very productive, and as George finishes baiting each pot, Calvin stacks them on the stern. "We'll try another spot farther upriver," says George. "This time of year, you've got to keep moving the pots."

The next line is farther inshore on the south side of the river. The first pot that Calvin attempts to fish is caught on something on the bottom. George wraps the line around the bow cleat as Calvin moves the boat back and forth, trying to jar the pot loose. Suddenly the line snaps. "That's twenty-two dollars gone when you lose one of them," says George.

This string of pots did produce a good catch of eels and catfish, though. Several of the pots from the previous row that George had taken up were thrown overboard to make the line longer. George is surprised to see the catfish. "We usually catch a lot of cats in the early spring after a wet winter," he says. "They like fresh water. We were catching two hundred pounds a day when we were working our way upriver." The Meades don't sell the catfish but some eelers do.

"Look what's coming down river." Calvin points to a dark rain cloud moving our way. Rain gear is quickly pulled out as the eelers continue to fish.

The storm hits and raindrops as big as quarters shower the boat and eelers. "I've got plenty of flotation in her," says George of his new boat. "I've been out here fishing for forty years, and I couldn't swim from here to the stern of the boat."

Throughout the day, Calvin pulls pots while his father dumps the contents into the live box, then rebaits them. The rain continues to pour relentlessly but has little effect on the two watermen. When the last pot is pulled about 10:00 A.M., George says it's not a bad day's work. He estimates the two hundred eel pots have landed about 270 pounds. "I'm never too far off my estimates," he says.

As the KenCraft moves into Sharps landing, the rain turns into a sprinkle. George jumps out of the boat and pulls his truck up close to the dock. The truck has a flatbed trailer with a live box. After the eels are transferred from the boat onto the truck, George takes them to Mt. Holly.

Round pots are used in the upper reaches of creeks and coves where
the water is calm. The dip net is necessary to handle the slippery eels.

Eels are moved from the boat into the Meades' aerated tank on their truck. Once on the truck, they are hauled to George Robberecht's eel plant at Mt. Holly.

Many eelers who do not carry their eels to the market each day build boxes out of marine plywood and wire, which float in the water. The eels are dumped into the box and stay there until one of Robberechts' trucks picks them up.

As the last barrel of eels is dumped into the box on the truck, George looks at Calvin and puts his arm on his son's shoulder. "Well, we made it one more time, Son."

The U. S. Fish and Wildlife Service and the National Marine Fisheries Service reviewed the status of American eel in 2007 and found that at the time Endangered Species Act protection was not warranted. The agencies received another petition in 2010 seeking to extend federal protection to the American eel. They found substantial information to warrant the initiation of a more extensive status review of the species. I have not heard from George or Calvin Meade since our day out on the water together. George Robberecht is deceased and his business at Mt. Holly has closed.

CHAPTER TEN

HAND TONGING
FOR OYSTERS

Over the years, I've covered the oyster fishery up and down the Bay and have gone out with many watermen who work hand tongs. Also, having grown up on the Rappahannock River, I have been watching those hardy souls scratching the bottom of the river for oysters almost as long as I can remember.

When it came time to do this chapter on hand tongs, I decided to go out with Roosevelt Wingfield because he so exemplifies the traditional Bay waterman with his work ethic and independent approach to life. When disease nearly wiped out the Rappahannock oyster crop in 1988 and most everyone else turned to other fisheries, Roosevelt was still going out every day sounding the bottom with a bamboo pole, trying to catch a mess.

Politics has long been a part of the seafood industry on the Chesapeake Bay. As early as 1661, Virginia's government in Jamestown issued a decree that all Indians had to purchase a license to harvest oysters. No one else was required to obtain such a permit. It was a deliberate move to starve the poor natives into moving farther inland. From all accounts, the move worked, and the English then had control over the seafood in the streams and rivers of the Chesapeake.

During those early years, the Chesapeake Bay was loaded with oysters, so much so, that it required only a walk to the shore at low tide to pick up a mess for supper. But as the population began to grow and the colonists developed a taste for the delicious bivalve, the beds up and down the Bay became more and more depleted, until the only oysters to be found were covered with deep water.

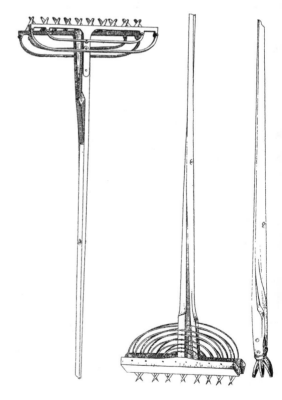

Early oyster tongs had wooden heads and shafts. Later local blacksmiths began shaping the heads from metal. (Shaft tongs and a nipper made entirely of wood were pictured in Goode's The Fisheries and Fishery Industry of the United States, published in 1887.)

Around 1700, shaft tongs, which allowed oystermen to stand in a boat and pluck the oysters from the bottom, were introduced on the Bay. The shafts and heads were originally made from wood. Later, the heads were formed from metal, but even today the shafts are made from wood in the traditional way. Early hand tongers in Virginia were either slaves, who were harvesting oysters for their masters, or a poorer class of whites, who were trying to scrape together enough to eat. However, this all changed after the Civil War.

The economy of the South was devastated by the war, and many people had to turn to the river just to survive. An 1880s U.S. Fish report by Richard H. Edmonds on the oyster interests of Virginia states:

Previous to the late war the oystermen of Virginia were composed of Negroes working for their masters and of a very rough class of whites. But at the close of the war, the demand for oysters was very great and high prices were paid. Many who had been reduced from wealth to poverty were glad to avail themselves of the chance to make a support by oystering, which was at the time a very profitable employment.

The four years of war, during which oysters had almost a complete rest in many parts of the state, gave them a chance for development, and when the trade revived the beds were well stocked with large, finely-flavored oysters. Men from nearly all occupations, representing all classes of society eagerly entered the business, and soon there were hundreds of oystermen where formerly there had been but a dozen or so.

Many of the most extensive farmers in the tidewater counties found that the conditions of labor had so greatly changed that to make a living it was necessary for them to devote all spare time to the oyster trade. A very noticeable fact in connection with the tonging interests of Virginia is the total absence of foreigners in the trade. Among the 8,860 tongers of Virginia (in the 1880s) there are, according to the statements of the county clerks, only about ten who are not Americans. The entire trade may be said to be virtually in the hands of native Virginians, since there are probably not 300 tongers in the whole State who were not born and raised there. The life of an ordinary tonger presents few attractions to induce strangers to enter his business. The work is very laborious, the remuneration only fair, and the injury to health from exposure is so great that few ever reach old age.

Hand tongs were made up and down the Bay and almost every waterfront community had a good supply of tongs available for sale. The local blacksmith would make the heads and a shaft maker would shape the wooden scissor-like shafts from either hickory or locust. The length of the shafts depended greatly on the depth of the rivers and creeks that the oystermen were working. There was also a short-handle tong with a small head used in shallow water that was called a nipper. These were

Many of Virginia's hand tongers, prior to and after the Civil War, were black. With little or nothing to call their own, former slaves were able to scratch a living from the state's oyster beds. (Courtesy of the Virginia Institute of Marine Science)

Nippers were a regular household tool during the early twentieth century. For many living along the creek banks, a short paddle out into the creek would yield a delicious supper. (Courtesy of the Virginia Institute of Marine Science)

Roosevelt Wingfield, fifty-six, has hand tonged for oysters most of his life. He is one of just a few watermen who use a traditional bamboo pole to sound the bottom for oysters.

more for home use in creeks and often children were sent out with a pair of nippers to catch a mess of oysters for the supper table. The long-handle tongs range from fourteen feet to around thirty feet in length and are still used today in Maryland and Virginia waters.

• • •

Though the charcoal gray sky, the fiery red haze just above the Northern Neck announced the start of another day. The roar of the engine from the deadrise sent a large raft of canvasbacks soaring into the sky. With wings flapping furiously, the canvas-colored ducks became tiny specks as they moved farther away into the morning sky.

Roosevelt Wingfield is a striking, muscular man of fifty-six years, who looks forty-five at most. In the tradition of his forefathers, he has worked hard to make a living from the river. Sometimes it's been good to him and sometimes it's been bad.

On this March day, Roosevelt is working a thirty-five foot deadrise workboat named *Barbara Ann*. Four sets of shaft tongs are sitting on the culling board as Roosevelt stands by the steering stick headed upriver to Long Rock on the Rappahannock. Normally, there are others on the boat working with him, but today he's alone. Oystering has been poor of late, and many have been forced to work on land.

"Yeah, it's been slow," said Roosevelt over the engine noise. "But, I've seen it slow before."

The engine slowed as the waterman arrived in the vicinity of where he wanted to work. There was a long bamboo pole sitting next to the shaft tongs. Suddenly, Roosevelt grabbed the pole. "This is what you call a depth finder," he said of the long pole as he began to sound the bottom. "It's just like a good pair of tongs. When it scrapes across the bottom, you can hear the music of oysters down there. Ya see, when the pole hits on a lump of oysters, it makes the same sound as when my tongs are working. Hear that? There's a small lump right there." He then shoved the pole into the bottom to mark the spot and got ready to tong up a mess.

Roosevelt picked a pair of twenty-foot shaft tongs from among the sets of tongs on the culling board. Each has a different shaft length for a particular depth of water.

With the sun still halfway up, another deadrise workboat came into sight. "Yeah, here comes Walter, late as usual. I get out here before the wind and all starts being funny. It's slick calm right now, but you wait until about nine o'clock or so when that tide starts changing. We'll be lucky to catch a handful."

Walter and his mate came alongside in the workboat named *Hard Times*. "Hey, oh there, Roosevelt, I done lost my stick. Is this a good spot?"

Roosevelt answered, "I heard some music on the bottom, Walter. Let's give it a try."

"You don't mind, do ya?" asked Walter.

"No man, we just as well keep it all in the family," said Roosevelt, as the two white men on *Hard Times* looked at one another and laughed.

Roosevelt's first lick brought up five large oysters and several little ones. "Look at the size of those boys," he said. "Now they've been on that bottom for some time.

"An oysterman, he's like a gambling man—one day he's a winner and the next he's a loser. Ya never know what you're going to make in a day," he said. "I've been working the water for thirty-five years and still ain't got rich yet."

The whole time Roosevelt worked from the washboards of his deadrise, he talked about oystering and his life. "My family came from the Norman Plantation over on the Piankatank River and I guess we've had oystermen in my family all the way back to slavery. We may even have had them in Africa, I don't know. My grandma told me when I was a boy where I come from. We lived over near Turk's Ferry on the Piankatank River and she said most of my ancestors worked in the fields or in the river."

Walter seemed to be bringing in a few oysters, while Roosevelt was catching more shells. "Walter is right on 'em. I'm over here on this snakey bottom. It's so many shells I can hardly get my tongs closed. Now you don't have to be but a few feet off a lump and the other fellow will make a day's work and you won't. Years back, oysters were everywhere. I'd come out with my father-in-law and we'd catch sixty-five or seventy-five bushels a day, but we weren't getting but $2.75 for a bushel. I'll be lucky to catch four bushels today, but at $25 a bushel, that's not too bad."

After about an hour Walter yelled, "I'm a-headin' on, Roosevelt. Not enough here for me. If ya see me staying in one spot for long, ya know I've found a mess."

"All righty boys, I'll see ya later," said Roosevelt still bringing up plenty of shells and a few marketable oysters.

"I started out oystering on the *Ol' Shamrock* as a culling boy, but that didn't last long," he said. "I was born to have a pair of tongs in my hands, so I didn't stay a culling boy long. I worked for twelve seasons on the Potomac and a bunch more on the James before it got so polluted over there. In the summer, I work in the woods logging. But, I'd rather be out here a-tonging than anywhere in the world. The *Shamrock*, she was a log canoe that had once had sails in her but when I worked on her she had a six-cylinder Chrysler to move her."

With the culling board filled with shells and oysters, Roosevelt jumped down from the washboard to cull his catch. "Look at those mussels all over this oyster," he said as he pulled the mussels off. "Carry those in and the man will holler. Boy, I'd fill a tub in a hurry if he'd buy them. Wouldn't I? "You take a man who's buying a piece of property, he gets rocks and stones, don't he—whether he wants them or not. But, you try selling a few oysters with a mussel or two on 'em and the man starts jumping."

"Dog stone," he said as he pulled off a little round tunicate or sea squirt and squeezed it. A tiny stream of water squirted from a small hole in the brown blob. "I don't know what they're really called, but we call them dog stones."

"Now we call this a snap." There was a long thin oyster in his hand. "She ain't no good because they shuck so slow. The man don't want them. You take shuckers trying to make a living on how many gallons they can shuck, they don't want a bunch of snaps that will slow them down."

The good oysters were thrown under the culling board in the boat, while everything else went overboard. When the culling board was empty, Roosevelt reached down and picked up a handful of salt and sprinkled it on the washboard where some ice had formed. "I can't swim the first lick. She'll take you away from here—the river will. I know, she took my son," he said as his voice cracked some. "I told him not to go out on that day, but he did it anyway and he fell overboard and drowned. He wa'n't but twenty-nine years old. Went down over on Smokey Point and came up almost the same place he went down. Believe me, boy, the river will take ya away from here, if ya ain't careful."

Back up on the washboard with tongs in hand, Roosevelt continued his day's work. Each lick seemed just like the last, and the oysterman never seemed to tire. All day he worked the shafts, back and forth, in a circular and an in-and-out motion to get as many oysters in his tongs as he could before closing them by bringing the shafts together. He appeared to use very little effort as he pulled the seventy-five to one-hundred-pound load to the surface. "Oh, look at that big one," he would say referring to a very large oyster. "I bet he's poor as a lizard inside," he said followed by a hearty laugh.

Roosevelt doesn't see a bright future in the oyster business and predicts these tools of the trade, a set of hand tongs and a culling board, will someday become museum pieces.

After Roosevelt moved to another spot, more oysters began to come into the boat.

This is a little better spot than before. If I stay here, I might make a day's work. I used to go out with my uncle a-oystering and he was a slicker. The buyers then wanted all your catch and some would stop buying from ya if ya didn't give them all ya had. Well my uncle would tong for a while and then shuck a few. He would hide the shucked oysters in a jar under the seat in his skiff. Come the end of the day, he'd sell the unshucked ones to the man and keep the others to sell to his neighbors. He made more money off those few pints that he had tucked under the seat than all the rest.

We had a lot of fun years back when the old folks were out here tonging. They used to tell some of the best stories in the world. Now nobody has time for anything except working.

As the morning passed, the tide began to change and the wind began to blow from the southeast. Roosevelt began to blow his nose between licks. "I don't care what kind of day it is, a southeast wind will may your nose run," he said. "A sou'wester, nor'easter, or whatever, there's no problem, but a sou'easter will stop a nose up every time."

It became more difficult for Roosevelt to work his tongs as the day went on because a "cross tide" and the wind seemed to be working against him. He ate a sandwich while he worked. "Sure aren't many oysters like it used to be," he said. "Just a few years ago, you could take a long lunch break and still catch plenty of oysters."

Every once in a while, he would dip his bare hands down into the cold river water. "If you've got cold hands the worst thing you can do is put them up against a stove. Stick them down in the water, that'll warm 'em up."

As the day wore on, a flock of Canada geese flew over forming a vee in the sky. It wasn't long after this that Roosevelt pulled up his tongs and headed for home.

There were three bushels in the bottom of the boat, which meant a seventy-five-dollar day. "The sad part of all this is, you're looking at a dying art," he said about his skill of hand tonging. "The young ones now can't make a living with hand tongs. It won't be long before all this will be a thing of the past. You wait and see."

Watermen still use hand tongs to work in the James River oyster seed fishery on Virginia Marine Resource Commission specified "hand tong" grounds. Few others, however, harvest oysters with hand tongs anymore. The oyster fishery has gone to using cages to grow oyster in and harvesting wild oysters with narrow 22-inch wide "hand" dredges. Roosevelt is deceased and his prediction that hand tongs would become a historical memory may very soon come true.

CHAPTER ELEVEN

OYSTER DREDGE

I happened to be down at Deagle and Son Marine Railway in Deltaville on a spring day in 1986, where, to my delight, I saw a battered and worn old skipjack up on dry dock. The helmsman's wheel was lying on the ground and the hull appeared hogged beyond repair, but incredibly several months later the Rebecca T. Ruark, *was back on the waves, looking as good as new.*

I swore then, if I could ever talk a publisher into taking on this project, the Rebecca *would be the focus of the chapter on oyster dredging. Her skipper, Captain Wade Murphy, turned out to be as colorful as the old girl herself.*

The introduction of new types of fishing gear has often produced some exciting times on the Chesapeake Bay, but none provided more lore and color than the oyster dredge.

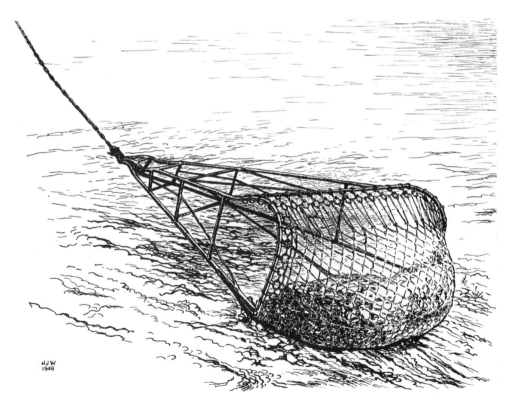

Oyster Dredge. (Courtesy of the Virginia Institute of Marine Science)

The dredge was introduced on the Bay around the turn of the nineteenth century when northerners, who had depleted their own oyster grounds, came south looking to harvest the bounty of the Chesapeake to supply an ever-increasing demand for oysters in northern cities.

At first, they came to buy seed stock from local tongers to carry back to grow out on their own grounds up north, but as the demand for oysters continued to grow, many northern vessels came south equipped with a new style of harvesting gear. The dredge created such a stir in Virginia that the legislature enacted a law in 1811 prohibiting any harvesting instrument for oysters except hand tongs. Eight years later law was enacted to prohibit out-of-state shipment of oysters. Neither of these laws amounted to much, though, because there was no enforcement.

The Maryland legislature followed Virginia's course and, in 1820, enacted laws to prohibit the dredge and out-of-state shipment of oysters. After the Civil War, however, Maryland changed its law to allow the use of the dredge, and Virginia passed a law that allowed the dredge on private grounds. This led to perhaps the most colorful and dangerous period in the history of the Chesapeake Bay fisheries. The oyster wars of the Chesapeake pitted hand tongers and dredgers against one another and there were many battles from one end of the Bay to the other.

The Maryland Oyster Police were formed in 1868 to prevent oystering after dark and in unauthorized areas. However, Virginia was wide open for the taking because the

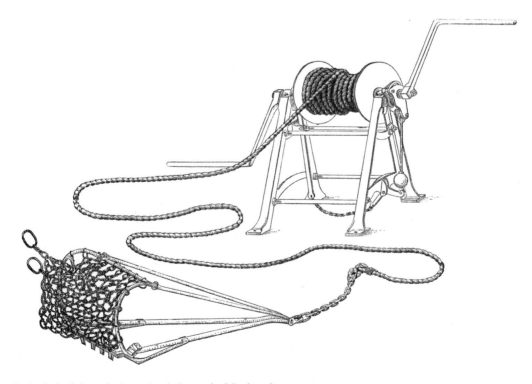

During the days before combustion engines, dredges were hauled to the surface with hand winches that required strong arms and a strong back. (From Goode's The Fisheries and Fishery Industries of the United States)

state had no police enforcement and as Maryland police got tighter on the dredgers and the oyster stock became more and more depleted, the oystermen began looking toward Virginia.

An incident that was typical in those days occurred in the winter of 1879-80, when forty Maryland dredge boats entered the Rappahannock River and began work. The local hand tongers, incensed at this depredation upon their beds, tried to drive the dredgers away. They were totally unsuccessful as the dredgers, who were well supplied with rifles, opened fire upon the tongers. For several weeks, the appearance of a tonger at any time was certain to draw a volley from the dredgers. The Virginia state legislature, in session at the time, decided to supply the tongers with a cannon, a large number of rifles, and a supply of ammunition. Before the arrival of these weapons, however, the dredgers left—loaded down with Rappahannock River oysters.

Virginians were not always unsuccessful, though. In 1850, a group of out-of-state dredgers entered the mouth of the Nansemond River and began work. They were working day and night and Sundays before Sheriff Hugh H. Kelley, commanding seventy-five volunteers aboard a steamer, captured twelve oyster vessels with their crews and forced them to proceed to court at Suffolk, where each captain was fined $33.50.

Before the Civil War, many Virginia slave owners were more concerned about losing their slaves than losing the oysters to Maryland dredge boats. Yankee captains were accused of encouraging slaves, who were often out tonging oysters for their masters, to join their crews where payment was a trip to the land of freedom. It got so bad that many slave owners would not send their slaves out to work on the river while the dredge boats were around.

Virginia had its own band of renegades, too. As late as 1949, the Potomac River oyster war resurfaced as a Maryland court sentenced two Virginia oyster dredgers to a year in prison and confiscated their boats, as well as fining a third dredger five hundred dollars. The three were caught moonlighting at the mouth of the St. Mary's River. A Maryland patrol boat gave chase and rammed their forty-two-foot workboats to shore amid rifle fire. During the heyday of the oyster canning industry millions and millions of bushels came across the docks in Baltimore, many of which were ill-gotten by dredge boats. Richard H. Edmonds, in an 1879 report on the Maryland oyster industry, wrote:

Dredging in Maryland is simply a general scramble, carried on in 700 boats, manned by 5,600 daring and unscrupulous men, who regard neither the laws of God nor man.

Some of the captains and a few of the men may be honest and upright, but it is an unfortunate fact that such form a very small minority. The tenure by which the captains hold their positions is such that they are almost forced to disregard the laws. Many of the boats are owned by unprincipled men, and I am informed that a number of them are even held by the keepers of houses of ill-repute. An honest captain who complies with the law by not working on Sunday, at night, or on forbidden ground, will take at least a week longer to catch a load of oysters than one who, disregarding the law, gets his oysters whenever and wherever he can. The first captain, upon his return, is informed in language more forcible than elegant that unless he makes as quick trips as the second captain his place will be filled by someone less scrupulous. With such a system as this carried out by a large number of the boat owners, what but evasion of the laws can be expected of captains?

All blame for violating laws does not, however, attach to the boat owners, as some of them are prominent gentlemen of the most upright character. It is the misfortune of such men that their captains have often been trained by less honest employers, and having once acquired a love of ill-gotten gain, it is difficult to keep them from continuing in the same course. As he usually has a share in the profits, it is of course to his interest to make his trips as quickly as possible; and while the boat owner may be opposed to breaking any laws, his captain may think and act otherwise.

The unscrupulousness of the captain is well assisted by the character of his men. These men, taken as a class, form perhaps one of the most depraved bodies of workmen to be found in the country. They are gathered from jails, penitentiaries, workhouses, and the lowest and vilest dens of the city. They are principally whites, many of whom are foreigners (almost every European country being represented), unable to speak more than a few words of English. When a crew, which usually consists of about eight men, is wanted, the vessel owner or captain applies to a shipping agent, who then gathers these men wherever they may be found, drunk or sober. As one large boat owner expressed it to me, "We don't care where he gets them whether they are drunk or sober, clothed or naked, just so they can be made to work at turning a windlass." The shipping agent having placed the crew aboard, is paid $2 for each man furnished. With such a crew as this, who neither know nor care for laws, the captain is of course able to work wherever he desires to. As may be supposed, the life led by these men on board of the vessels is of the roughest kind. When sleeping, surrounded by vermin of all kinds; when working, poorly clad and with every garment stiff with ice, while the wind dashes the last freezing spray over them, hour after hour winding away at the windlass, pulling a heavy dredge, or else stooping with backs nearly broken culling oysters. Returning from a trip, the men take their little pay and soon spend it in debauchery amid the lowest groggeries and dens of infamy to be found in certain portions of Baltimore. It is a gratifying fact, though, that even amid such surroundings as these, there are some few respectable and honorable men. This is more especially the case on the boats owned in the lower counties of Maryland. The crews of these are often gathered from

Built in 1886, the Rebecca T. Ruark *is one of the oldest working skipjacks left on the Bay.*

the surrounding neighborhoods, and even as a class are not as degraded as those on Baltimore vessels.

• • •

Tilghman Island lies in Talbot County, Maryland, nestled between the Chesapeake Bay and the Choptank River. Tilghman is home for one of the oldest working vessels on the Bay. The *Rebecca T. Ruark* was originally built and rigged as a sloop on Taylors Island, Maryland, in 1886. The *Rebecca*, as she is fondly called by skipjack admirers, once had the traditional sloop-style, gaff-rigged topsail. But like many of the early sloops, the *Rebecca* was converted to sharp-headed skipjack rigging, a style that still survives today in Maryland waters, where the last commercial sailing fleet in America operates. The *Rebecca*, however, is most certainly a sloop, as her hull reveals the full rounded bilge and full bow that denotes the early sloops.

The *Rebecca* and her owner and skipper Captain Wade Murphy offer a touch of Americana that would leave any admirer of American heritage spellbound. Her survival and that of the other twenty-some skipjacks that dredge for oysters under sail in Maryland are solely due to an 1865 law that restricted oyster dredging to sail.

Captain Wade Murphy is owner and skipper of the Rebecca, *as she is fondly called by skipjack lovers.*

In 1967, this law was modified to allow the use of push boats for power on Monday and Tuesdays.

It should also be noted here that the aforementioned information on the character of the early captains who worked the Chesapeake Bay dredge boats is no reflection on those hardy, dedicated men who now make up Maryland's dredge fleet. They are admired and their boats are loved by all.

Captain Wade is no exception. A Tilghman Islander born and bred, Wade is the third generation of his family to dredge for oysters under sail. At 4:30 A.M. on a Monday in February, Wade and his crew of two were getting ready for the *Rebecca* to make yet another journey into the Bay as she's done for the past 102 years. Moored in Knapps Narrows, a small canal that separates the island from the mainland, the vessel lies against a dock in Tilghman as a cold misty rain falls.

Since it was a Monday, the skipper and his crew would work under the power of a push boat. Oystering had been so bad in the winter of 1988-89 that no one had been working under sail. "Just ain't worth it," said Wade as he made the push boat ready and cranked up the little boat's 350-horse-power Oldsmobile engine. There is no combustion engine on the *Rebecca* other than for pulling the two dredges. The push boat is attached to the stern of the vessel with a block and tackle. The bow on the push boat has a split piece of tire (bow fender) over it to protect it from the stern of the sailboat, while underway. "There just haven't been any oysters this year. At least, not enough to justify paying a crew and coming out here except on power days," said Wade.

One of the crewmen untied the mooring lines, while the other cranked up a small stove in the house to get some heat and to cook breakfast. As the *Rebecca* slowly moved through the narrows bound for the Chesapeake, Wade talked about his thirty years of owning and working aboard skipjacks. "Thirty years ago when I first started working, there were eighty skipjacks working the Bay. Now there are about sixteen that are actually working," he said with one hand on the wheel and the other in his pocket. "Yeah, my granddaddy and daddy dredged for oysters, so I guess I was just destined to get in the business."

As the *Rebecca* moved into the Bay, the aroma of fried eggs, sausage, and scrapple filled the small house and rushed up through the cabin door to hit Wade in the face. "I don't want my egg hard there, mate," said Wade to the crewman below. "Make the yoke a little hard with a little lace around the edges.

"I bought the *Rebecca* from Emerson Todd. He was in his eighties when he finally retired and sold her to me. I tell ya, I love this old boat. She's seen many a wave break over her bow."

As the mist of rain turned into a steady sprinkle, Wade went below to eat his breakfast while another crewman took over the helm. "We've got three hours, so you might just as well get comfortable," he said. The state of Maryland had recently opened up some new oyster bottom near Annapolis for the dredge boats, and Wade thought there might be a good day's work there.

Push boats are used for power on Mondays and Tuesdays, while the law requires that sails be used to power the skipjacks the rest of the week.

A natural storyteller, Wade began to relate some of the stories that had been passed down about his family. One involved his grandfather, James Murphy.

My granddaddy drowned, dredging oysters on a schooner, when my daddy was thirteen years old. That meant Daddy had to go to work and it was a rough business for a boy. The story goes that, about eighty years ago, James Murphy lived here on Tilghman and there was a black kid living here too. My grandfather was on a trip up the Bay when he came home to find that this negra kid had tried to break into his house. Well, he went out and found him and like to killed him. After that, the negra disappeared and everyone figured they'd seen the last of him.

Well, many years later, my grandfather picked up a couple of black boys on the western shore to help him dredge on this trip. One of them looked sort of familiar but he couldn't exactly place him. The story goes that on that trip my granddaddy was lost at sea, supposedly slipped overboard, but everybody figured that that negra, who looked sort of familiar, was the one he had nearly killed some years back and that he had pushed him overboard. What made it even more suspicious was when the boat came back to Tilghman, that negra got off before anyone here could get a good look at him. My granddaddy was forty-six years old when the ol' Bay took his life. His body washed up on the western shore and supposedly he was identified there by a thirteen-year-old child who recognized a tattoo on him.

He [my grandfather] must of been a real son-of-a-booger, because another story was passed down about the way he won my grandmother's hand in marriage. Supposedly, he and a man named Faulkner were after her hand at the same time and Faulkner won. It wasn't long after the marriage that Faulkner and James Murphy went out in a boat together and Faulkner fell overboard and drowned. The legend has it that he was pushed over by my grandfather, and a little while later he [my grandfather] married Faulkner's widow.

"Them were days, weren't they?" Wade said with a big grin on his face.

"Ya ever notice cookin' tastes better out on the water than anywhere else. You couldn't get better tasting eggs in a high dollar restaurant in Baltimore," he said, finishing up his breakfast.

"Raining out there, mate?" Wade yelled to the crewman at the helm.

"Comin' down steady, Cap'n."

"My Daddy, Capt. Wade Murphy, Sr., was a fine man," he said with pride. "He worked almost right on up until he died. I remember going over one day to his house after he got old and I told him about the free cheese that the government gives out to the elderly. 'Come on, let's go down to the firehouse and get some of that cheese for ya, Daddy,' I said. I knew he wouldn't take it, but I wanted to see what he'd say."

"'I ain't going down there! I don't take no handouts!' he said to me."

The sounds of hot grease crackling in the frying pan, good conversation, and the constant gentle rain hitting the roof of the house made time go quickly. "Where are we, mate?" asked Wade to the helmsman. "Looka there! Daybreak in another hour and we'll be a-oystering."

Conversation jumped from family to oysters, to crabs, but it always seemed to come back to *Rebecca*. "I think she's the only working sloop hull left on the Bay," said Wade. "I was told she once had a two-masted schooner rig, but she's mighty small for a schooner. I never knew her when she was sloop rigged, but I'll tell ya, she's a sailing trick. You take a day when there's plenty wind and plenty oysters, I can catch just as many under sail as with the push boat."

There was red haze in the sky just before sun-up; *Rebecca* and her crew were not far now from the grounds just off Annapolis. "I was sixteen when I went to work full time on my daddy's boat," said Wade. "I was in the tenth grade when I decided to quit school. I wasn't doing nothing anyway in school, I figured. Well, it was full-time sail in those days—no power days. The first day I was out it was blowing a northeaster with a hard freezing rain. The next day was the same thing. I almost went back to school the next day but it cleared off. I believe if we'd had two more days of bad weather, I wouldn't be here today," said Wade with a chuckle.

"All right boys, we're here," he said to the two members of his crew. "Where are the [oyster ground] markers?" asked Wade, talking to himself. "They got to be a mile-and-a-half offshore."

Wade finally found some markers but wasn't sure if they were the right ones. He radioed several of the other captains, but since it was new ground no one was sure where the beds were located. "I guess we're going to have to leave here boys," said Wade after searching for the markers for about thirty minutes. "I can't take a chance on getting a thousand-dollar fine."

The skipper pointed the *Rebecca* in the direction of the Bay Bridge. "I know where there are some oysters over near Kent Island, off from the old ferry landing," he said.

As Wade sailed up the Bay, there was chatter over his CB radio as one skipjack skipper asked another why he hadn't brought him some crabs. A few crabs are caught in the dredge in some areas of Maryland, but it is unlawful to market them. Captains often take them home for steaming. "I would have brought ya some, but they weren't hardly worth bringing home," he said.

"You're lying," said the other skipper. "I heard they were so good you near 'bout choked on their fat."

Wade laughed, "Damn they were fat crabs, wa'n't they."

Finally, the *Rebecca* and its crew were over the oyster grounds as the six-cylinder Chevy engine was cranked up to run the hauler that raises and lowers the dredges. It was 7:10 A.M. and the two crew members put on rubber knee pads to protect their knees as they culled oysters. The two dredges, one on each side of the *Rebecca*, were than lowered into the Bay.

Wade explained that he has five different types of dredges and that the type of bottom dictates which style he uses. The gum dredge is one that has no teeth and is used on real hard (stone) bottom. Tooth gummers have real small teeth and a blade. They are used where the stone is small. The round bar dredge has longer teeth and is used for oystering on bottoms that have shell stock, and mud dredge is effective for really soft bottoms. It has long teeth to get under the mud.

"We're going to be using a round bar today," said Wade, "because we're going to be working in some shells."

The first lick was very discouraging, but a second haul brought up forty-two large oysters. Wade tossed a buoy over the side to mark the area where he made the catch. "A boat coming, Skipper," yelled one of the hands.

"Lord, I know it's not the law today, as messy as it is out here," said Wade pulling out some binoculars to get a better view. "It ain't the law, boys."

"Last week, I pulled one, I'll tell ya," said Wade. "The police came out in a Whaler [while it was] blowing a solid gale. I said. 'I know they're not going to board me today,' but sure enough they did."

"They always ask how much a bushel of oysters is bringing first off, before checking our catch and I always tell them a little lie because they don't want us to be making too much money. I said twenty dollars a bushel. We were actually

Wade lends a helping hand to a member of his crew as the haul yielded forty-two large oysters, one of the best hauls of the day.

getting twenty-two dollars. Well, he paused and then asked, 'Will ya sell me three and a half bushels?'" 'Damn,' I thought to myself. 'I hate to sell those oysters for twenty dollars,' but I had to do it or they'd know I was a liar. I lost seven dollars on that deal. That'll teach me."

With the Bay Bridge just off in the distance, the crew of the *Rebecca* continued to work. The rain would stop and start, but the crew constantly worked the dredges. Early on, one dredge hit a "hang" on the bottom, which was the reason given for the other one landing more oysters. They thought the dredge might be bent, but neither one was bringing in many.

"Damn, we ain't done nothin'," said Wade. "We would have done better working at McDonalds."

"I just can't find a spot," he said. "I've seen the day when we could catch 150 bushels in two hours. This Dermo and MSX [two deadly oyster diseases that have recently played havoc on the Bay's oyster] have done us in, but I'm looking for it to come back slowly."

"I've got those boys in stones up to their elbows and they still have smiles on their faces," he said. The dredge began to bounce some and Wade explained that the *Rebecca* was working over a stone bed.

Wade's push boat or yawl boat was built in 1974 in Dorchester County, near Cambridge, for the sum of four thousand dollars. He also owns another skipjack named the *Sigsbee*, which he thinks was named for the admiral of the battleship Maine, whose name was Charles W. Sigsbee. "I bought the old *Sigsbee* for three thousand dollars twenty-five years ago. Now a new yawl boat would cost twice that," he said.

"I would like to get on one little spot and make a day," he said with sincerity. "It would take about thirty bushels to make for a halfway decent day."

The *Rebecca* was headed for home at 4:00 P.M. and there were not nearly thirty bushels on deck. A short while after the crew started the two-and-a-half-hour trip home, the sun came out for a brief moment and shone on Bloody Point Lighthouse. As the skipjack cruised past the lighthouse, the sun reflecting on ol' Bloody Point light offered a rustic Bay scene.

The sunlight was short-lived as fog began to hover over the Bay. Wade had his Loran set on the first and second markers to Knapps Narrows, but suddenly he called down to the crew. "Problems, boys," said Wade. "Watch that depth finder." First 6' 2" flashed up on the screen, then 5' 7", then 5' 2". "We can't go much lower," said Wade.

Suddenly, the finder showed the depth at 4' 6" and dropping. Wade cut the engine down and moved slowly. "I don't know which side of the channel I'm on," he said. "The channel will fool ya here. There's shoal water on each side of ya." The finder showed 3' 2" before it started going back up—3' 8", 4' 2", 4' 7, . . . 5' 8". "We're home free, boys," said Wade.

With the fog and night converging on the *Rebecca*, Wade inched his boat along, as the Loran directed him to Knapps Narrows. The worst was yet to come, even though

A crewman takes a break while the dredges are on the bottom.

At the end of the day, the crew of the Rebecca *had landed only fifteen bushels.*

the *Rebecca* was within a mile of the first buoy into the narrows that was close to home. "I know one thing, I've never seen it (fog) no thicker," said Wade.

Everyone, except Wade, was stationed on the bow of the *Rebecca* to watch for that first buoy. It was very difficult to see, even with a light flashing on the buoy, but it was to be the easiest one to find. The second one was much more difficult. Wade pulled out a spotlight, which was of little help.

Suddenly, out of nowhere voices were very close by and the sound of another push boat was right on top of us. "Russell! Russell!" yelled Wade over the CB. "We're ahead of you so watch out."

Russell Dize is skipper of the skipjack *Katherine*. The next thing we knew the *Katherine* was up ahead of us. "I think he's passed us," said Wade. "I didn't see him."

"Are we moving?" asked Wade. "I can't tell."

A member of the crew assured him that the *Rebecca* was not aground. "Well, we might not be, but the *Katherine* sure is," he said as the sound of her engine roared into reverse.

"I swear I can't see a thing," said the skipper.

It took the better part of an hour to find the buoys leading into Knapps Narrows, but once the *Rebecca* made it to Harrison's Oyster House there on Tilghman, the fog lifted and the stars shone bright.

"Look at that sky, would ya. I can't believe it," said Wade.

The crew unloaded a pitiful fifteen bushels and received eighteen dollars a bushel, but all agreed they had seen worse.

Sixteen hours had passed when the crew of the *Rebecca* finished their work and headed for home. Wade assured the men it would be better tomorrow, but when they both left he said, "Lord, I hope it's better tomorrow for all of our sakes. That's a lot of work for fifteen bushels of oysters. Don't you think so?"

The *Rebecca T. Ruark* had made yet another day on the Chesapeake.

There are fewer than a dozen skipjacks working in Maryland's oyster dredge fishery today. Captain Wade Murphy still owns the Rebecca, *but uses her mainly for charter. The dredge is still used in Virginia on private oyster grounds and on Virginia Marine Resource Commission specified state public grounds.*

 # PATENT TONGING

Long before I'd laid eyes on Dink Miller, I'd heard the story of the Miller twins, Virgil and Dink. Virgil was a handsome baby, but Dink was as ugly as Virgil was handsome. One day a friend arrived at the Miller's door to see the pair of newborns. Mrs. Miller, somewhat embarrassed by Dink's ugliness, told her friend that the twins were upstairs and she'd bring them down one at a time. She went up and brought Virgil down first and the friend cooed over the handsome child. Then she went back up and brought Virgil right back down in place of Dink. "They're identical," she said "Aren't they handsome?"

The first time I met Dink, he told me this tale that I'd heard before, and as far as I know, he tells almost everyone he meets who know Virgil and himself. His hearty sense of humor and success as a clammer are why I asked him to be a part of this project.

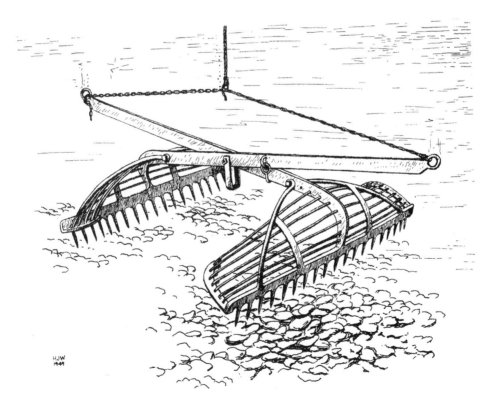

Patent tongs. (Courtesy of the Virginia Institute of Marine Science)

When Maryland and Virginia restricted the use of the dredge, many oystermen were limited to working in relatively shallow waters with hand tongs. Some means of harvesting oysters in deep water needed to be found. In the late 1800s, the need was answered when a Maryland native and two Virginians invented a type of tong for deepwater tonging that came to be known as patent tongs.

The first patent on the new style of tongs was issued to Charles L. Marsh of Solomons, Maryland, in 1887. Marsh, a blacksmith, lived along the Patuxent River, where some of the deepest oyster bars on the Bay exist. Marsh claimed, and later proved, that his ingenious invention could harvest from three pecks to a bushel of oysters in a lick, and from thirty-two to one hundred bushels a day. The blacksmith also wrote in a letter, dated September 1890, stating that he had manufactured some twelve hundred pairs of tongs, which he sold for sixteen dollars a pair over the three-year period.

In April 1890, the patent office issued a second patent on deepwater tongs to Joseph A. Bristow and William M. Dixon of Virginia. Bristow ran a country store in Stormont [a few miles from Urbanna], and Dixon was a blacksmith from Mathews County. The main difference between Marsh's tongs and the Bristow/Dixon style was the shape of the tong head and the catch used to open and close the tongs. The Bristow/Dixon tong head is shaped with a right angle, while Marsh's tong head is more round. Both apparently worked quite well, because there are variations of each in Maryland and Virginia even to this day.

It is not known whether Bristow and Dixon knew of Marsh's invention when they applied for their patent. However, the patent office obviously saw enough difference to issue the 1890 patent. The Virginia tongs also gained international fame at the 1898 World's Fair in Chicago when the invention won a blue ribbon.

There was little known of the Bristow/Dixon tongs until 1984 when Bristow's great-grandson, John M. (Buddy) Moore, was cleaning out an old chicken house on the family farm in Stormont and came across a crate. Inside was the actual pair of tongs that his great-grandfather had shipped to the World's Fair. The tongs have a wooden release latch on which the names of the patentees are inscribed. The wooden latch would float upward when the tongs were in the water, releasing the latch and allowing the watermen to close the tongs on his catch.

An advertising brochure for the tongs read:

Deep Water oyster tongs—the only right angle heads, and consequently the only perfect working tongs invented. The only tongs that the weight, or anchors, pull equally from each arm, and thereby prevent tipping or turning over while getting in the bivalves. Can be used for taking oysters, clams, mussels, sponge or coral in any depth of water. Shipped to all parts of the world on short notice.

It was also revealed in family papers discovered at the same time that Bristow provided the brains behind the operation and Dixon the skill of making the tongs.

A letter of agreement between Bristow and Dixon, dated July 10, 1890, stated that "Bristow contributed more time and labor in discovering" the tongs, while Dixon was in "possession of facilities for the manufacture" of the tongs.

The first patent tongs in Maryland and Virginia were pulled to the surface by hand using a hand winders. The hand winder was later replaced with a winder powered by a small donkey engine. In 1958, Maryland watermen began using hydraulic patent tongs. William Edward Barrett of Calvert County, Maryland, and Rayner Wilson, a blacksmith in that area, developed the first hydraulically operated patent tongs. These are still used in Maryland waters today. However, Virginia law prohibits the use of hydraulics to hoist the tongs from the bottom. Virginia watermen have perfected a system using used auto parts to hoist their tongs. This mechanical system runs off the main engine. Most have a foot-operated clutch pedal that controls a three-speed (Ford or Chevy) transmission which is connected from the main engine to an automobile brake drum. This enables the tonger to start and stop the tongs and run the gear at different speeds.

Charles Marsh, Joseph Bristow, and William Dixon left behind a legacy that has been passed on through generations and generations of Chesapeake Bay watermen. They truly were men of vision.

It takes an early riser to catch a patent tong boat, but I found the experience, in January 1989, well worth the loss of a little sleep.

• • •

"Well, let me tell ya, fellow, you're out a-clammin' with the granddaddy of them all on the Chesapeake Bay."

"Yep, you're right there," came another voice over the CB radio. "Dink is the oldest clammer around. I hear tell he was at the Last Supper."

"Hell, man, Dink's older than that," came another crackling voice. "He's as old as the mud on the bottom of the Bay."

Laughter exploded over the CB as Dink Miller of Deltaville headed out of Dividing Creek on Virginia's Northern Neck at 5:30 A.M. in his classic Chesapeake Bay forty-two-foot wooden deadrise clam boat, the *Mary Joan*, bound for Tangier Lump in the Bay.

"Yeah, yeah, I hear ya boys. You're right, I'm the oldest, but I'm also the best looking of the whole bunch of ya," said Dink coming back across the CB.

At sixty-one, Dink is one of the oldest clammers around. He started working clams back in the late 1940s right after he bought his boat. The *Mary Joan* was built by Ed Hudgins of Onemo, Virginia, in 1948. "She's got a solid log keel in her," says Dink. "Lord, boy, she's gotten me out of a many a spot on this Bay."

Dividing Creek is a small tributary that empties into the Bay. Ordinarily it's not a home port of a clamming fleet, but with the recent slump in the oyster industry and an accidental discovery of some clams in that area last spring, the creek is now home for about eight clam boats.

Dink Miller, sixty-one, is one of the older of Virginia's hard clammers.
Dink started working a pair of patent tongs in the 1940s.

The Mary Joan *is a classic Bay deadrise workboat that Dink had built in 1948 by Ed Hudgins of Onemo, Virginia.*

For several years, clammers have known there was a strike of clams off Tangier Lump, near Tangier Island, Virginia, in the middle of the Chesapeake Bay, but last spring when a gill netter brought up a cluster of small clams from just over the edge of the lump, in seventy feet of water, a new ground was discovered. At first glance it seemed a minor find, but watermen soon realized there were plenty of clams for the taking in the deep ship channel.

"These are all fairly new clams," said Dink having now left the creek and reached the Bay. "Ya see, hard clams grow best in salty water and the recent drought has helped us clamming boys.

"The water is salty and we're seeing clams in places we have never seen them before."

Dink also realizes that there are more folks looking for clams than ever before. "Twenty years ago, I was the only one this side of Gwynn Island messing with clams. Now, everybody on the Bay wants them.

"We've even got one coming all he way from Richmond, Virginia, now to go clamming," says Dink about one of the younger watermen. "He goes back and forth every day (a 120-mile round-trip drive). He's a snapper, ain't he? Lord, boy, a crippled black duck gets more sleep than he does."

Dawn was still to come as Dink watched his Loran. "I was down on the York River dredging oysters when I learned about clamming. Some of the boys were doing it there and I gave it a try."

Dink sold his clams then to a buyer named Dan Elliott. "Back then, you couldn't sell no little ones (top necks). We'd throw them overboard. Now we can't sell no big ones (chowders). It was just backwards. There were more clams, too. I can remember down on the James River in the 1950s we would catch sixteen thousand little ones a day, now we're lucky to catch sixteen hundred. We were getting eighty cents for a hundred [clams] then. Don't sound like much, but we could do something with a dollar then."

The market price for clams on this day had top necks (clams about the size of a silver dollar) selling for fourteen cents and cherries (clams that are slightly larger) at seven cents. There was no market for the larger chowders.

Tangier Lump was still a good distance away as dawn broke over the horizon. "We're going to get some rain today," he said as voices began to crackle across the CB.

"Hey, boy, ya going to put me on a hot goose today?" asked one of the watermen.

"Yeah, man, I plucked that hot goose yesterday," came another voice.

Dink explained that the second clammer had caught a big load of clams. "When they say 'I'm on a hot goose' it means they're on some clams," he said with a smile that never seems to leave his face.

As the full light of day came, it was clear the day would be overcast at best. Suddenly, Dink throttled the engine down. "Well, boy, we're here," he said. "Now I'll show you how to catch a mess of clams."

Dink's clam rig is typical of the mechanical gear used in Virginia waters to harvest hard clams. His rig runs off the main engine, but Dink recalls when "donkey" engines were used to haul the patent tong. "Now that was some work. All we do now is pour it on the main engine. Anyone can work these rigs. All ya got to have is a strong back and weak mind," said Dink with a laugh. The clammer covered himself with a wet suit and went about the task of catching clams.

A GM (four-cylinder, 53 cubic inches per cylinder) engine hummed along as a chain weight over the stern helped slow the forward movement of the vessel to just the right pace.

Each lick seemed to produce a few clams, but not what Dink thought it should be. "The tide ain't right," he said as the rain began to fall.

The up-and-down motion of the tong continued until lunch, when Dink decided it was time for a break. There were five bags of top necks caught by lunch. Each bag holds two hundred clams.

"Well, we got us a thousand," he said, pulling out his sandwich. "I hope we can get another thousand by quittin' time."

The rain was steady and many of the clammers were inside by their CBs. "I wish I hadn't come out here today," said a voice over the radio.

With a loud laugh, Dink grabbed the mike and said, "Boy, if I had your money I'd go home too."

Throughout the day, Dink worked in the Bay's cut channel raising and lowering his patent tongs.

Clams continued to come on board at a steady pace when suddenly, at about mid-afternoon, the boat jerked down toward the water as Dink made a lick.

"Rock . . . big one," he yelled over the engine noise.

A rock the size of a basketball surfaced in the dredge. "Darn it," said Dink as he tossed the rock overboard and pulled a broken tooth from his tongs "Cracked the weld."

Throughout the day, the clammers on the CB alerted one another of oncoming ships. "We got to get out of the way," said Dink. "We're in the ship channel."

About that time, a Toyota automobile carrier, the size of three basketball courts, came barreling down the Bay. The CB started blasting. "Get out of the way, boys, here comes a big one."

"What do you think she'd do to ya if she hit ya?" asked Dink. "Might bruise the ol' boat . . . ya think?"

At around 3:30 P.M. Dink pulled up his tongs with eighteen hundred top necks and two hundred cherry clams on board.

With two thousand clams, he headed for home in the thickest of fog. His Loran setting was on the first buoy into Dividing Creek and was 5.2 miles away.

"Boy, she's thick, ain't she," he said. "I hope we can find our way in that creek."

The only movement on the water was an occasional duck lifting off to clear itself from the oncoming deadrise.

Dink had little rest, pausing only for lunch and between hauls, but he landed two thousand clams before calling it a day.

"Boy, I hope this Loran is on target or we could end up in Maryland," he said with that smile that never went away.

Finally, the first buoy of Dividing Creek was in sight but the others were covered by the fog. Dink inched his boat along until each buoy was in clear view. "I guarantee I'm going to put a reading on every one of these buoys," he said, shaking his head.

Back at the dock, Dink examined his catch. "We done all right, boy. We caught us a good mess! Not as a good as I have done, but not bad."

Dink loaded the bags full of clams into the back of his pickup truck and hauled them off to a buyer in Deltaville.

Virginia's wild clam patent tong fishery is for the most part inactive today as aquaculture (farmed clams) have taken over the lion share of that market. Wilbur Denvy "Dink" Miller died April 24, 2008. His wife, Shirley, asked me to speak at his funeral and I did so out of the great respect I have for Dink, who loved life and loved to work the water.

CHAPTER THIRTEEN

RUNNERS (BUY BOATS)

I remember when I was a youngster growing up in Urbanna, there were buy boats named Grace, John Branford, Muriel Eileen, *and* P. E. Pruitt. *They were just part of the everyday decor on the creek in the 1950s. Like so many other things, no one really paid much attention to these large freight vessels until the age of buy boats had pretty much passed and they were gone from the creek.*

I first did a story on buy boats for a magazine in 1985, but I have admired them for most of my life. Paul Pruitt, who graciously agreed to help on this chapter, is as knowledgeable on buy boats as anyone on the Chesapeake. He has also been one of those folks who has encouraged me over the years to record the history of the Bay and has set a fine example in life for others with his kindly, good-natured approach to living.

When considering the "ol'" working vessels of Chesapeake Bay, most people think of log canoes, schooners, sloops, rams, bugeyes, and skipjacks. But another such vessel, one that's still plying the water of the Chesapeake, is the deadrise "buy boat," which some refer to as the "bay boat" or "run boat," or "runner," or "deck boat."

The first buy boat on the Bay was probably a one-log dugout canoe that an early settler used to scull or paddle out into a cove, where he would barter for fish or oysters with native Americans. There was, however, not much need for buy boats in the early colonial days of Virginia and Maryland. During those years, virtually all plantations and towns were situated on or near a body of water. Slaves could easily be used to work the Bay for its fish and shellfish, and the less wealthy could catch their own seafood with relative ease.

But, with the coming of more settlers and the forced relocation of the American Indian away from the coast, the nation began to spread inland. As centers of population and commerce evolved, fewer and fewer people had the capability to catch their own seafood. Many began purchasing fish and oysters from local watermen, either directly off their boats or from the back of an oxcart or horse-drawn wagon.

Then a few entrepreneurs began buying wholesale from watermen and selling retail to the general public. Some had their own storefronts, while others had large boats that they filled with fresh seafood purchased from pound netters or shaft tongers. They would then carry the product back to a dock in a city or town, and sell it to anyone willing to pay the price.

Hand tongers gather around the buy boat Margarett *delivering their daily harvest of oysters. Buy boats, such as the* Margarett, *are used in the oyster industry to purchase oysters from oystermen and deliver them to packinghouses where the oysters are shucked for market. (Photo by John Frye, taken in the 1960s)*

As fish, crab, and oyster sales began to expand on the Bay, oyster shucking houses, crab and herring processing plants, and various other seafood facilities evolved, too.

These early plants, however, were often some distance away from the rivers and coves where particular species were being harvested. And, in those days, watermen were working the Bay in twenty-five-foot to forty-foot sail-driven log canoes, boats that were certainly not suitable for carrying heavy catches over long distances on a daily basis.

Land transportation was primitive at best, and roads were poor. A trip to market some sixty miles over land was completely impractical for a watermen with a load of fresh fish and no ice or refrigeration to keep it from spoiling. The buy boat provided the answer to the need for some means to gather and transport seafood, and it played an important role in the development of the Bay's seafood industry.

Various types of sailing vessels, including schooners, sloops, and bugeyes, were used as buy boats prior to the introduction of the internal combustion engine. A description of buy boats from an 1880 U.S. fish report:

> Connected with the tongers, and each dependent upon the other, is a branch of the trade conducted by vessels generally known as runners, of which

there are owned in this state (Maryland) about two hundred, carrying about eight hundred men. The oysters caught by tongers are either sold to these vessels, and by them carried to some market in the state, or they are bought by boats owned in other states and carried to northern cities.

The runner will anchor near some tonging ground, an empty basket or a small flag will be hoisted to the masthead as a signal that she is ready to receive oysters. In one or two days she will be loaded and is at once off for a market. On some occasions half a dozen or more runners may be seen in the same locality surrounded by forty or fifty canoes. As soon as a tonger has caught as many as his small boat will carry, he sells out to the runner and returns to work. The men employed on runners will average about $18 a month, including their board, which, with the pay of the captain (about $50 a month), will amount to $166,400 for a season of eight months, that being the length of time that these vessels are engaged in carrying oysters.

Early on, runners came from up north. For instance, in the mid-1880s, the Van Name brothers, who ran an oyster business by that name on Staten Island, New York, for over a half century, regularly sent Capt. Dave Van Name down to the York River on the Chesapeake in a schooner. He would buy oysters and sail them back to the family operation in New York.

The oyster industry of this period was not alone in using schooners as buy boats. Tangier Island entrepreneurs bought fish from local pound netters and hauled them to the docks in Washington D.C., where they were sold off the boats.

At the end of the nineteenth century, the oyster industry on the Bay was in its heyday. Owners of the early shucking houses, however, were often involved in a variety of different endeavors. Besides their oyster operations, some also had a striker house and a tomato canning factory along the shore.

Many operators owned their own sailing craft, which bought and hauled oysters in the winter months and seed oysters and herring in the spring. When they weren't handling seafood, some of the schooners would haul canned tomatoes to Baltimore and maybe a load of local lumber to Norfolk. Since overland trucking had yet to evolve, there was plenty of business.

But it was with the introduction of the internal combustion engine that the buy boat came into its own. When it became available, many of the old sailing craft were refurbished to handle power and were set up like today's buy boats, with the house aft, a high deck, and a sturdy mast/boom configuration. Although the early engines had a considerable impact on the seafood industry on the Bay, power plants like Lathrop, Atlas, and Fairbanks-Morse could not push the large (fifty-five-foot and over) vessels very fast. Indeed, during the 1920s and 1930s, many buy boats had a sail for auxiliary power and to provide stability when loaded and underway.

• • •

Paul Pruitt has worked on and owned buy boats throughout his working career as a Bay waterman.

Paul E. Pruitt of Urbanna (formerly of Tangier Island) worked as a young man with his father aboard a buy boat. He later owned a good example of the type of boat, the fifty-nine-foot *P.E. Pruitt*, which was later named the *Thomas W.*

This traditional buy boat had a square sail measuring sixteen feet on the gaff. "It was a lot prettier than a sharp (jib-headed) sail," said Paul, who had his sail made at a loft in Crisfield. "We'd hoist it sometimes going across the Bay," he recalls. "But those sails were right much trouble. When there would come a hard summer rain, they'd mildew if we didn't get them up soon to dry right after the storm.

"When we got decent power, most everyone stopped using the sail," said Paul. "It would help, though, to keep the boat steady and to keep her from rolling. It also helped us go."

In addition to her sail, the *P. E. Pruitt* had a three-cylinder, thirty-six-horsepower Lathrop—"one of the best ever made," according to Paul. "I once ran her from North Carolina to Baltimore in thirty-eight hours freighting watermelons, and she was steady plucking," he said. Though substantial in overall length, Pruitt's vessel carried only about eight hundred bushels of oysters, while larger buy boats would hold fifteen hundred bushels. Still, she was more than equal to her many tasks, one of which turned out to be freighting potatoes from Onancock, Virginia, on the Eastern Shore to Washington,

The Thomas W. *originally the P. E. Pruitt, was still plying the waters of the Bay in 1985, working in the winter crab dredging fishery. Paul had her built at Crisfield in 1935. He sold her in the early 1970s and went to working crab pots in a much smaller deadrise.*

D.C., for twenty-five cents a barrel. The *Pruitt* also carried spuds to Crisfield, where they were loaded onto a train.

E.S. Pruitt, Paul's father, owned another buy boat, a fifty-five-foot, Poquoson, round-stern, log canoe with a fourteen-foot beam powered by both a two-cylinder, twenty-four-horsepower, Lathrop engine and a sail. The *Three Brothers*, as she was named, was used by the Pruitts to buy oysters, crabs, and fish, the latter coming from haul seiners near Crisfield and pound netters from New Point, Virginia. "I remember the time we bought 330 bushels of fish and iced them down with seven tons of ice," said Paul.

"Before Daddy started the [E.S. Pruitt] fish house in Baltimore, we would sell our fish there off the boat," he recalls. "Then they passed a law so we couldn't do that anymore. Daddy then rented the fish house for ten dollars a week, which made it even better for us because everyone else had to quit."

During the summer crab season, the Pruitts freighted hard crabs from New Point to Cape Charles, and in the winter they would haul oysters from the Potomac and Rappahannock rivers to the John Handy Co., in Crisfield. This establishment was a large shucking plant that produced a thousand bushels daily and was serviced by no fewer than four buy boats.

When Paul's father died around 1940, the E.S. Pruitt Fish House closed. Paul, however, continued to work his buy boat. In later years, the *P. E. Pruitt*, was used to buy bait for crab potters in Maryland. "I would buy alewives (menhaden) and small trout from pound netters near New Point and sell it to watermen on Smith Island, Maryland," said Paul. "The trout were too small for market. They were not the best crab bait, but the islanders would take anything they could get then.

When I first started buying fish from the pound netters around New Point, we were paying a half cent a pound for spot, croaker, and trout. But the fishermen all got together and had a big meeting and they wouldn't sell to us for any less than a penny a pound. Sometimes it went up to two or three cents, but it was never very high, way back. Spanish mackerel and flounder brought the biggest money—ten cents a pound.

Speaking of Christmas, one of the closest calls I ever had came during one of those hard winters in the thirties. I don't remember exactly what year it was, but it was before I was married. We had been out on the *Three Brothers* a-buying oysters. I was itchy to get home to Tangier before Christmas, so I decided to catch a steamboat out of Baltimore, because Daddy didn't want to leave right away. Well, it got good and cold and most everything was froze up solid. But the steamer, the *Eastern Shore*, was leaving anyway. She was an ol' side-wheeler that had seen her better days but she had a steel hull that would break the ice and I figured she could get me to Tangier.

Well, boy, was I wrong about that! As we headed on down the Bay, the hull of the steamer hitting up against the ice sounded like thunder during a bad summer storm. We were rolling this way and that. Then we got down to about Sandy Point Lighthouse and the ice shoved us up into shore, where we ran aground. To make things worse, the tide started pushing the ice up over the stern until it was so high I couldn't see over it. It was time to abandon ship and they didn't waste any time about it. They lowered us down in lifeboats and we had a time getting ashore because of all the ice.

When I got back to Baltimore, I was glad to see the ol' *Three Brothers* and my daddy's fish house. It took a while for the ice to leave and I felt stranded in Baltimore for most of that winter. But to tell ya the truth, I wouldn't ever ride on the ol' *Eastern Shore* again. She may have sunk after that, I don't know.

Yeah, I've seen a lot, when it comes to buy boats. But, boy, I'll tell ya something, everything has a season just like it says in the Bible. The steamboat, the sailing vessels— they had their season and they're all about gone. It's the same thing with the buy boat. Its season is near 'bout over.

Captain Paul Pruitt died December 28, 1996, at the age of 84. In 2003, Chesapeake Bay Buyboats was published, a book that I wrote dedicated to those wonderful deadrise boats and the culture surrounding it. Although Captain Paul was not alive to see it, he played a major role in helping me understand the significance of buy boats in regards to socioeconomics and the watermen's culture of the Bay.

CHAPTER FOURTEEN

OYSTER CAMPS, WATCH HOUSES, AND GUARD BOATS

Almost before I was able to walk, I had heard of my great-grandfather's oyster camp on Robinson Creek. George Heath had run a camp and store and raised his family on four acres just outside of Urbanna. One of his children was Minnie Heath Blake, who was my maternal grandmother. Another was Oleathia Heath Carlton, my great-aunt. Aunt Leaf, as I have known her all my life, was the inspiration for this chapter.

She told me early on about the camp and watch house that she visited as a child. If it was not for her, surely these tidbits of information on the oyster fishery would have been lost forever, because I doubt very seriously that I would have known to ask for information from others.

Following the Civil War, the economy of the South was devastated. Many a Confederate soldier arrived home in 1865 to find older folks and children barely able

This oyster watch house near Wachapreague, Virginia, on the ocean side of the Eastern Shore was once owned by Spinny Davis and was called the Davis watch house. It is now owned by the Virginia Institute of Marine Science. The structure is in disrepair but is a good example of the style of buildings that were once used up and down the Bay to stand watch over oyster grounds.

to look after themselves. But, for those who lived on the tributaries of the Chesapeake, the saving grace was often the rivers and creeks that flowed nearby. Besides the land, the water was the only source of food during those hard times.

Although many stories have been passed down about the tight times right after the war, this one probably reflects as well as any the realities of those days.

Charles H. Palmer, Sr., of Urbanna, had gone to war in 1862, with all the glorified hopes of helping bring victory to the South. Those dreams were soon shattered when the youngster, early in the war, caught a ball in his jaw at the Battle of Frayser's Farm (Battle of Glendale) in the Seven Days Battles near Richmond. He served out his tenure in the Confederate army working in the war offices in Richmond. After the city was evacuated and burned by fleeing Confederate troops, Palmer was captured and taken to the Union prison camp at Point Lookout, Maryland.

Sometime after General Robert E. Lee surrendered at Appomattox, the Yankees began releasing groups of prisoners on certain days. The release date was determined by alphabetical order of the first letter in the prisoner's last name. When the day finally came that all the men whose last names began with "P" were released, Charles made the journey home to Urbanna. When he arrived, he could hardly believe his eyes. His old home, which had once been neatly kept, was in shambles; his step-mother and father were nearly starved and frozen in the unheated house.

Like everyone else arriving home, Charles turned to the creek and river for help. Down on the shore was an old punt that he had used as a boy to fish and crab. His sculling paddle was still in the bottom of the boat and a pair of old oyster tongs in the shed. He took these and sculled out to the mouth of Urbanna Creek with the intention of catching a mess of oysters to eat. As Charles made a couple of licks, to his surprise and delight, he brought up some large oysters and several big chunks of coal. Unbeknown to him, a Yankee vessel had been captured by Rebel troops and sunk off the mouth of the creek during the war and its hold had been full of coal, now available for the taking. Over that winter, the Palmers had plenty of oysters to eat and coal to keep them warm. [Most likely the coal came from a Union schooner named *Golden Rod* captured "laden with coal" by rebel sailors and brought to Urbanna in August 1863.]

Many families like the Palmers, who had homes along the rivers, coves, and creeks of the Bay, began to depend heavily on oysters for food. The family oyster bed "just out yonder" in the water was an important part of the family's property and poachers were not treated with kindness. Interestingly, these family plots were not legal, but the practice continued to grow. By the 1890s, there was concern that there would be open warfare between oyster tongers trying to make a living off public grounds and those so-called oyster growers, who by then were claiming more and more grounds.

Oyster growers were taking oyster grounds most informally as markers were hardly ever used and no rent was being paid to the state. Also, large, out-of-state oyster firms were taking grounds for their own purposes. Whoever had the strongest arm was usually the one who ended up with the grounds. A man who had been tonging a rock for years and years suddenly had the end of a rifle telling him to stay away. These problems often ended up in court where, in most cases, the tongers would win.

But as more and more bloodshed occurred, there was an obvious need for the state to intervene in some manner. This was supported by many state officials and, in the early 1890s, the Virginia legislature authorized Lt. James Bowen Baylor, of the United States Coast and Geodetic Survey, to survey 143,000 acres of public grounds to help put an end to the bloodshed. Baylor was also instructed to survey another 110,000 acres to be set aside for private growing. These acres were to be owned by the state, but could be leased by growers for an annual rent. By 1894, Baylor had completed his survey and boundaries were then established for public and private oyster grounds in Virginia.

Over the years, oystering on public and private rock in Virginia led to several interesting practices. In the years before combustion engines, the sail-driven log canoe was the main vessel used by watermen. Since public grounds on some rivers produced more catch than others, watermen would often travel far to those more productive rivers.

With the poor overland transportation of the times, watermen could not travel to and from home on a daily basis. So, scattered along the banks of the more productive oyster-growing rivers were "oyster camps," or "shantytowns," where oystermen would live while working the river.

Later, as the present-day house/pilothouse configuration on deadrise workboats evolved, many watermen lived on their boats. But the sail-driven canoes were open boats and few had any type of house at all. When the combustion engine came along, masts were pulled from the old canoes and Model T and A engines (sometimes cut in half and reworked) were installed toward the stern, which allowed a small pilothouse forward.

As large numbers of oystermen came to the shores of these rivers, the oyster growers found that more and more of their oysters, then on their own legal private grounds, were disappearing. Since the state had not established any means of preventing such problems, the growers soon resorted to their own system of protection. They began building "watch houses" and using "guard boats" to patrol the grounds, particularly at night when most of the poaching occurred.

• • •

Oleathia Heath Carlton, now ninety, lives in the same house where she was born, on a small slice of land wedged between Robinson Creek and Heath's Cove, just a short way from the Rappahannock River. Her father, George Henry Heath, was a Civil War veteran who somehow came up with four hundred dollars not long after the war—an enormous sum of money for those days—to purchase the four acres and house where Oleathia now lives.

"Exactly how Pappy came up with four hundred dollars in those times has been a mystery to the family," said Oleathia. "To say the least, Pappy was an entrepreneur. One of the first things he did when he moved here was to start building shanties

During the August storm of 1933, a watchman and his wife were living in the Davis watch house. The story goes that the storm struck with such force that the watchman, a man named Justice from Locustville, Virginia, had to tie his wife to one of the pilings to keep her from being blown away. The watch house survived the storm and the Justices were spared.

along the shore, so during oyster season oystermen could come from Gloucester, King & Queen, Essex, and Mathews counties to rent from him. Once they started coming, he opened a little store and they naturally were his best customers during the oyster season." She continues:

Back then, it was all sail and they would sail from their homes in canoes. They didn't bring much. Don't guess they had much. They would bring hand tongs to work with, either a pine-tag or corn-shuck tick mattress to sleep on, and some brought their own stoves to cook on and to keep warm by. Pappy had some stoves in a few of the shanties. Some had chimneys but most of the time they'd stick a stove pipe through the wall to get the smoke out. If there was a chimney, it was on a shelf. [To save on bricks, chimneys were often built starting halfway up the wall rather than from the ground.] It's a wonder some of them didn't burn down, but the oystermen spent very little time in the shanties because they were on the river most of the time.

The shanties were built of board and batten and were all white washed. There was nothing inside except bunks built along the walls and a rough

Oleathia Heath Carlton

table. For chairs, they used old fish boxes and they had coal oil lamps for light. The roofs had wood shingles and there was no plaster inside. The oystermen would tack newspapers on the inside walls for insulation from the cold.

We had different size shanties. Some were one room, some two, and one had three rooms. Most of our people were Negroes and we looked forward to seeing the same ones every year. Back then, when I was a child, they [blacks] were all called uncles and aunts. They weren't really our uncles and aunts but we called them that. My favorite was Uncle Mum Montague. He was a small man and, oh, so nice and friendly. He always seemed to have the biggest smile on his face.

I recall that a photographer once came to camp. One would come once a year to take and sell photographs. When it was Uncle Mum's turn to get his picture taken, he couldn't get his thumbs right. I thought that was funny because most people can't get their hair right, but he couldn't get his thumbs right. He wiggled them and wiggled them until finally the photographer just snapped a picture.

Most of the oystermen were just like old friends and we children looked forward to seeing them every fall. They'd go home about Christmastime because the river was frozen and we'd have a long spring and summer before they would return.

Life in the oyster camps was not always pleasant and Oleathia recalls two tragic incidents that ended in sadness at her father's camp:

My brother, Joe, was seven years old when he found a loaded gun in one of the shanties. People carried guns on the water in those days because there were oyster pirates around. Everybody carried cash because they were paid with it and there were some dishonest men who would steal it if they had the chance. Well, this one man had left his gun on the table. Joe picked the gun up and it went off killing him on the spot. Oh, Pappy mourned over Joe. He picked up the gun, ran down to the cove and threw it into the water. Do you know that man came back looking for the gun and was mad because Pappy threw it in the creek.

There were nine of us children and Joe was number three. That was a rough time around home. Let me tell you.

Another sad thing that happened was when a young Negro boy drowned. We had a lot of young boys who worked on the canoes as culling boys. They were between eight and twelve years old. Many weren't there because they wanted to be either. You probably heard stories of the way men were forced to work on sail [dredge] boats and when the job was done they were paid off with the boom. [During the years when dredging for oysters by sail was in its heyday, men, often down on their luck, were "shanghaied" into working aboard a oyster dredge boat. Once the job was done, the more evil captains would sometimes kill them by maneuvering the boom of the rig into knocking them overboard, rather than pay them off.]

Many of the culling boys were kidnapped off the streets of Baltimore. The poor parents never knew what happened to them. This boy, who drowned, was one of those. He went down to the shore to get some water. There was an artesian well where water would bubble up out of the ground. Somehow, he slipped off a dock and drowned. When they found him, they tied him to a stake in the water to keep him from drifting away. Back then, the sheriff was the only one who could take him out of the water. For some reason, he took his own time getting there and that poor boy was left tied to that stake for several days. When they pulled him out, nobody even knew his real name.

"Camp life wasn't always easy, was it?" she said in deep thought. "Pappy passed away when I was five years old. He died in 1904 at the age of sixty-eight. Mamma kept the camp going for several years after that, but after a while they [oystermen] just stopped coming. I missed them—especially old Uncle Mum."

Not long after George Health passed away, Eva, his oldest daughter, was married to a Mr. Miller from Mathews County. Mr. Miller was a watchman on an oyster watch house not far from the Health's home place. Oleathia recalls, with fondness, going out to visit her sister, who, after the wedding, moved into her new home, which was built over the water:

Eva was the oldest of the nine children and she would be 101, if she were alive today. The watch house was on the other side of Balls Point at the mouth of Lagrange Creek (on the Rappahannock) and I used to love go out there. Of course, I was just a child and I thought Eva was so lucky to live out in the river. I'm sure, though, that we just went out on nice days.

The one-room watch house was built on big pilings and had a walk deck all the way around it so Mr. Miller could view the oyster grounds from every direction. The inside was very much like the one-room shanties that we had at the camp, but Eva had it fixed up real nice. There was a wood cookstove and the furnishings were better than those in the camp but it was rough living compared to today.

Oh, how I looked forward to going out there. Mamma would carry baked bread, pies, and other things out to them. I can remember us rowing out in the boat and I can still recall the sweet smell of the water around us mixed with Mamma' home cooking. Oh boy, were those good times. Eva didn't stay there long. They moved to Mathews and, oh, how I missed the Sunday afternoon boat rides to see her—so did Mamma and the rest of the family!

• • •

John Morey, seventy-eight, of Signpine, Virginia, built one of the last watch houses on the York River in 1953. A year later, Hurricane Hazel took her away.

I built her for Will Travis. He had a shucking house on Timberneck Creek [in Gloucester County] and he had some very productive beds just off from Mt. Folly on the York River. Someone had been taking a lot of his stuff [oysters], so he needed a good watch house.

The house was built on big pilings and I remember it was a real muddy bottom. When you put a piling down in soupy mud, you shove them down as far as you want and leave them through one flood tide. After that, the piling won't settle any more.

We worked from a twelve-foot wide by thirty-two-foot long barge. We'd carry all we needed on the barge for a day's work and then came on home in the evening. That way we wouldn't have to go back and forth for stuff.

The watch house was twelve feet by twenty-four feet and had two rooms. There was a kitchen and bedroom inside. The inside had sheetrock on the walls and there was quarter-inch plywood on the outside. There pilings were creosoted and made from rough pine. The roof was covered with wood shingles and the house was finished off right nice inside. A man would go out and stay a week at a time so they wanted it to be comfortable.

It was painted white naturally because white doesn't draw heat like some colors. You never see a boat painted green or black because those colors draw heat and will cause it to rot very quickly.

Inside the watch house, there was a four-burner kerosene stove for cooking and an oil burner for heat. Also, there was a six-foot-wide walkway around the house and four large windows on each side for a good clear view of the grounds. A man didn't have to go outside and look, he could see everything from inside the watch house.

[Hurricane] Hazel took her away, though. She wasn't there but one year. After the storm, we went over to see what was left. We never found a piece of her. We went to the shore where a northeaster would normally carry her, but there wasn't a piece of her anywhere to be found.

Will Travis had forty thousand bushels of oysters planted on those grounds, but Hazel caused most of them to die. After the storm, oysters were ricked six feet high in spots. I don't know how, but Hazel picked the oyster up off the bottom of the river and stacked them up. That was some storm. It was the last watch house I was to build. After Hazel, things just seemed to go from bad to worse in the oyster business.

• • •

J. J. (Jimmy Jones) Belvin of Bena, Virginia, has worked the water for most of his eighty-six years. Over the years, he has worked aboard some of the more famous vessels on the Chesapeake including, the *H.H. Conway*.

John Morey

During the latter part of the his career, Jimmy Jones worked for J. H. Miles & Company Inc., an oyster packing firm in Norfolk. He was skipper of the buy boat *Oysterman*, which was used by the company to buy and dredge oysters. Miles and Company had over eight thousand acres of oyster grounds under lease, from Ocean View to Mobjack Bay. While working for Miles, Jimmy often delivered supplies back and forth to Mile's watch houses on James River and to their guard boats on Mobjack Bay.

"One of the watch houses was right at Thomas Rock not far from the James River Bridge," said Jimmy. "I used to carry stuff out to the old man who worked it. I'd take him groceries and whatever he needed. There were several watchmen and one would stay out there until he got tired and another one would go out and watch."

They had to watch it like a cat watches a mouse because those tongers would try to sneak over the line. I think there were about seventy-five acres of ground there and it was a real good rock. The watchman had a little bateau with an outboard motor that he would use to go tell the tongers to get away from the line. If somebody went over, he would tell them to move and that it would make things bad on them both if they didn't.

The tongers knew he had a little something in there to protect himself with, either a pistol or a rifle. So, they would usually do what he said. But, you best believe if he didn't have that protection there would be trouble. You take three or four big oystermen on a boat, they could jump on him and whip him good.

The watch house was built on pilings out in the river and the watchman had to keep watch night and day. Sometimes he would leave on Saturday and come back on Monday because the tongers didn't work on weekends. There was a pier on one side of the watch house with steps leading upward to the walkway. The walkway went all the way around the house. The one at Thomas Rock had two rooms and a nice roof. It didn't leak a drop. It was comfortable and he [the watchman] had plenty to eat.

"Captain Rufus [Miles] saw to that. That's one fine man. He treated me good as my Daddy would," said Jimmy about his former employer.

Now, they had two guard boats. They were both about forty feet long and ten feet wide and driven by a gasoline engine. There was one in Mobjack Bay and another on the James. They would use boats where it was not suitable to have a watch house. The guard boats had a small house so, if the weather got bad, a man could get in out of it. There was no pilothouse though, like they build on plank boats today. The guard boats were used on the larger grounds like the three thousand acres in Mobjack Bay. You can't cover much with a watch house on three thousand acres, but a boat can get you around pretty quick.

The boat could also go where the tongers were working. If a bunch of oystermen were tonging in a spot, the boys in the guard boat would go anchor and watch and see if they went over the line. On large grounds the boat was the best, but on smaller grounds most people built watch houses. They were more comfortable and were there night and day, good weather or bad.

I never worked a watch house or a guard boat. I would think it would be mighty lonely work, but in those days you did whatever you could find to do. They were tight times.

I've hauled and planted as much as a hundred thousand bushels of seed oysters from the James River in one season on the old *Oysterman*. Before that, I ran the *H.H. Conway* for Captain Johnny Ward of Deltaville. She was built as a sailing schooner in 1883 and was named the *William Sommers* then. Ol man Harvey Conway bought her and changed her name. [The Conways were from Cambridge, Maryland, and had a fleet of vessels, many of which were named for members of the Conway family. The *H.H. Conway* had been converted to power when Jimmy was her skipper.]

I never knew any of Captain Rufus's watchmen to have much trouble, but you best believe if he hadn't had them out there, somebody would have robbed him blind.

Watch houses were used up and down the Chesapeake as well as on the ocean side of the Eastern Shore of Virginia. There are a few worn and battered houses still standing around the Bay, left as a reminder to us all that the oyster industry was once a thriving business.

Oleathia Carlton, John Morey and Jimmy Jones Belvin are all deceased. Spinny Davis's watch house near Wachapreague is all gone except for two poles. Mud flats and an occasional snow goose, occupy the site.

CHAPTER FIFTEEN

PLANTING SEED OYSTERS

My phone rang late one night in 1985. It was James H. Ward Sr., of Deltaville. He invited me to go out on his vessel, the Nellie Crockett, *the next morning bright and early to do a story on planting seed oysters. I was unable to go on that particular day, but asked him to give me a call when he came to town again, and I'd make every effort to do the story.*

Almost a year later, my phone rang again. It was James, and this time I was able to work things out so I could go out with him.

The first New England sailing vessels arrived on Chesapeake Bay around 1800 to try a new experiment. They were sent to see whether Bay oysters could survive the long voyage by sail back to New England and be successfully planted on northern oyster beds. The New England oyster industry was in decline and dealers there were looking for an alternative means of supplying a steadily growing demand for oysters in large northern cities.

Since the mid-1700s, due to the fact that much of their natural oyster stock had been depleted, New England oyster growers had been successfully planting seed and growing or bedding it on their own grounds. Aware that the Chesapeake held some of the most productive oyster grounds in North America, these packers decided to send vessels down to buy market-size and seed oysters from the James River and elsewhere. This was, perhaps, the first effort to grow bay oysters on beds set aside by man.

In an 1880 report on the nation's oyster industry, Ernest Ingersoll calls this experiment a success—at least initially:

> At its height, between 1850 and 1860, from 100,000 to 150,000 bushels were laid down in harbors near Cape Cod annually, which, if a fair proportion survived, would yield 300,000 to 400,000 bushels when taken up in the fall. The breaking out of the war of the rebellion, however, so interfered with the getting of oysters in the Chesapeake and so increased the expense that the business began to decline.

Ingersoll also describes the planting procedure used then:

> Fishing [vessels] or coastal vessels were chartered to go and get the oysters, which the captain buys from tongers in Maryland and Virginia, who surround

his vessel the moment he anchors, and rapidly pass up their measurefuls, receiving cash in payment. As soon as loaded, he sails away homeward. The round voyage takes from 25 to 30 days between the Chesapeake and Providence, [Rhode Island,] and a proportionately shorter time to nearer ports.

Vessels sailing to northern ports carry from 2,500 to 5,000 bushels at a cargo. When arriving at her destination her crew is re-enforced by as many additional men as can conveniently work upon her decks. Where feasible, she simply cruises back and forth across the designated ground and the oysters are shoveled over board by means of six-tined, shovel-shaped forks. In other cases, her cargo is expeditiously unloaded onto flat-boats, from which it is thrown broadcast upon the beds, while the schooner is hastening back on a second voyage. As a rule one vessel is chartered by several planters, each of whom pays in advance his part of her expenses and purchasing fund, and receives a proportionate share of the cargo.

After the Civil War, business with northern growers resumed, but many local oystermen, after seeing the success of the New England growers, began to plant their own seed and harvest them when they matured. This procedure was so successful that in 1894, the Virginia legislature authorized Lt. Baylor to survey the public and private oyster grounds in Virginia waters.

• • •

About the same time Ingersoll was writing his much-acclaimed report of the U. S. oyster industry, William Henry Ward, of Crisfield, was running seed oysters from one end of the Bay to the other in sail-driven sloops. His son, Will Ward, followed in his footsteps by hauling seed for nearly seventy-five years in the old schooner *Lula M. Phillips* and up until his death in 1989 Will's son, James H. Ward Sr., was hauling oysters on the Chesapeake in the buy boat *Nellie Crockett*.

When I visited with James in 1986 he said:

My daddy was eleven years old when he started working for my grandfather. He went to the fifth grade and then quit to work on the boats. My grandfather had several small sailboats. I think they were skipjacks and sloops. One of them was named the *Louise Travers*.

Grandfather would sail with my father from Crisfield to buy seed oysters on the James River, but in those days he was also using his boats to haul loads of potatoes in hundred-pound sacks, tomatoes in bushel baskets, watermelons, and lumber. Daddy used to tell me that Grandfather would also go around and buy junk iron and haul it to Washington, D.C., and Baltimore to sell. He told me once about the times they would sail to Gloucester County, Virginia, on the York River to buy junk and there he would often go ashore just to any old house. There, Grandfather would almost always come away with some good

The buy boat Nellie Crockett *is loaded down with seed oysters bound for private oyster beds on the Rappahannock River near Water View. The planting of seed is a tradition on the Chesapeake that goes back to the 1800s.*

hospitality and a free meal. Things were a lot different back then. Today, you'd get shot as soon as you set foot on somebody's property that they don't know ya.

I went to work on the *Lula M. Phillips* full time when I came out of the service in 1946. Besides hauling seed oysters, we were hauling some lumber, grain, and whatever else we could find. But the war [World War II] changed our business a lot. Trucks began hauling many of the things that we hauled. In fact, later on, about the only thing left for us were seed oysters. What lumber we were hauling came from Totuskey Creek on the Rappahannock River. It would take three and a half days to load up, twenty-four hours to get to Baltimore, a day to unload, and about twenty-two hours to get back to Totuskey for another load. We'd always unload on a Friday and go right back. It didn't make any difference then if it were Saturday or Sunday, we'd work right on through. Daddy had a 75-horsepower Fairbanks-Morse engine that was a lot bigger in size than the 450-horsepower I've got in the *Nellie Crockett.*

The *Lula M. Phillips* was built as the two-master schooner *Annie M. Leonard* at Oxford, Maryland, in 1877. Captain Will bought her in 1934 and ran seed in the

James H. Ward Sr., was owner and skipper of the Nellie Crockett
until his death in 1989.

Phillips until he retired in the early 1970s. She had been converted to power when he purchased her.

James and his father bought the *Nellie Crockett* in 1955. James bought his father's share out in 1966 to become full owner.

> Captain [Andrew A.] Shad Crockett of Tangier Island had her built in 1925 in Crisfield. He was hauling the same things my father and grandfather would haul—potatoes, tomatoes, watermelons, lumber, and seed oysters. I'll tell ya the truth; this ol' boat has been a good friend. Many a time, I've come down the Bay on those rough nights, ice making up on the rigging and deck, but she's always brought me home. I don't load her down, though, in the wintertime. I carry about 1,850 bushels in the winter and about 2,000 in the spring. The season lasts from the first of October until June 15. You've got to be careful in the wintertime because ice builds up on the boat when it goes up and down. I've seen six inches of ice on deck and that's a lot of weight. It pays to be conservative with a load in cold weather.

James still buys and plants seed the same way his father did and his father before him. He buys all his oysters from hand tongers. James buys most of his seed from the tongers on the James River, but has also bought some from tongers on the Piankatank and Great Wicomico rivers. Traditionally, these three Virginia rivers have produced the majority of the seed oysters used on the Bay because the salinity level is perfect for producing seed, but not particularly good for growing oysters to market size. The Rappahannock, Potomac, and York rivers, on the other hand, have the correct salinity level for growing large market-size oysters.

I know I do it the same way as it's been done for a hundred years, I guess. There are new ways of unloading. Some take a high-pressure water hose and blow them off the deck, while some growers have conveyors on barges that scatter the seed, but I do it the ol' fashion way of broadcasting it with strong backs and shovels.

Interestingly, Jame's method is not much different from the procedure described in Ingersoll's 1880 report.

I generally spend Saturday cleaning up the boat after a haul, so that at 3:30 A.M. Monday morning I'm on the boat making ready to go. I get outside Jackson Creek about 4:15 A.M. and it takes me about five-and-a-half hours to get to Deep Creek on the James River. If I've got a fair tide it doesn't take quite that long. When I get to Deep Creek, I go to the dock there to fuel up, buy ice and food, and by 10:15 A.M., I'm at my spot, all anchored, ready to buy oysters.

I've got several tongers that sell just to me. Some are old-timers who sold to my father. I'm real lucky to have good oystermen to buy from. You take on a good day, I can buy a thousand to eleven hundred bushels of seed. But most days, I guess we average five hundred bushels, so it takes three or four days to make a load. I got a power hoister, which my grandfather didn't have, to haul the measure up on deck. They used to have to haul the seed up from the log canoe with block and tackle by hand. Another difference today is I don't see any log canoes anymore. Most everyone now is using deadrise workboats. I can get two boats on each side of the *Nellie Crockett* and unload all four boats in a hurry.

On one of his October trips, after loading 1,822 bushels onto the *Nellie Crockett* from Deep Creek, James arrived at 1:00 A.M. on a Friday, in Urbanna, to pick up a crew of six men and wait for high tide. The load was to be delivered to grounds near Punchbowl Point on the Rappahannock. These are relatively deepwater beds, eight to ten feet at high tide, which offer plenty of depth for the Nellie Crockett to maneuver. [She draws five feet light and seven feet loaded.] At 8:30 A.M., the captain and crew left Urbanna on a rising tide.

On the way, James explained that, because of the depth of the water, seed could be broadcast from the deck of the *Nellie Crockett*. The large buy boat cannot touch bottom while seed is being spread because if mud is stirred up it could cover the

The seed is planted in the same manner that it has been for centuries, by board-casting oysters and shell over the grounds.

oysters and cause them to die. Therefore, in many areas farther upriver on the Potomac, Coan, Patuxent, etc., three small boats are generally used to scatter the seed. There oysters are taken off the *Nellie Crockett,* placed on smaller vessels, and spread across the beds by about a dozen men. "The small boats are able to get up in the corners and in areas that the *Nellie Crockett* can't go, but in deep water I can do it as well as the small boats," says James.

On arriving at the mouth of Parrotts Creek, James placed a call to the leaseholder of the grounds on his VHF radio, notifying him that the *Nellie Crockett* and its crew were ready to deliver. Shortly thereafter, he arrived to assist James in the unloading. They both stayed in the pilothouse as the buyer directed the *Nellie Crockett* across his 14½-acre oyster rock.

The vessel circled back and forth across the beds as the six men (three on each side) shoveled the oysters into the Rappahannock. With only an occasional break to light up a cigar, the men worked for an hour and a half steady until the load was all overboard. When the oysters were delivered and payment made, the *Nellie Crockett* headed back to the James River to load up once again.

When James first started delivering oysters with his father, they were selling seed to planters for fifty to sixty cents a bushel. Now, James charges about $4.50 a bushel

With only an occasional break, the men unloaded the Nellie Crockett
in an hour and a half.

for seed delivered in Virginia and about $6.38 a bushel in Maryland, where there is a
higher tax on seed oysters and more freight cost than in Virginia. He said:

> I deliver seed all over the Chesapeake—Maryland and Virginia. It's something
> that I've done all my life and I'm proud of my heritage. It's been an honest
> living for me, my father and my grandfather and I guess I'll keep on doing it
> as long as I'm able.

James Ward died of cancer in 1989 just before Harvesting was released in 1990. Today, the
Nellie Crockett *is owned by Theodore (Ted) Parish of Georgetown, Maryland and in 1994 was
designated a National Historic Landmark.*

CHAPTER SIXTEEN

BUILDING A CHESAPEAKE
BAY LOG CANOE

I was first introduced to William M. Rollins, Sr., in 1983. A relative of mine, Carroll C. Chowning Jr., in the marine engine business, had visited his shop in Poquoson, Virginia, and seen Bill's log canoe under construction. He relayed the news to me and the next day I went to Poquoson to see for myself.

I could hardly believe that I'd found a Chesapeake Bay log canoe builder who had learned the craft from an old-time master builder and was actually building a canoe. That first visit was the beginning of numerous visits to Rollins Boatyard; with Bill's help, I did several articles on his canoe that appeared in national and regional publications.

Five hefty logs, an old broad ax, a foot adz, a strong back, and a knowledge of Chesapeake Bay boatbuilding that spans three hundred years, that's what it takes to build a Chesapeake Bay log canoe.

No one knows this better than Bill Rollins, the last of the log canoe builders in Poquoson. Seventy years ago, when the log canoe was the primary vessel of Bay watermen, Poquoson was one of the Chesapeake's major boatbuilding centers. In those days, numerous backyard canoe builders were scattered along the marshy banks of the Back River near the mouth of the York. Bill's shop is the only one left.

Bill has been exposed to the tradition of log canoe building nearly all his life. As a sun-browned, barefoot youngster, he spent a lot of time watching and listening to the old-time boatbuilders in his neighborhood. Then, between the summer of his junior and senior years in high school, Bill worked for Clyde Smith, a noted builder of log canoes. It was under Smith's tutelage that he mastered the art of building these craft.

Old man Captain Clyde built the prettiest canoe in the country, and I modeled mine right after his. If a canoe has pretty lines, you can't tell the difference from the bow and the stern. Captain Clyde's were mighty pretty. It would take him about nine months to build one and, even then, he had to have plenty of help with the chopping to get it finished. When he worked at Bennett's Railway in Poquoson, he had a helper named Rooster. Rooster had a good eye for canoes too. So much of building a pretty canoe is having an eye for it.

I worked with Captain Clyde in the summer of 1943 at J.S. Darling's Railway in Hampton, Virginia. My Uncle Ed worked there and he got me the job. It was a good place for a boy to learn. Captain Clyde was a master builder and I

Indians were using log canoes when the first European settlers arrived in the New World, and Chesapeake Bay watermen used them to harvest the Bay well into the twentieth century. The Holly June *was the last canoe built in Poquoson, Virginia, once a center of log canoe building in the state.*

learned what I know from him. All the boys I worked with there are dead now. Even the young ones are gone. It's hard for me to believe all the canoe builders have passed away.

Bill later worked for the National Aeronautics and Space Administration (NASA), and for thirty years he only built boats in his spare time. Now retired, he operates his yard full time.

He and his son, Will, had talked for quite a while about building a log canoe, but didn't know where to find logs of the necessary size. They finally located five hefty yellow pine trees in Providence Forge, Virginia, and had them cut on a full moon.

The old-timers around here would always cut on a full moon. The sap travels up and down through a tree with the moon, so when you cut on a full moon there are fewer mildew problems with the finished product.

We selected five logs that were between eighteen and twenty inches in diameter, just right for a twenty-six-foot canoe," said Bill. "A twenty-inch-thick log gives you a right good size pole. Three of the logs were straight, while two had slight curves in the trunks. (See photo 1 on page 149.)

The center log or keel log requires the biggest tree and it must be relatively straight. The logs next to the keel are called garboard logs and these should also be straight. The bilge log, however, form the sheer of the boat and should be hewn from logs that are slightly curved (see drawings A, B, and C on pages 150 and 151).

The bilge logs fall into the curve of the boat and, believe me, if they've got the right curve it saves you from having to do a lot of chopping.

Yellow pine is all we've ever build canoes from because the tree is big, straight, and soft enough to hew. There are canoes built out of yellow pine that have been around for over a hundred years.

Years back, those big pine logs were not easy for canoe builders to move around. We used a tractor when they were outside in the yard and we used a block and fall to turn them when inside the shop. But the old boys did it different. In the evenings, they would get a bunch of men from the country store down the way or from around the neighborhood and they'd all push and shove to move them where they wanted them. That's something we've lost today—neighbors helping neighbors. There was a fellowship among men in those days. It was a fun time when they would all laugh and spin yarns and chaw a little tobacco. There was work to be done but it was also a time for a little socializing too.

The keel log is squared on all four sides and then shaped on the bottom, as in drawing A on page 150. The garboard log is squared on two sides where it butts to the seams of the keel and bilge log, and the bilge log is squared on one side where

it butts up against the garboard log. The logs are hewn to match each other, as seen in photos 2 and 3 on page 152. They are all shaped with a board ax, a foot adz, and a handsaw. To get a smooth, tight fit among the logs, Bill sets the logs up and runs through each seam with a handsaw. As he saws, tiny shims must be put behind the cut, so the logs won't fall down and pinch the saw.

The logs are cut rough but by sawing through the seams, the saw makes a matching cut. Once all the way through from fore to aft, it should give the logs a smooth fit.

The fit should be reasonably tight but after the hull is put in the water it swells together and if any weeping is left it can be caulked.

Once the logs are shaped, each side is bolted together with $^{7}/_{8}$-inch galvanized bolts as in drawing C on page 151. Ten bolts, five on each side, are equally spaced throughout the hull to fasten it together. "The old boys didn't do it this way," said Bill. "Way back, they used pins or trunnels of locust wood and later they used steel bolts. Each log was individually fastened to the next log, whereas we counterbore into the bilge log and keel log and run one bolt through all three."

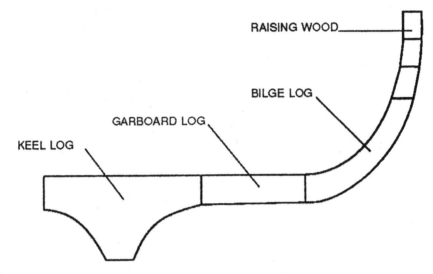

RAISING WOOD

BILGE LOG

GARBOARD LOG

KEEL LOG

Drawing A

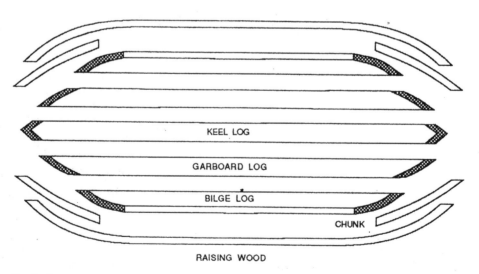

KEEL LOG

GARBOARD LOG

BILGE LOG

CHUNK

RAISING WOOD

Drawing B

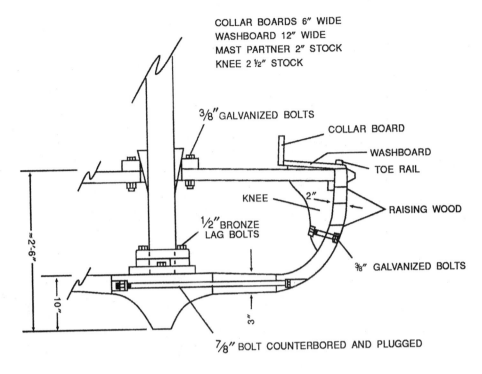

COLLAR BOARDS 6" WIDE
WASHBOARD 12" WIDE
MAST PARTNER 2" STOCK
KNEE 2 ½" STOCK

3/8" GALVANIZED BOLTS

COLLAR BOARD

WASHBOARD

TOE RAIL

KNEE — 2"

RAISING WOOD

1/2" BRONZE LAG BOLTS

3/8" GALVANIZED BOLTS

≈ 2'-6"

10"

3"

7/8" BOLT COUNTERBORED AND PLUGGED

Drawing C

After the hull is together, the inside has to be chopped out and smoothed down, as in photo 4 on page 153. The garboard log is chopped with a foot adz until it is 3 inches thick and the bilge log is chopped down to 2½ inches. Bill is able to get it to the proper thickness by using the same technique as the canoe builders of old.

Say, I want the bilge log to be 2½ inches thick the entire way. I drill ½-inch holes, 2½ inches deep all along the bilge log from the bottom. Then, I take ½-inch wooden dowel rods 2½ inches long and drive them in the holes.

Once this is done, I get inside the hull and start chipping and chopping. When I chop down to where I hit the top of a dowel, I know I've gone deep enough. You can't fool them old boys. This method came right from the colonists.

The next step is to shape the bow and stern. Since it is nearly impossible to get five logs to all meet on the ends, Bill has to square off the bilge and part of the garboard log so "chunks" or short planks can fill out the pointed "deadrise" ends (see photo on page 154 and drawings B, page 150, and D, page 154). The chunk is made of yellow pine and is fastened with ½-inch galvanized drift bolts, driven through the chunk into the hull.

Photo 2

Photo 3

Photo 4

At this point the twenty-six-foot-by-seven-foot hull is faired and smoothed to look like a finished hull. The next step is to raise the sides to the desired height. Bill does this by installing "raising" wood along the top edge of the bilge logs and chunks (see drawings A, B, C, and D). The raising wood is made from two-inch-thick yellow pine, and five to six-inch galvanized drift bolts are used to fasten the wood to the bilge log.

Once the raising wood is in place, knees, two feet apart, are fastened with ⅜-inch carriage bolts to the inside of the bilge log and nailed to the raising wood (see drawing C and photo 6). The knees are cut to shape from 2½-inch white cedar, which is different from the way the old builders would shape knees, Bill told me. Years back, canoe builders would search the woods for a branch or limb that was still fastened to the trunk of a tree. "They would cut and chop it out in one piece to form a ninety-degree angle," said Bill (see photo 7, page 156).

The advantage of cutting it out in one piece is that the grain is running two ways and the knee does not have to be pieced together. Anytime you cut wood against the grain, it leaves a weak place and the old boys knew this. The knees must be strong because they support the washboards. Oystermen stand

Photo 5

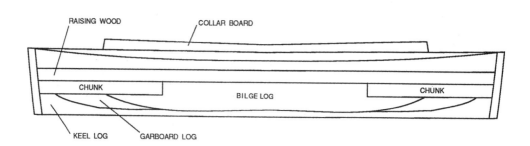

Drawing D. (Drawing by Ray V. Rodgers III)

on the washboards of a boat as they work [hand tongs]. They must have a strong platform.

The washboards are fastened with nails to the top edge of the raising board and knees (see drawing C, page 151, and photo 8, page 157). Bill makes his washboard twelve inches wide, which was pretty standard on early canoes. "It often depended on the size of a man's foot," said Bill. "The washboard had to be wide enough so a man's feet could fit between the coaming (collar board) and the toe rail. If a man had big feet, he'd order a wider washboard. You don't see too many men though with feet over twelve inches long," said Bill with a chuckle.

A six-inch-wide collar board is attached to the inside edge of the washboard and a one-inch-wide toe rail runs along the top outside edge (see drawing C). "We used white cedar for the washboards, collar, and toe rail and covered it all with a coat of fiberglass, but the old boys used yellow pine for it all," he said.

The stems on the bow and stern are made from fir. The bow stem is thirty-eight inches long and the stern stem is thirty-five inches. The stems are fastened with ½-inch drift bolts, countersunk and plugged. "I made sure there is no metal exposed to the weather on the stems," he said [see photo 9, page 158].

Once the basic hull is finished, Bill takes a chain saw and cuts a 3½-foot-long, ½-inch-wide slot through the keel log for the center-well (see photo 10). The centerboard was fabricated by Bill out of ¼-inch stainless steel plate and the center box is 4 foot by 2 foot and is $^5/_{16}$-inch thick. The center box is made of fiberglass, but naturally in the old style it was made of wood (see photo 11 and drawing E).

The mast is twenty-six feet long and the boom is thirteen feet long. Both are made from white cedar. "It was always a rule of thumb that the length of the mast and the length of the keel log be the same," he said. "Now, I know some canoes built for racing have taller masts, but a work canoe most always had the same length mast and keel." The mast is 5 inches in diameter at the base, while the circular shape is carried up to the top where it is 2¾ inches in diameter.

"There are two ways of attaching the mast," explained Bill. "Nine out of ten builders bring the mast up through a seat, which is what I do. Others would chisel a hole in the keel, where the mast would fit tightly down into it." In both styles, a "mast step" or box is built around the base of it to give additional support (see photo 12, page 161). The mast step is attached to the hull with ½-inch bronze lag bolts, drilled into the keel log.

Bill also installed a mast partner, which is made from two-inch fir stock and attached around the mast where the seat and mast come together. The mast partner is fastened with $^3/_8$-inch galvanized carriage bolts and three wedges are fitted between the mast and mast partner (see drawing C, page 151 and photo 13, page 162). "Wedging a mast goes back to Bible days," said Bill. "By driving wedges between the mast and mast partner, it gives the mast room to breath. It allows expansion and contraction when the mast is under pressure of hard winds. When it gets really rough, the lee wedges will loosen up and they must be tapped back down with a maul."

Photo 6

Photo 7

Photo 8

Photo 9

Photo 10

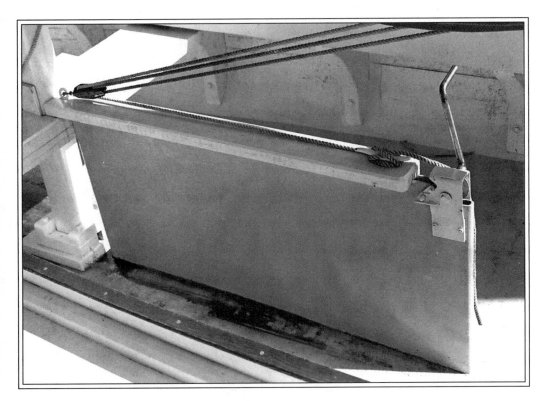

Photo 11

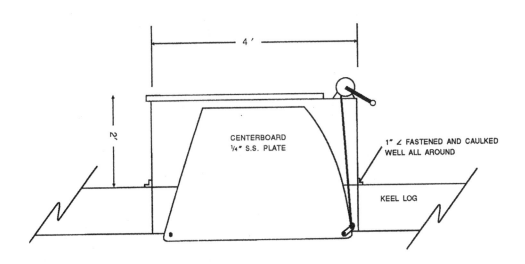

CENTERBOARD
¼" S.S. PLATE

1" ∠ FASTENED AND CAULKED
WELL ALL AROUND

KEEL LOG

4 '

2'

Drawing E. (Drawing by Ray V. Rodgers III)

Bill used a modern Marconi sail rig as opposed to older styles. "There were a thousand different rigs on the old canoes. Every builder did something a little different, but most had wooden hoops around the mast with the edge of the sail fastened to the hoops so it could be raised and lowered. They had some awful-looking sail rigs on those boats."

The rudder is cut from ¾-inch exterior plywood and covered with several layers of fiberglass (see photo 14, page 163). "The old boys had to dowel their rudders together because they seldom had a single board wide enough to make a rudder [see photo 16 page 164]." The tiller is made of oak and boxed into the top of the rudder.

The two-inch-by-four-inch, five-foot-long bowsprit is made from a piece of white oak and extends out three feet from the end of the bow. All standing rigging is ¼-inch stainless steel cable. The turnbuckles and other hardware are also stainless (the photo at the beginning of the chapter of Holly June shows how the boat is rigged). A galvanized chain bobstay and sprit braces extend from the sprit to the bow (see photo 15).

Bill installed seats fore and aft with lockers for storage under the bow and stern decks. "Most of the old canoes had some space under the bow for storage and generally enough room for a man to get in out of the weather," he said. "Once they started using motors, the masts were cut off and there was enough room for a little pilothouse. Early motors were placed as far aft as possible so there was room amidship for the culling boys to work.

I built this canoe as a tribute to the old-timers who built these things that I knew as a boy. Those were different times, and although it seems like a long time ago, it really hasn't been that long ago. I thank the Good Lord for giving me the opportunity to learn those old-timey ways from men such as Clyde Smith and others. They're gone now, but my canoe is a symbol of a way of life that was fair and honest. They were simple ways—a man did a hard day's work and the river and the Bay looked after him. A man's worth was determined by his goodness as a human being, not by the amount of money he made.

I miss those times. I guess we're better off now in some ways. But, they were truly wonderful days on the Chesapeake.

When Bill Rollins passed away, Bill Hight, who worked with me on the book Chesapeake Bay Buyboats, *and myself attended his wake in Poquoson. At the funeral home sitting on top of his casket was a model of the* Holly June.

Photo 12

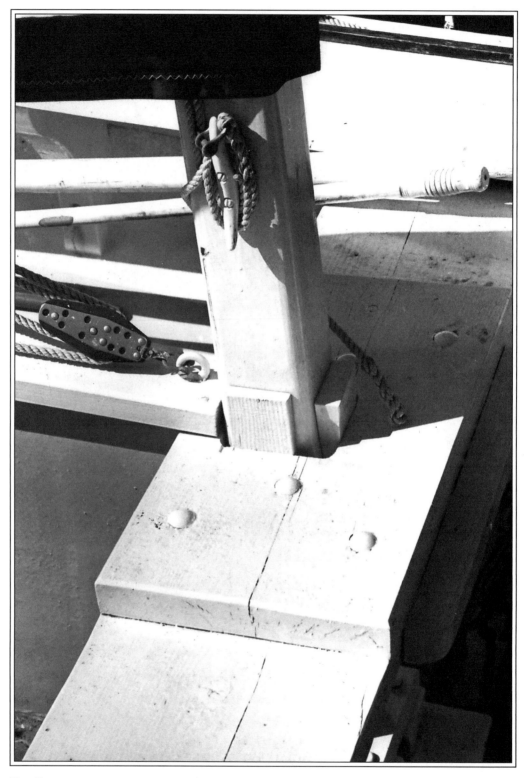

Photo 13

Photo 14

Photo 15

163

Photo 16

CHAPTER SEVENTEEN

THE MEN WHO SAILED
LOG CANOES

When I first started working on this chapter I thought it would be difficult to find men who had worked aboard sail-driven canoes. I was aware of one—my grandfather Raymond Blake—and I heard from him over and over again about his younger days aboard "sailing canoes."

I was surprised, however, to find that there were many others still around who had worked aboard vessels. So many, in fact, that I couldn't include all of them in this narrative.

My grandfather died in 1989 at the age of ninety. He had lived his life completely; his roots had been the land and the water and he had spent most of his life working them. Well into his eighties, he could still tong up a mess of oysters as fast as a man half his age. This chapter is dedicated to his memory.

These sail-driven log canoes are typical of the style used on Chesapeake at the turn of the twentieth century and before. (Courtesy of Dr. A. L. Van Name, Jr., and the Mariners Museum)

The earliest workboat used in the New World was the Chesapeake Bay log canoe. Log boats were being used by Indians who inhabited the shores of Maryland and Virginia when the first settlers arrived on the scene in 1607. Early drawings show First Americans in single log canoes spearing fish and harvesting the then-bountiful waters of the Bay.

Early on, Indians would burn out and scrape logs to make primitive single log canoes. Over the years, however, the Chesapeake Bay log canoe evolved into a very efficient means of transportation and was used extensively by watermen to fish, crab, and oyster.

When most of the virgin timber along the banks of the Chesapeake was cut, the white man began to use three, five, and even seven, logs fastened together with trunnels (locust pins) to reach the desired size of the canoe needed to work the water. The success of the canoe is evident by its longevity. The Chesapeake Bay log canoe was used by Bay watermen well into the twentieth century and when combustion engines came along many were converted. Some motor powered canoes were still in use during the 1960s and 1970s.

Those men who worked log canoes under sail had a different lifestyle than today's Chesapeake Bay watermen. During the first few decades of this century, in many rural areas of the South, hard times were very much a part of the lives of the people. Generations had seen little improvement in their standard of living. Many blacks had either been slaves or were the children or grandchildren of slaves. Most blacks and whites alike lived in a form of poverty that allowed them few material luxuries, but seldom left them hungry at mealtime. Going to school was not a top priority for many of those living in these areas and most young boys, eleven to twelve years of age and younger, would go to work to help the family make ends meet. Their choice of jobs included working in the woods cutting and stacking cordwood, pulling fodder in the fields, or culling oysters on a log canoe. Many worked with their fathers, while others were guided by their mothers as to when they went to work and who they worked with.

• • •

For Clemmon Brown, it was his mother who directed him to go to work at the age of nine culling oysters on a sail-driven log canoe.

Clemmon reminisced :

Well, just about every little barefoot black boy had to go to work when he was old enough. When I was nine, I went to work on a twenty-six-foot sail canoe that belonged to Charles Burrell. After each day, he would give me a dollar to carry home to the family and ten or fifteen cents for me to keep. He was the first one to teach me to cull oysters and when I was young I would work until it got real cold in the winter; then Mama wouldn't let me go anymore.

Clemmon Brown

Charles Burrell was a good man and he talked to me a lot while we worked. He schooled me about things that I've since learned to be very important. He'd tell me things like "you've got to have respect for yourself first to have respect for others." I guess he was in his late thirties back around 1918 when I was working for him.

We had four or five sandbags in the boat that we would throw up on the washboard when the canoe was under sail and leaning to one side. The bags would keep her from tipping over. I can hear him now, "Get it over there! Get to over there, boy!" he'd say. I'd grab a bag and tote it to the other side of the boat. It weighed about fifty pounds, which was heavy for me.

Charles would pack his lunch in a jar, and Mama would fix mine. We had plenty to eat. I'd carry chicken or fried ham, jelly biscuits—plenty of food. He kept a jar of blackstrap molasses under the bow deck and we would sop our bread in it. That was dessert mostly. Most of the boats had a jar or can of molasses tucked under the bow and it was extra good on hot biscuits.

We were always concerned about bad weather and a many a time when it got to storming we'd beach the canoe and run for the nearest tree or shelter if there was one nearby. Then, we would wait until the storm was over and head back out. On bad weather days when we wouldn't oyster, Mama would send me to school. I learned to read and write in a little one-room schoolhouse. I would walk to school and it was about eight miles round-trip. I went until I was fourteen years old and then went on the river full time.

Oysters were selling for about twenty-five or thirty-five cents a bushel and sometimes we couldn't sell them at that. Big buy boats would come in the river and raise a flag to let us know they were buying, and if they raised another flag it meant they were paying a nickel more than anyone else. Towards the last of the season, we could hardly give them away. If the wind was dead, we would scull and row from Mud Creek (on the south side of the Rappahannock) across the river to Morattico to sell oysters for twenty-five cents a bushel. We had more oysters than we could eat and with the season going out we wanted every penny we could get.

We had two sets of tongs on board. One had twenty-foot shafts and the others were twenty-two feet. One of my jobs was to make sure there was a good mop on board all the time. I'd go in the woods and find a good piece of hickory to pull a hickory mop from. I've pulled a many a one and they would stay nice and soft to wash the boat up with. We never had to buy one because I could make them, but a lot of the boys had to buy theirs. The mop makers would have them in the bow of their boat with the mop heads sticking up so everyone could see.

During the 1920s, there were so many canoes on the river you couldn't look around and not see one. Oystermen would come from all over to catch a mess on the Rappahannock. Most every creek had an oyster camp where the boys would come from Mathews and Gloucester counties or Tangier Island and rent a shanty for the winter. Usually a storekeeper would have the shanties for rent because it was also good for store business. All those boys brought with them are the clothes on their backs, tongs, an old tick mattress filled with pine needles to sleep on, and a quilt or two to cover them up on cold winter nights.

•   •   •

At ninety-five and a half years of age, Henion Brown remembered well the days of sail-driven log canoes. Henion worked with his father in a small open canoe and also in a larger "deck boat," the hull of which was made from logs. The deck boat, named *Annie*, was about forty-five feet long. Henion's earliest recollection goes back before the turn of this century when he was but a lad.

When I was real small, Daddy had a small canoe that he used to fish his pound nets in the York River and Chesapeake Bay. Sometimes when we were coming home, he would start cleaning a fish, and I would be steering her home. He was a great sport and loved to race. Racing was a great thing in those days and there was no record of Daddy ever losing a canoe race. If there was another boat ahead of us, he'd look back at me and say, "Son, catch 'em." I'd say, "I'm doing all I can do, Daddy." "Give her to me, boy," he'd say and take the helm and shoot right on by the other canoes. He'd always laugh and say, "That's how you do it, son." Daddy was a real small fellow with a black mustache, but he was quite a man and he could handle a canoe.

Another time I recall was around 1901 when I was with him and some other men haul seining on the York River. We were in Daddy's canoe catching mostly menhaden. Daddy would sell the menhaden to farmers for fertilizer and would get ten cents a bushel for them. You figure they would catch about a hundred bushels, so they would get ten dollars and the four men would split that. It was a good day's work back then, but now it ain't pocket change. I was sitting up in the bow and I saw this with my own eyes, so I can tell ya it's the truth. Back then, there wa'n't no bridge across the York River. Everything was ferried across in a rowboat. A drummer came down to the shore in a horse and buggy. Four colored men unhitched the horse and pulled the buggy into the big rowboat. They rowed the buggy and man across and came back and got the horse. They tied a red kerchief around the horse's eyes and tied a big rope around his hips and made him jump in the boat. They then rowed him across. I wouldn't have believed it if I hadn't seen it myself but I guess that's how they did everyone who wanted to go over to Yorktown in those days.

Years later, I was digging a well for an old man there in Guinea Neck in Gloucester County, and I was telling him about what I had seen. He said he

Henion Brown

had worked there with the colored men for several years and a many a horse had jumped overboard. He'd tell you the truth too, Captain. He was a fine man.

Another time Daddy and I were pound netting in the Bay when the worst storm I ever saw came up. It was April 4, 1903, and I can tell you this, I've seen some bad ones since, but none as bad as this one. When it hit, we were in the little canoe working one of Daddy's five-pound nets. We were able to reach safety in Hampton, but Daddy was worried about the other boys working in the Bay. When it finally cleared enough so we could get back out, we sailed out to the nets to try and find them. We found most of their boats had capsized, but they had tied themselves to the net poles, so they wouldn't drown. One old fellow was still chewing a wad of tobacco when we picked him up. Daddy asked him how he could spit because he must have been underwater most of the time. He said he had a big chew when it all started and he would take a spit when the sea would leave him up above the surface. I tell ya, that was some storm.

Henion learned at an early age how to mend a net and he would often help his father with the mending. There was always a little box aboard his father's canoe with line and shuttles to do the mending.

All of us used wooden seine needles. I never made one, but Daddy always had several around. The old boys around home would make needles from dogwood. That's the strongest wood there is, you know. Dogwood is what the cross that Christ was crucified on is made from and they tell me God made sure no one would ever be crucified on a dogwood cross again. It takes a big tree for a cross. God made sure dogwood trees would never be big enough again. But I'll tell ya this, it makes the best fish needle in the world.

The fish were plentiful when Henion was a youngster working with his dad.

I've been out there when the roar of the fish under the boat sounded like a bunch of airplanes overhead. I believe you could throw your breeches overboard on a hook and you'd catch a fish. I've sold thousands of pounds of fish for half a cent a pound. My daddy used to catch plenty of sturgeon weighing two hundred and three hundred pounds. Later on, we stopped catching them.

After Henion's father died in 1905, the canoes were sold, but Henion continued to fish pound nets until he was in his eighties. Although he never owned a canoe, he worked for Isaac Fass in 1907 on a buy boat, buying oysters from oystermen in log canoes on Mobjack Bay.

We were buying clean culled oysters for thirty-five cents a bushel and some of those boys had forty and fifty bushels on board. When we were buying we'd

McKinley Wilson

come into a creek and raise a flag to let the oystermen know we were buying. I only worked for him for one year and made about fifteen dollars a month. When I think about log canoes, I think about my daddy and those pretty days when he'd be in the boat cleaning fish and I'd be at the helm sailing her for home. It don't seem that long ago.

• • •

When McKinley (Mac) Wilson was seven years old he went to work for his father culling oysters on a log canoe. Mac's father had a small canoe that he kept in Lagrange Creek on the Rappahannock River.

When Daddy was alive I worked mostly on good (weather) days and would go to school sometimes, but when he died in 1912, I had to go to work full time. I worked on the river during oyster season and dug sweet potatoes and whatever else I could find the rest of the time. Canoes was all we had back then and my fist job after Daddy died was a-culling oysters on the *Miss Emma* owned by Willie Carter. I was making six dollars a month and board. The *Miss Emma* was thirty feet long and had a mainsail and a jib. Most all the big canoes had sandbags to keep them from taking in water. The bags were made from either canvas or burlap. The men would get their wives or old women to sew them together. The weight of the bags depended on the crew. If young boys were working on the canoe, the bags weighted about thirty-five pounds, but if it was a man crew, they had seventy-five-pound sandbags on board.

When I was small, we would sell the oysters to big sailing schooners that would come all the way from New Jersey, Baltimore, and Norfolk. We liked the New Jersey buyers for a couple of reasons. Usually they would pay two or three cents more for a bushel of oysters, but mostly captains liked the red hooch they had on board. They'd have the booze to entice the guys to sell to them. The boats from Norfolk did that too, but they had white moonshine liquor and there was plenty of that around home. When the Jersey boat came they would hoist a bottle of whiskey up the mast with the flag to let you know they were there. When you went aboard they would give you one drink and then you had to buy whatever else you wanted. Some of those boys would buy a pint and hardly be able to get home. It was red liquor, and it was some kind of good. All the red liquor was bottled and sealed. There were no screw tops, all corks. Captain would pay fifty cents for a pint and twenty-five cents for a half-pint. The captain would treat the culling boys good, so I'd get a nip once in a while.

There was always a jug of water and a jar of molasses under the bow. Most every boat had molasses and we'd dip our bread in it at lunchtime. When the jar would get low, Captain would fill it up again. We worked hard, but it wasn't too bad. In the fall, we all worried about thunderstorms. A many a time I've seen the river full of canoes turned over when a bad storm came up. Some of the canoes were over forty feet long and would carry two hundred bushels of oysters. You know bugeyes were made from logs and some of them were sixty and seventy feet long.

There was no (local) land market much for oysters when I was young. A farmer might buy a bushel for Christmas, but you could go around the shore and catch all the oysters you wanted. Lord, they were everywhere, until this pollution started. Now the creeks are a dumping ground. I had me a pair of nippers (short shaft tongs) and have gone out in Lagrange Creek and caught five and six bushels. I've picked up ten bushels with my hands. There was plenty of oysters back then and the Rappahannock was solid full of canoes.

Every creek had a little shantytown where oystermen would rent a shanty for the season. Some even stayed until it got cold. It wa'n't like it is today. The only way home was to walk or sail and if there wa'n't no wind, you had to scull home. So, they would come over and stay the winter in these shanty houses. They'd bring a bed tick filled with corn shucks or pine needles, their tongs, and a couple jars of molasses. The rest they could buy at a store. I knew some of them. Most of the boys would walk home for Christmas just to be with their families. If they lived forty or fifty miles away, that was a good long walk.

Later on we got motors and the sailboats were all gone. I liked the motor because you could get where you wanted to any time of day, but there was something special about those old sailboats. It was something to see, all those boats with sails raised. You see, the Rappahannock River oyster was king back then and everybody wanted him. He's still king as far as I'm concerned; there just aren't as many of him to go around anymore.

• • •

Raymond Blake was born in 1898 in a little log house at Nohead Bottom, Virginia just a few miles from the mouth of the Rappahannock River. When Raymond was fourteen years old, he went to work full-time with his father oystering during the season and farming the twenty-eight acres the Blakes owned around their homestead in the spring and summer.

Daddy had a thirty-two-foot, three-log canoe that we would oyster from. Around the first of September, he would take the sails out of the outbuilding and stretch them all out in the yard to see if there were any repairs needed. Then, we would go down and check out the boat. The canoe was a typical Virginia-style vessel with a sloop-type rig with the jib set on a short bowsprit. It's different from the Maryland canoes that have two masts, with a pivot jib set on a long sprit supported by a long head and rails.

Shortly before September 15, we would install the mast and centerboard. You see, at the end of the season we would take the sails home for storage and would pull the canoe up on skids on the shore, pull the mast and centerboard out and put them far enough up on shore so that the tide wouldn't take them away. We didn't use the boat for anything but oystering, so when the season was over she was through for the rest of the year.

The sails were made from the best canvas we could get. Daddy didn't like a lot of patches in his sails."

Everybody used sandbags back then. When we would tack into the wind and Daddy would shift her the other way, I'd grab a bag and throw it up on the high side gunwale. I learned how to tong oysters while Daddy was eating his lunch. I was the culling boy, but whenever lunchtime rolled around I'd jump up on the washboard and try my hand at catching a mess. Well, on this one day, I tonged up fifteen oysters with one lick. Daddy stopped eaten' and came over and counted them out. He said then, "I'm a putting a pair of tongs in here for you tomorrow." From that day on there were tongs in the boat for me."

Raymond Blake

When Raymond was twenty years old, modern technology began to catch up with the log canoe as combustion engines were being introduced to commercial workboats. Raymond's father then bought a new boat about the size of the old one, but she had a one-cylinder Palmer engine in her.

I liked the motor because on a slick calm day, you could get home quicker. When we had the sail, I've had to row, while Daddy sculled and a many a time it was after dark before we got home.

When we had the sailboat we would sell to buy boats that came out of Carter Creek on the Northern Neck, but when Daddy had the motor-boat we would take our oysters to Burhan's Steamboat Wharf, near Whiting Creek where we kept the canoe. Everybody used to joke about how tight my Daddy was with money. He was tight, too, but we didn't always have much, so he spent what he had on the things we needed.

This story I'm about to tell you actually happened but over the years it grew little by little. I was about twenty-five years old and I had just bought my first canoe. She cost me seventy-five dollars, had a five-horsepower Minus engine and was the first one we had owned with a round stern. All of them before had had a pointed stern. I really wasn't used to her yet. We had been out oystering and took what we had caught to sell at Burhan's. I went in to get the money and as usual they paid me with silver dollars. I had money in both hands when I came back to the boat and slipped off the stern and fell right down into that icy water. Lord, it was cold. Everybody came running and Daddy was the first one there. He yelled down at me, "Hang on to the money, boy; don't let it go." Well, you can guess what everybody said after that. The word got around that the only thing Daddy was concerned about was losing that money. By the way, I didn't lose a cent. They pulled me out and took me inside the building on the dock and I stayed by that wood stove until I dried out. That story was told over and over and every time it got worse and worse, but I'll tell ya this my Daddy was a fine man. He never made much money but we always had food on our table and clothes on our backs.

I remember another close call when we were working near Burhan's. Daddy and I were working a rock not far from the wharf on a cold, misty day when from out of nowhere the steamboat *Potomac* was heading right for us. I yelled at Daddy, "She's going to hit us." Then I heard some screaming, "Get out of the way! Get out of the way, we've lost steering!" Daddy took his tongs and shoved on the side of the *Potomac* and pushed us clear. Later on, the captain apologized, and said he couldn't steer her at all. I've often wondered what he did when he got to the wharf. That was a close one.

Daddy taught me well. I oystered and farmed my entire life. Those log canoes were tough, sturdy boats. We would put a little copper on the bottom and paint her up real nice and she was a pretty thing, moving across the water. I can't really say I miss those old devils, but I do miss the times Daddy and I had a-working together. When you are young, you don't think about things ending, but they do.

I venture to say there is no one alive today who commercially harvested oysters, fish, or crabs from a sail driven log canoe. This chapter captured the last voices of those times.

CHAPTER EIGHTEEN

MAKING HICKORY
OYSTER MOPS

I don't recall ever seeing a barrel of hickory mops in the corner of a country store, although, I have a feeling that when I was a child they were there. I just didn't notice. However, I did take notice several years ago when I went to interview an older watermen near Water View, Virginia. When I arrived, he was scrubbing down his boat with a mop made of corn shucks.

He told me that he had always used mops made either of corn shucks or of hickory. After some investigation as to how widely these mops had been used in years past, I discovered that just about every old-timer in my area who had worked out of a Chesapeake Bay log canoe had used one, and there were several active mop makers still alive and well. McKinley (Mac) Wilson was one of those I went to visit.

When early settlers first set up housekeeping along the shores of the Chesapeake Bay, brooms and mops made from hickory or white oak were a standard household item used by colonists to sweep their floors or to scrub down their boats. For the next three centuries, various styles of mops and brooms were made here. Interestingly, the old type made from hickory lasted well into the twentieth century.

Many Bay oystermen during the early 1900s used these mops to scrub down decks, washboards, and culling boards on their log canoes. Mac Wilson is one of the few left around the Chesapeake Bay who still recalls how they're made. Mac has been making oyster mops out of hickory for the better part of seventy years. He started making them back in 1919, the year he got married.

Back then, Mac and his father worked the water in a sail-driven log canoe that they used to tong oysters in the Rappahannock River. But, when the weather was bad and it was impossible to oyster, Mac would stay home and whittle up a mop.

I learned how to make hickory mops from watching other watermen make them. Back in those days, a lot of people were making them and most all the country stores had a barrelful in the corner that were for sale.

During those days, Mac would sell one or two a week and would charge whatever a bushel of oysters was bringing at the dock that day.

If a bushel was bringing thirty-five cents, then I'd get thirty-five cents for a mop. Thirty-five cents was not bad money back then. That was good extra money for a part-time job.

I've sold oysters for as little as a dollar for three bushels. But even then, that was good money. Most of the time Daddy and I would catch twenty to twenty-five bushels a day hand tonging. The only land job I had back then was on a dairy farm for a while. I worked from sunup to sundown and made twenty-five cents a day and got a bucket of milk a day. So you see oystering wasn't so bad.

Mac worked at Hampstead Dairy Farm just a half mile walking distance from his home. Mac's main competition years ago was the corn-shuck mop.

Some boys like the corn-shuck mop because they didn't scratch up a paint job. But, they didn't last as long as my mops either. You get out there with the ice forming on the washboards and see what happens to a corn-shuck mop compared to my hickory one. The ice will tear up a corn-shuck, but not my mops. They keep on scrubbing for a long time.

In the early fall, Mac goes out into the wood near his home and selects hickory trees that are just right for making mops. He cuts trees that are as big around as a baseball for medium- and large-size mops and smaller saplings for smaller ones.

Finding good hickory is becoming an ever-increasing problem for the mop maker. "Hickory grows slow," Mac says. "It takes ten years for it to get to the size I need to make a good mop."

During Mac's search for good hickory, he usually starts in the thickest part of the forest because there it is well protected from the elements and usually has good, soft hickory trees for mop making. "The best place to get good hickory is deep in the wood, because the north wind can't blow on it," says Mac. "Hickory that grows on the edge of a field where the north wind can hit it has a hard side and makes the strands hard to shape into a mop."

Mac also selects trees that have few knots near the base. His mops are peeled-strand brooms where the strands remain attached to the handle from which they were peeled. "Pulling strands around a knotty pole is not an easy job so I always look for trees that are smooth at the bottom," says Mac.

He uses only three tools to make his mops: a pocketknife to shape each strand, a hatchet or drawing knife to skin the bark, and a rasp to smooth the handles.

Watermen no longer buy Mac's mops, but folks who want an antique style of mop have been steady customers over the years. "They don't mind paying fifteen to twenty dollars for one," he said.

Mac starts by skinning the bark from the end he plans to make the head from. The bark is skinned off about twelve to fourteen inches up the hickory pole.

Photo 1

Photo 2

Photo 3

Photo 4

Photo 5

After skinning the pole, Mac begins forming the mop head with his pocketknife by
cutting and then pulling small strands (about 1/4 inch wide) of hickory (see photo 1, page
180). Depending on the size of the mop head desired, the strands are between eight and
twelve inches long. Mac keeps pulling the strands until the tip is about the size of a dime,
then he cuts it off (see photo 2, page 180).

The mop maker then measures up the handle by pulling one hickory strand back
(photo 3, page 181); adds three to four inches to it and then skins the bark off from
that point to where the mop head starts. He then turns the strands back toward the
sweeping end and ties them together loosely (photo 4, page 181).

Photo 6

With his pocketknife, Mac begins cutting strands and pulling them down the handle toward the mop head (photo 5, page 182). When enough strands of hickory have been pulled down over the head, Mac unties the leather and pulls all the strips down to shape the mop. Next, on the larger mops, he weaves a string in and out of the head to hold it in place. On smaller ones, he ties a string around it to hold it tight (photo 6 page 183).

He then skins all the bark from the handle and uses a rasp to smooth the handle down (photo 7, above). "When most of my mops were going to oystermen, I didn't smooth the handle down on them much," says Mac. "But now, because most of them

Photo 7

are going to women who want to put them up on the wall, I try to get them good and smooth."

Mac Wilson recalls how life was on the Chesapeake as a waterman at the turn of this century and how his craft of mop making is part of that rich heritage. "I don't know anybody who does this anymore," he says. "The old boys who used to make oyster mops have all gone. I guess I'm one of the last ones left."

Mac is deceased and I don't know anyone who makes mops out of hickory now. When I interviewed Mac in the early 1980s, Eugene Burch of Remilk was still making a mop or two out of hickory and Emma Williams of Samos was making mops out of corn shucks and selling them to watermen. They are both deceased.

MAKING A WHITE OAK SCULLING PADDLE

During the late 1950s and early 1960s, Woodland (Guinea) Rowe's carpentry shop was located on Cross Street in Urbanna. There was always a batch of newly shaped wooden crab net handles and sculling paddles for sale, leaning against the side of the cinder-block building.

Sometime in the 1960s, Woodland closed his shop and opened a small shop behind his home on Obert Street in town overlooking Perkins Creek, more or less to give himself something to do in retirement. When it came time to do this chapter on sculling paddles, I remembered those paddles, leaning against Woodland's old shop and asked if he would make one more for old time's sake.

In years gone by, when there wasn't enough wind to fill a sail, sculling was used to power many of the Chesapeake's small craft. Log canoes, bar cats, and crabbing skiffs were, as often as not, powered with an old sculling paddle.

While there is no longer much demand for sculling paddles, Woodland Rowe on occasion still makes them and has been doing so for "near on" sixty years. Woodland joked:

> Years back, the only way to get anywhere when the wind was still was to scull, row, or get out and swim.
>
> When I was a small boy, I remember the men around Guinea Neck would sail their log canoes to Norfolk to pick up supplies that we couldn't buy around home and many a time they'd come home by sculling the whole way.

Sculling paddles were made from a variety of different woods, but white oak seems to have been the preferred stock.

> White oak is the best as long as you're not trying to make it from an old snarly piece. I've made some from pine too, but they don't last as long.
>
> Lord knows when I made my first paddle. I was probably in the first grade or so. I'd go down to the local boat yard and watch the old-timers work. I've made everything from a schooner mast to a coffin.

During the time when they were in wide use, eight-foot long sculling paddles would bring two or sometimes three dollars apiece. "That wasn't a bad price and there was plenty of demand for them. I've made a boatload of them in my time—I have."

Photo 1

Photo 2

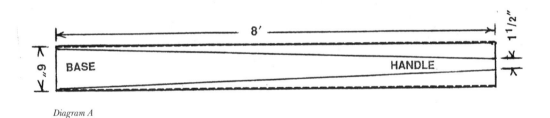

Diagram A

Woodland starts with an oak board 8 feet long, 6 inches wide, and 1½ inches thick. "Make sure you pick a piece of wood that doesn't have a knot near where the paddle will rest on the stern. This is where it suffers the most stress when in use and a knot is a weak spot in the board."

The next step is to mark the paddle on the face of the board. Woodland said this can be done with a straight edge and pencil, or a chalk box, but he prefers using a straight edge and an old-time knife, what he calls a "racer knife," to mark the board (photos 1 and 2 and diagram A, pages 186 & 187).

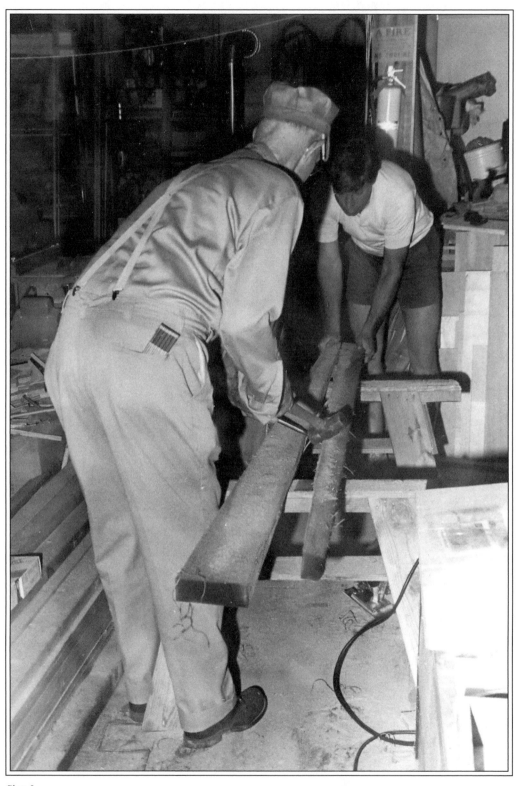

Photo 3

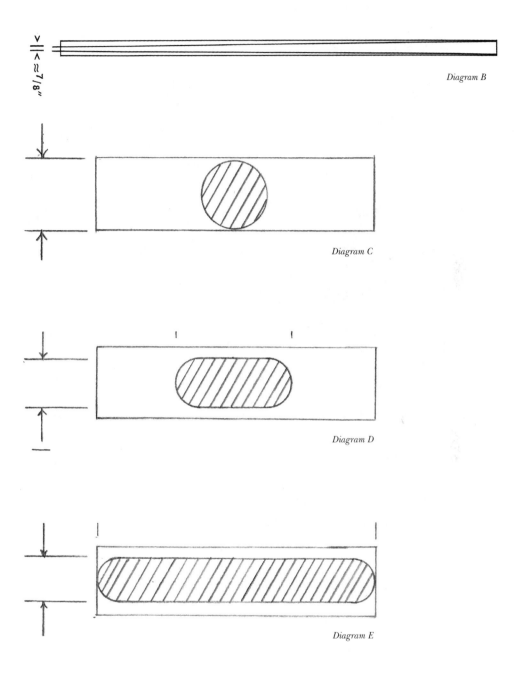

Diagram B

Diagram C

Diagram D

Diagram E

I bought the knife in Baltimore years ago to strike a waterline on the side of a boat. I guess it's an antique because I've never seen one quite like it before.

Photo 4

7/8" 1½"

Diagram F
Drawings by Ray V. Rodgers III

Photo 5

The markings on the board should show the paddle to be 6 inches at the end and 1½" inches at the paddle end. The paddle is 8 feet in length. Woodland then cuts off the wide edges on each side of the marked lines on the board (photo 3, page 188).

The paddle is then turned on edge and the thickness marked. Woodland measures 1½ inches at the handle end and $7/8$ of an inch at the paddle end (see photo 4, diagram B, and cross-sectional diagrams C, D, and E).

The board is then cut on edge (photo 5 and diagram F). If the saw does not have the capacity to cut through the board on edge, Woodland uses a chisel or hatchet to remove the slab that remains (photo 6).

Photo 6

Once the slab is removed, the rough paddle is shaped. It is now square and bulky on the handle end and thick on the paddle end. The paddle maker then uses a foot adz, hatchet, broad ax, or electric plane to clean the faces of the paddle (photo 7). He also uses an electric plane or drawing knife to work the handle round and smooth.

The handle should be about 1¼ inch to 1½ inch in diameter (see cross-sectional diagram C). This does, however, depend on the size of the user's hands. "I don't mind my own paddle being 2 inches thick at the end of the handle, but not many men have long fingers like mine," said Woodland holding up his hand.

As Woodland works his way down the paddle, the round shape gives way to the rectangular shape of the base, the end that goes into the water. The edges of the base should have about a ½-inch radius along the length of the paddle, from the handle to the foot. The foot on the paddle is between ¾ inch and 1 inch thick. The taper, from the tip of the handle to the tip of the base, is about ¼ inch to ½ inch on each side and is a straight line as opposed to an arc.

Woodland emphasizes that the measurements are not cut in stone and should be adjusted according to the size and strength of the user. "If it's a good-size man with

Photo 7

broad shoulders and hefty arms, he can handle a bigger sculling paddle. You've got to think about the man who's using it when you make it."

Although Woodland has very few calls anymore for paddles, a man recently came by and ordered two, one for himself and one for a museum in Newport News.

"I remember when everyone around sculled here and there," he said. "Many of the old boys would take a burlap bag, wet it, and put it on the stern post to help keep the paddle steady as they sculled.

"The fastest sculler I remember was old Loving Henry Dize of Tangier Island. He could go faster in a sharp-end skiff than anyone I've ever seen," said Woodland.

With the paddle complete. Woodland shows off the finished product.

"It's hard for me to realize that those days are gone. It seems like just yesterday a sculling paddle and a puff of wind was all we had to drive our boats—time does fly," sighed Woodland.

Ralph Woodland Rowe died on December 12, 1993 at the age of 84. His obituary listed him as a retired building contractor but most around town remember him for his ability to make wooden crab net handles and sculling paddles.

CHAPTER TWENTY

CRAB NETS

As a young boy, I mudlarked for crabs in the small coves around Urbanna Creek. My crab net was always a lightweight store-bought net, from Taylor's Hardware store in town, but most of my competition in those days came from professional crabbers who used homemade handles and nets.

I first met Captain Hugh Norris in the early 1980s, and since then I have done several stories on this charming, wonderful old waterman. On many occasions when I would stop by to pick his brain about something I was working on, Captain Hugh would be sitting around knitting a crab net bag, and, if he finished it while I was there, he wouldn't stand for anything, but for me to take it home.

Just before Captain Hugh Norris started a career as mate and skipper aboard his first of several Bay sailing craft, he learned to knit crab net bags. It was back in 1914 when Hugh was just fifteen that he first learned how, and he's been making them the old-time way ever since. A neighbor taught him to knit the bags by hand. "I used to go over under the shade of a big oak tree and watch him work," says Hugh.

His neighbor worked aboard a menhaden fish steamer and part of his duty was to maintain the big dip net used to haul fish from the purse net up into the fish hold on deck. So, he was well versed in the knitting of several different types of nets and was a fine teacher for Hugh, who was interested in learning the skill.

Since those early lessons, it is hard to say exactly how many nets Hugh has made for both commercial and recreational crabbers.

I didn't make many of them when I was working on the schooners, but when I came home and started working the water, I made many for myself and he other boys around too. Those were the days before crab pots, and trotlines were the best means of catching an ol' jimmy hard crab. Everybody working a trotline needed a crab net to dip crabs off the line with, and I made nets for a lot of them boys who couldn't do it themselves. I worked a trotline in the 1920s and 1930s from a log canoe, and I'd catch as many as twenty barrels a day. Every crab had to be caught in a dip net, so you can see why a good net was an important tool of the trade.

Nets were also made for crabbers who netted for soft-shell crabs and peelers.

Since 1914, Captain Hugh Norris has been making crab net bags for area watermen. Today, he still carries on his craft in his living room at his house on Jackson Creek in Deltaville.

When there was plenty of eel grass around, a lot of the boys made their livings by poling around shore, catching soft crabs, peelers, and jimmies too. For them I made a net with a long handle and a deep bag. They'd stand on the box of a skiff and use the handle to shove along shore.

Smaller dip nets, with short handles and shallow bags, were also made for crabbers who waded along the shore and those who culled and sorted crabs in shedding floats. Although Captain Hugh still makes bags for any type of crabber, he no longer sells a complete crab net. Years back, he would get the metal bows, which the net was attached to, from a store in Crisfield, Maryland, and make the handles from yellow pine he would select from the woods nearby.

Captain Hugh still makes the bags at his home and sells them mostly to watermen who prefer old-style nets. Sitting on his living room sofa, Hugh proceeded to demonstrate the skill he learned over seventy years ago. But, before getting down to business, he shuffled through a cardboard box full of twine and other items related to knitting his nets.

Dip nets were once the main tool for harvesting soft-shell crabs and peelers on the Bay, Many watermen would pole along the shore in a skiff and, if necessary, wade in the water to catch a mess. (Courtesy of the Virginia Institute of Marine Science.)

"You know, you can't learn this in a half-hour. But let me show you how it's done. Now, where did that thing go?" he asked himself as he continued to look though the box. "Oh, here it is," he said, pulling out a solid brass fish needle, or shuttle. "This is what I learned to knit my first bag with. The man who taught me how, gave it to me to learn with. Land sakes, that was a long time ago."

Captain Hugh starts getting ready for the spring run on dip nets during the winter months. On good clear days, he drives down to the local boat yards that repair the winter crab and oyster dredging gear and picks up off the ground the small metal rings that have fallen from the dredges.

"I use these for my centers," Hugh says, holding up a rusty metal ring that has a 1½-inch opening. "If the rings are broken, I get them welded back together."

Hugh wraps the rings in electrical tape or "tire tape." "It's the same type of stuff we used to use to patch tires on the old cars," he says. "The tape keeps the ring from rusting real bad." He also says if you want to get "fancy," brass rings make good centers for the bags.

"I make my nets out of nylon or regular (number 18) cotton twine," he says. "I like working with cotton because it doesn't slip on the ring like the nylon." When occasionally he does use nylon, Hugh applies glue to the knots attached to the metal ring. (This is not done when cotton twine is used.) Nylon also will unravel on the cut ends, so Hugh burns each end with a match to prevent this problem.

Short-handled dip nets were used by watermen who would mudlark for crabs in shallow guts and coves. Captain Hugh would knit the nets and make the handle length according to the desire of the buyer. (Courtesy of the Virginia Institute of Marine Science)

"The first thing you've got to do is put your string on the needle." Hugh held the shuttle in his left hand and while holding the string onto the needle with his thumb, began wrapping the string around the shuttle (see photos 1, 2, and 3). Hugh carries the string through the crescent-shaped guide at the bottom of the shuttle and back up around the needle on the opposite side. He continues this until the shuttle is full (photos 4 through 8). "Don't overload the shuttle as it will make the tying of knots more difficult," he cautioned.

"I could make a bag in a couple hours, but it hurts my hands so bad," Hugh says. "So, I just take my time and work on them when I want to. There's no reason to rush."

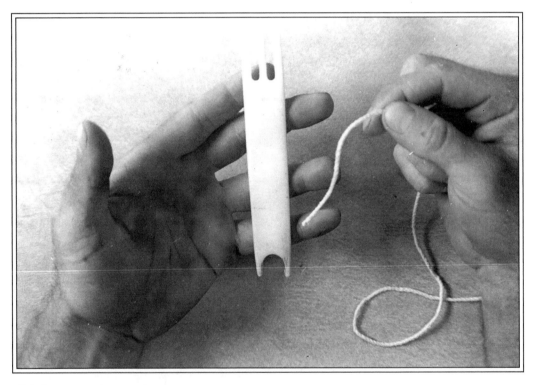

Photo 1

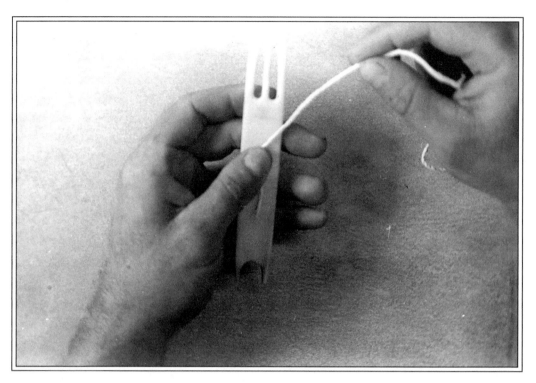

Photo 2

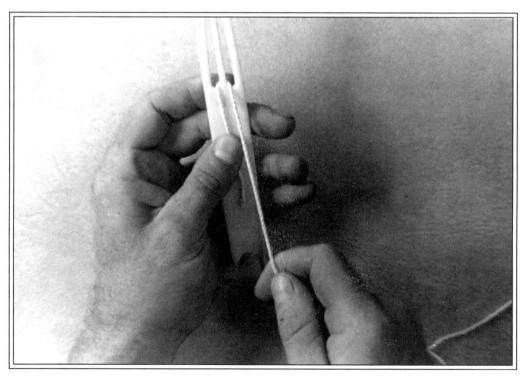

Photo 3

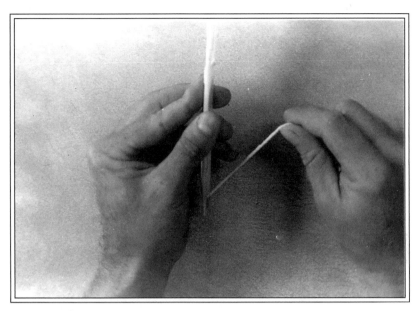

Photo 4

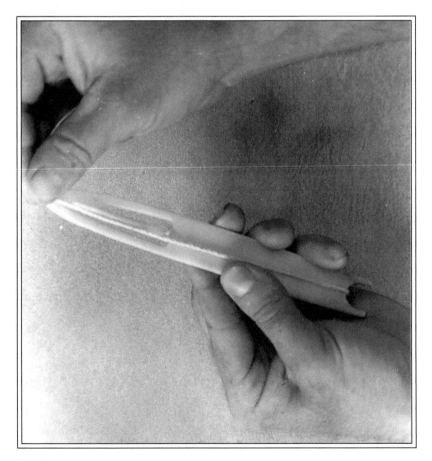

Photo 5

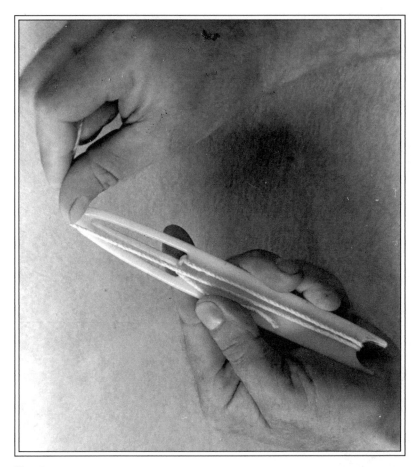

Photo 6

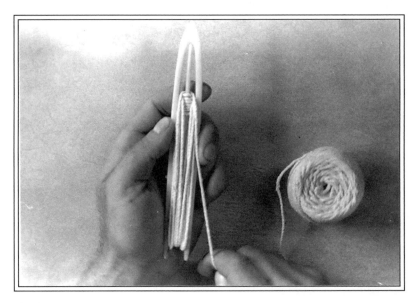

Photo 7

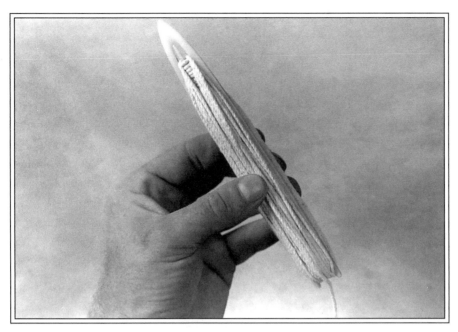

Photo 8

Photo 9

Captain Hugh starts the bag by securing the center ring to the arm of an old goosenecked rocking chair in his living room (photo 9). "I like using my ol' chair because I can move it anywhere I want to get a comfortable working position," he says.

Photo 10

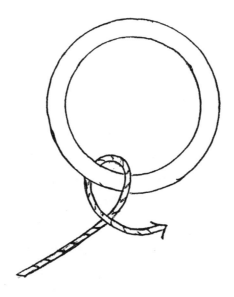

Drawing A. (Drawing by Ray V. Rodgers III)

Hugh then proceeded to make the net. In step 1, he passes the needle through the center ring from top to bottom with his right hand, while holding the ring and the end of the string in his left hand (photo 10, drawing A).

In step 2, Hugh has a single loop, or marsh, around the center ring that he held between his thumb and the forefinger of his left hand (photo 11). He then pulled the loop of string around the forefinger of his left hand and duplicated the procedure

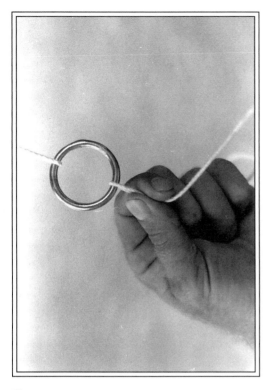
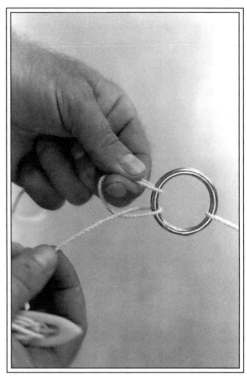

Photo 11

Photo 12

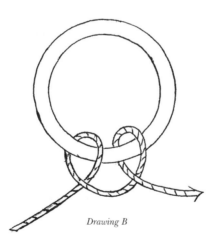

Drawing B

in step 2 (photo 12, drawing B). When this knot is pulled tight, it should be two half hitches as shown in photo 13. The first knot will be referred to as A knot. All the knots around the ring are the same, with loops of equal size between each pair of half hitches (drawing C).

Photo 13

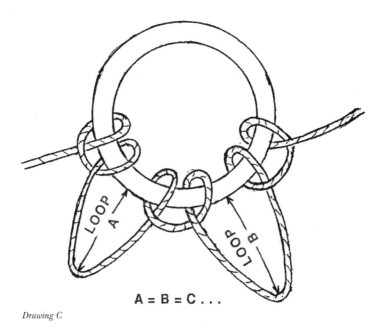

A = B = C . . .

Drawing C

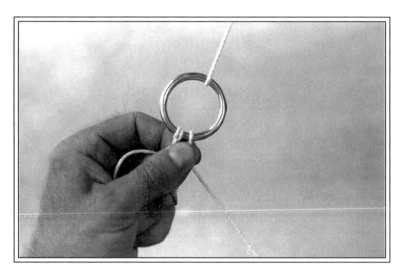

For step 3, Hugh pulls the loop of string around the index finger of his left hand and passes the needles through the top of the center ring as described in step 1 (photo 14). Then he pinches the loop between his thumb and forefinger (photo 15) and then knits a second half hitch (photo 16). When this knot is pulled tight it should resemble what is shown in photo 17.

Photo 16

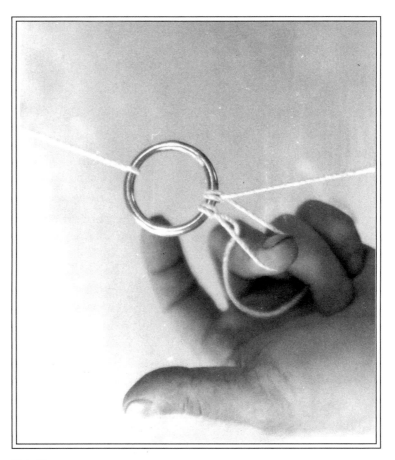

Photo 17

Photo 18

In step 4, Hugh duplicates the procedure in step 3 until the entire center ring is completely and tightly covered. "You want the knots as tight as you can get them," he says, "because more loops give you a fuller net. The first loop is used as a gauge and each loop thereafter should be measured by the size and length of the preceding loop," he explained.

When the entire ring is covered it should resemble photo 18, and the maker should be back to A knot. To get from the first to the second row, Hugh feeds the needle

Photo 19

Photo 20

Photo 21

Photo 22

through A loop as shown in photo 19, using the ring finger of his left hand to gauge the length and size of the second row of loops (photo 20).

Where the string passes through A loop, Hugh pinches the loop between his index finger and the thumb of his left hand (photo 21). He then passes the string around the forefinger of his left hand, places the needle through A loop from the bottom

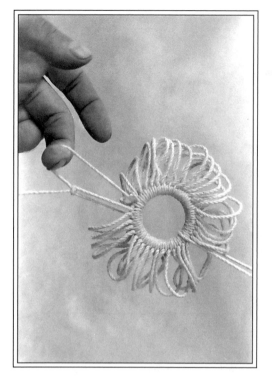
Photo 23

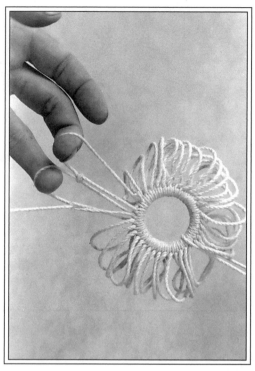
Photo 24

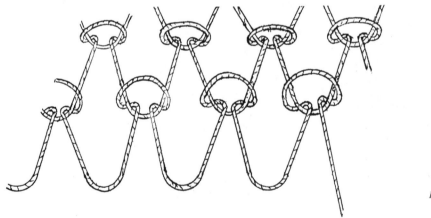
Drawing D

Drawing E

and brings the needle inside the loop formed by the string around the forefinger of his left hand (photo 22).

When the knot is pulled tight in step 5, it should look like photo 23. This knot is a flat knot (drawing D). Although the flat knot will work fine, Captain Hugh said

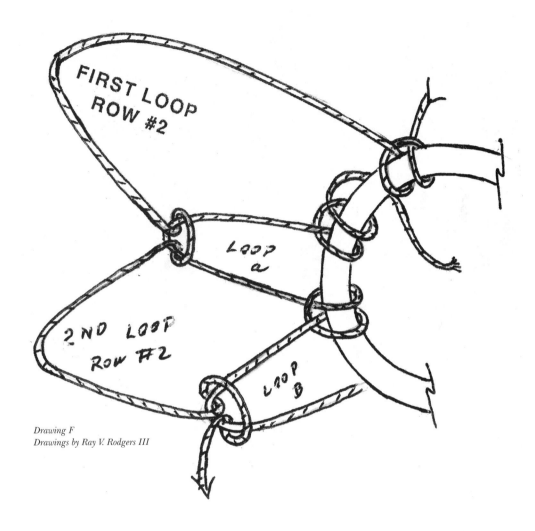

FIRST LOOP
ROW #2

LOOP
a

2ND LOOP
ROW #2

LOOP
B

Drawing F
Drawings by Ray V. Rodgers III

sometimes he uses an old knot he was taught as a boy. He referred to this knot as a "she knot" (drawing E). "Either knot will work just fine," he says.

In step 6, the rest of the net is completed by continuing to make loops around the net. The size of each loop is determined by the preceding loop (photo 24, drawing F).

Hugh completes the net by continuing step 4 through 6 from row to row until the net reaches the desired diameter. Sometimes before he finishes the net, the shuttle will run out of string. When this occurs, he simply reloads the shuttle and splices the new string to the loop where he left off by using a square knot or becket.

The shallow dip net was made by Captain Hugh for a crabber who uses it to harvest soft-shell crabs and peelers from crab floats.

When Hugh's net has reached the desired diameter he empties the shuttle and rethreads it with two strings at the same time. He then ties one more round of loops around the outside with the double strings. "I always double my last row because this row is tied to the bow," he says. "This last row needs more strength than the other rows because it take more stress."

The nets are made in different diameters, depending on what their use will be, says Hugh. "The boys who are shedding soft crabs, they want a shallow net because old soft crab can't move around like a jimmy. But, if a man wants to catch a hard crab, he wants a deep net."

Captain Hugh has seen a lot of changes on the Chesapeake Bay in his lifetime, and he's concerned that the skill he learned as a boy could well be lost. "Somebody best learn how to make these bags," he says. "Because when all the old boys like me are gone, there won't be nobody left who knows how."

Hugh Norris is deceased but there are fisher folks in villages such as Tangier Island, Virginia and Smith Island, Maryland where crab net bags are still used on a daily bases and made by local craftsmen.

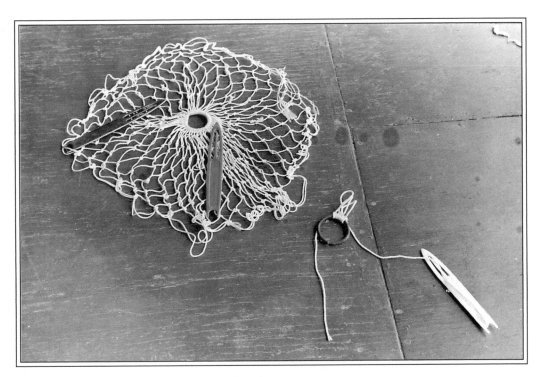

At the start of the spring crab season, Hugh's nets are in great demand,
and as soon as one is done, another is started.

CHAPTER TWENTY-ONE

TROTLINING FOR CHESAPEAKE BLUE CRABS

In 1988, I was asked to go on assignment to Maryland to do a story on trotlining. I ended up calling Lester Lee of Kent Island, Maryland, and he suggested I go out with his son Bobby "Tucker" Lee.

When I arrived at Kent Island, I looked up Tucker. He told me in no uncertain terms that I best be at his boat at 3:00 A.M. He said something to the effect that he'd had a bad experience with a journalist sometime back. I was afraid that I might miss his boat because he didn't seem very enthusiastic about taking me. I decided then that instead of getting a motel room for the night, I'd park my car in front of his boat at Kent Narrows and wait for 3:00 A.M. It was a long night, but worth every minute of it. Tucker and I both ended up enjoying the day.

Whack! Whack! The pounding of a hatchet against wood echoed across the water. The noise and the misty rainfall sprinkling on the harbor of Kent Narrows makes for an eerie setting, one ideal for a mystery novel.

The setting is familiar to Bobby "Tucker" Lee, as every morning about 3:00 A.M. during crab season he prepares to go out into the Chester or Wye rivers or Eastern Bay to trotline for the Chesapeake's blue crab. His first job as a trotliner is to prepare his lines with bait, and on this particular day Tucker is working extra hard because of the "bull lip" he purchased from a local beef slaughterhouse.

"I'll tell ya the truth there, fellow, this stuff is the toughest meat that God ever made," he said, sitting on a plastic bucket pounding on the meat with a brand-new hatchet. "I had to go out and get me a new hatchet just to cut it up."

It was taking three and four swipes to cut one small piece off the tough chunk of meat. The bull lip appeared to be more than just the lips of bulls because several pieces had holes that had once contained eye sockets. All the meat had obviously come from the facial area of cattle. "Putting beef steak on the line, we ought to catch some crabs," said Tucker who paused with the hatchet high in the air. "It takes four times longer to cut this stuff up as it does eel. It takes one whack with old eel and you're done with him."

This is one of the few times Tucker has used bull lips for bait. The traditional bait is eel, but over the years, trotline bait has come in many different forms. Tripe, pinheads (small croakers), and calves' ears were used by early crabbers. Small croakers were particularly good because they would remain firm longer than other fish.

But eel has always been the first choice of watermen, and years back, usually during February and March when the water was clear and cool, crabbers would pole along the shore and gig for eels buried in the mud. Watermen could recognize eel holes and almost always a big eel was landed. Since there was very little refrigeration then, eels were generally salt-cured in barrels and stored until crab season began.

Another reason Tucker likes eel is because when a line comes up empty, an eel bone will tell him whether or not a crab is down there. "You take bull lip now," he explained. "If the line comes up without bait, I can't be sure if the crab ate it off or the knot came untied, but with eel, if there's a bone on the line, I know there are jimmies on the bottom."

The reason for Tucker's using bull lip is a ninety cents a pound price for eel. "That's too much to pay for eel," says Tucker. "Some of the boys are using turkey necks. That's not bad bait either. It will last a couple days."

The trotline is one of the oldest methods used to harvest Chesapeake blue crab. Prior to the introduction of the crab pot in 1928, trotlines were the main gear used by Maryland and Virginia watermen to catch crabs in the spring, summer, and fall. A nineteenth-century fishing report by Richard Rathbun stated that the main method of harvesting blue crab on the East Coast was by trotlining crabs from deep water to within reach of a dip net, by means of pieces of meat attached to a long line.

Prior to the introduction of the crab pot in 1928, the trotline had been the main method of harvesting blue crabs for centuries. (Courtesy of the Virginia Institute of Marine Science)

Although the crab pot is the main means of harvesting crabs on the Chesapeake today, the trotline is still a viable gear for many Maryland watermen because state law requires the use of trotlines in most rivers, creeks, and coves. Crab pots are legal on the Maryland portion of Chesapeake Bay and in some rivers. The regulatory measure is designed in part to prevent overfishing of these waters where some of the largest jimmies on the Bay grow.

Any connoisseur of Chesapeake Bay crabs knows about the giant jimmies harvested from the Wye and Chester rivers and Eastern Bay. The question of why they're so big has been a topic of debate for centuries. Mike Oesterling, retired gear specialist with the Virginia Institute of Marine Science, says, "Crabs in low-salinity waters are generally larger than crabs in water with high salinity. These rivers of Maryland have a just right brackish water content that causes crabs to grow very large. This is evident in other areas besides the Eastern Bay region of Chesapeake Bay," says Oesterling, as some of the largest crabs he has seen came from Lake George on the St. Johns River in Florida. "This is another area where crabs live in water with a just right salinity level," he says.

Tucker, fifty-three, has been working a trotline since 1953. His father Lester Lee, is a renowned crabber and Tucker learned the skill from him. "Daddy taught me all I know. We do it a little different now from when he was a boy. He started out using snoods, six-inch drop lines with the bait tied to them that were attached to the main line every so many feet. The old crabbers would pull the boat over the line and dip crabs from the bow of a skiff. Today, the bait is tied directly to the main line, and the line is fished from the side of the boat."

As he continued to chop the bull lip, Tucker continued, "I've baited a many a crab line. My brother and I used to race to see who was the fastest. We'd race to do everything. Daddy was right there with us too. Shoot, he wa'n't nothing but a boy then himself."

Tucker carries several pickle barrels on his workboat. Inside each barrel is a liquid brine solution covering a bushel basket filled with a half mile of twenty-pound-test line. There are two-inch strips of eel tied to the line every two feet. Tucker began pulling some of the old eel off and tying the bull lip on in its place. He uses a slipknot (drawing A, page 219) to attach the bait to the line.

The brine solution in the barrel helps preserve the bait and line and supposedly attracts crabs to the trotline. Starting from scratch, Tucker says he mixes eighty pounds of salt into water to get the pickle solution and then adds five pounds daily to keep the salt content "just right." At the end of each trip, the line is stored in the solution overnight. "Daddy will float a potato to tell whether or not the pickle is ready," he says. "When the potato floats, the brine solution is ready for the line and bait."

When Tucker had baited most of the line to his satisfaction, he moved about the boat preparing things to get under way. The crabber moors his boat at a state-sponsored facility, set aside just for watermen, at Kent Narrows. By 4:00 A.M., there are boats moving here and yonder, and some carrying trotline rigs. "We're going over to Love Point," he said draining the pickle solution from the barrel into a white bucket. "I don't think anybody will be over that way." Love Point is the farthest northwest point on

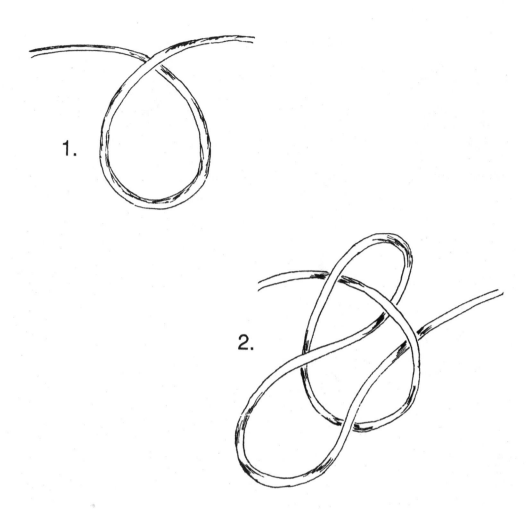

1.

2.

3.

pull

pull

Bait

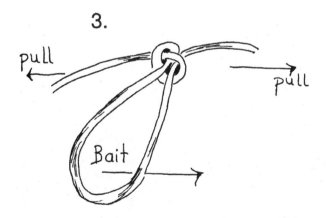

Drawing A. (Drawings by Dee Lantz Chowning)

Bull lip is baited directly to the main line of Tucker's trotline. Years back, snoods, six-inch drop lines, were tied to the main line and bait was attached at the bottom of the snood.

Kent Island. "There's a place over there where I've caught a lot of crabs during this time of year. I heard some of the boys talking, and they said they were going over to Hell Creek on Chester River, so maybe we'll be alone."

One of the hazards of working a trotline near another one is the possibility of getting tangled, and Tucker explains this has become even more of a problem since the "chicken-neckers" started working the rivers and creeks. Chicken-neckers are weekenders and summer folk who run trotlines for pleasure. "Sometime back in the early sixties, we started calling them chicken-neckers because they used chicken necks for bait," says Tucker. "They really aren't so bad. Most of the time, I worry more about getting tangled with commercial boys than those weekenders."

Tucker's boat is typical of many deadrise wooden workboats on the Chesapeake in that it appears somewhat unkempt but is obviously sturdy and functional. The engine house leaks and the rain falls on the 305 GMC engine. Before even trying to crank her up, Tucker pulls the carburetor and fiddles a bit. He cranks her up, and she starts on the first try. Lines are let go, and Tucker heads toward the mouth of the Chester River.

As the boat reaches the mouth of Kent Narrows, the sky is overcast so Tucker slows the vessel down and contemplates which direction to head. Finally, his decision made, he points the vessel toward Love Point, his original destination.

The rain has stopped, but the moisture gives a slight chill to the early morning air. As the boat moves toward the Chester, Tucker fiddles about the boat. He packs ice down in the cooler and ties a few chunks of bull lip to a line. He is always aware, though, of his location and stays close to the outside helm station, making sure everything is in order. Although the sky was still black as pitch, Tucker said, "Looks like we're going to miss that storm. I almost went somewhere else because of that sky. But, we'll be all right," he said reassuringly.

Tucker's trotline rig is fairly typical of those fished in Maryland waters. He uses number 1 cotton, untreated line, and each individual line is about one-half to three-quarters of a mile long. At the end of the line, a chain is attached to hold it on the bottom. A twenty-foot rope pendant is tied to the chain from which a plastic Clorox bottle is tied for a buoy. From the buoy another twenty-foot anchor line is tied to hold the gear in place. The anchors range from cinder blocks to old automobile parts. This configuration is on both ends of the trotline. Years back, wooden barrels were used for buoys (see drawing B, page 222) and even further back the ends of the lines were tied to stationary stakes (see drawing C page 223).

Other equipment includes a hinged wooden prop stick attached to the starboard washboard at about amidships. Made from a two-by-four, the three foot prop stick swings out over the water and is used to guide the line along while it is being worked. At the end of the stick is a horizontal brass roller and two vertical stationary pins on each side of the roller to keep the line from slipping off.

Trotline rigs vary to some extent from waterman to waterman. For instance, many crabbers use household rolling pins on the end of the prop stick to guide the line. Another variation is a hydraulic line hauler to haul lines at the end of the day. The

Automobile starters, like the one above, are often used to anchor a trotline.

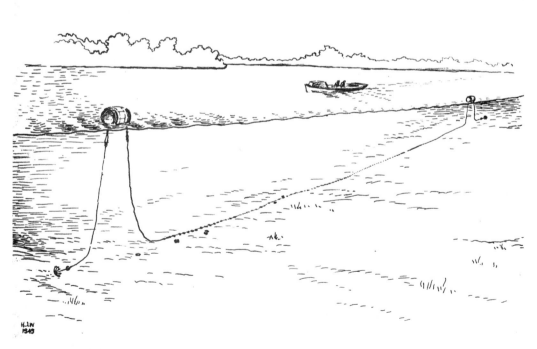

Drawing B. (Courtesy of the Virginia Institute of Marine Science)

Drawing C: This late-nineteenth-century drawing shows a trotline that is held in place by tying the ends to two stakes. Also notice the six-inch snood lines dangling from the main line. Bait was attached at the bottom end of the snood. Snoods like this are no longer used; today, watermen tie their bait directly to the main line. (From Goode's The Fisheries and Fishery Industries of the United States, *1887)*

A hinged prop stick is standard equipment on all trotline rigs.

On the end of the prop stick, rolling pin rollers are used by many trot liners to guide the line as it is being worked.

sheaves on these haulers are identical to crab pot haulers used by Maryland and Virginia watermen, but there is no arm used on trotline haulers. The sheaves are generally mounted flat on the washboard or on a forty-five-degree angle.

Another configuration used by some trotline rigs is a "tow-board," which is mounted on the stern. This is a wide board that is adjustable so it can either be lowered into or raised out of the water. When lowered, it slows the boat down when working a line in a strong following sea. If the boat moves too fast through the water, the crabber doesn't have time to dip a crab off a piece of bait before moving to another. Instead of a tow board, Tucker uses another popular method, a drag basket, which is a bushel basket tied to a line that is dragged behind the boat to slow it down.

The dip net is also a source of contention among watermen. Some prefer using wire net bags as opposed to Tucker's twine net. "I like mine better because I can lay it down on the washboard, but the wire nets have a big belly and can roll right overboard when they set them down," says Tucker. The standard dip net has a sixteen-inch bow and a seven-foot handle. Tucker says some watermen use longer handles, but they have a tendency to break off easily.

A little before 5:00 A.M., Tucker arrives at his spot. With dawn still to come, he points into the darkness. "Over there's Love Point, and yonder is a creek that we'll

Some watermen use tow boards mounted on the sterns of their Bay workboats to slow the boat down as the line is being worked, while others, like Tucker, use a drag basket. A drag basket is simply a bushel basket that is tied to the stern. When it is thrown overboard it drags through the water and slows down the forward motion of the boat.

make a lay in front of. We catch the best crabs near the mouth of small creeks. We'll be in a good spot."

There is no one else in sight, and a little before dawn Tucker throws the cinder-block anchor overboard and then lets the rest of the line out. The first lay is in seven to eight feet of water just off from the mouth of the creek. As the sun peeks from behind the clouds, it looks like it will be a good day after all. "I told ya we'd miss that storm, didn't I? I ought to go on TV and be one of those weathermen. I can tell ya what's a happening as good as they can," muses Tucker.

He extends the prop stick, makes sure everything is ready, then begins to fish the first lay. "Crabs don't bite much before six, but we'll give it a try," says Tucker.

The crabber pulls the line to the surface, hooks it with the net, and lays the line over the roller. With the boat in low gear, Tucker moves down the line. Almost every time a crab is spotted, he hollers, "Here comes one. Boy, look at that one. He's a biggy, ain't he!" This enthusiasm never stops throughout the day. "By golly, there are two on that one!" he yelled once.

Tucker's cat-quick stroke with the net has been mastered over years and years of working the lines. Once he swooped down on the line and a monster jimmy came to the surface only to fly up out of the net and land back in the water. After a loud laugh, Tucker screamed, "He was so big he wouldn't go in the net!"

As the sun begins to warm up, Tucker talks about his many years of working a trotline. Once when he was working the Wye River, he landed $2,500 worth of crabs in one week. There was the time he was working a line near an old crabber who advised him to move a little farther over because he would catch a "boatload." Sure enough, crabs were hitting on every bait. Tucker got the old man and both fished Tucker's line; when one stopped, the other started until they had landed thirty bushels apiece. "I had never seen it like that before or since," he says.

Tucker talks about the hard times, too. "Yep, a waterman will tell ya about those good times, but believe me, there has been many a time I've come out and not made expenses." Tucker says it costs him about $300 a week to operate, so he likes to harvest $160 worth of crabs a day. On this particular day, no. 1 jimmies are bringing $30 a bushel.

In the morning, the first two bushels are caught in a hurry, but Tucker predicts it will slack off about flood tide. Sure enough, after flood tide, it seems to take forever to get the third bushel. Determined to get a fourth bushel, Tucker works into the afternoon.

With each lay, Tucker catches fewer and fewer crabs until there are only three or four caught on each try. "Look at the size of those boys, though," says Tucker. "We ain't catching many, but if we keep trying, we'll fill that last bushel."

Before the afternoon is half over, Tucker has the bushel basket filled and we're headed for home. "Well, I didn't get my $160 today, but we made a little money." Besides the four bushels of no. 1 jimmies, he has a half bushel of white jimmies and females.

Tucker passes a pound netter and the men wave to each other. Behind the rustic scene of the man working his net with gulls hovering and swooping is the shoreline of Kent Island. Portions of the skyline are cluttered with freshly built condominiums.

At the start of his workday, Tucker guides the baited line over the side.

With a cat-quick stroke, Tucker lands a big jimmy in his dip net that is knitted from twine. Some watermen prefer their nets shaped from wire.

Tucker hollers and points to land. "That's what it will all be some day—chicken-neckers and condominiums." He tilts his straw hat back on his head, shakes his head and heads on in to Kent Narrows.

Tucker Lee is deceased but the commercial Maryland trotline fishery is alive and well and still catching some of the largest Chesapeake Bay blue crabs.

CHAPTER TWENTY-TWO

A LONG-TIME TROTLINER

I first read about Lester Lee and the chicken-neckers in the book, Beautiful Swimmers. *Like everyone else, I enjoyed William Warner's writings about this colorful Chesapeake Bay watermen.*

By the time I got around to writing this project, Lester had stopped crabbing and was recovering from a hip operation. He was unable to take me crabbing, but his wonderful memory and colorful way of recalling his younger years as a trotliner were more than I could resist. We had several interviews and I spent one night in his home. Lester is a rare treasure—a person who can make you laugh so hard you want to cry, but at the same time leaves a serious message with you that will last a lifetime.

Kent Island was settled in 1631, the first English settlement in Maryland. Since those early days when Capt. William Claiborne landed on the banks of Cox Creek and built Kent Fort, many Kent Islanders have made their living from the water. Some harvest the bounty of the "Mother of Waters," the Chesapeake, while others work the rivers and bays nearby.

Lester Lee, one of the oldest of Kent Island's watermen, got his start at the young age of eight, when he took one of his uncle's old worn-out trotlines and stretched it across Crab Alley Creek to catch a mess of crabs. From that day to this, Lester Lee has been a trotliner, and ,although a recent hip operation has sidelined him, he still thinks about working the lines.

"Yep, I was a youngster the first time I worked a trotline," said Lester from the river bank looking out over the very waters where he first started. "I caught a few crabs out there and later on started doing it for a living. There wa'n't the market then that there is today for crabs. There wa'n't no Bay Bridge and a thousand cars a day coming over here either."

The Bay Bridge connects the western part of Maryland and the Eastern Shore. The eastern end of the bridge empties onto the banks of Kent Island, bringing loads of people on weekends to enjoy the quiet "good living" of Eastern Shore life; the bridge also allows quick access for crab buyers to sell their product to seafood outlets in Baltimore and Annapolis.

Years back, we sold our crabs by the barrel and would ship them to Baltimore on the ol' *Smokey Joe*. She was a steamboat and we would catch her

Lester Lee is one of the oldest trotliners on Kent Island. He holds
one of the largest jimmies he ever caught. It was twenty-two inches
long from claw to claw and he decided he would have it mounted.
"It's not the biggest I ever caught, but it was big enough I wanted
it mounted," he said.

at the steamboat dock at Love Point. We had to catch the train at Bluff Point on Wye River, roll the barrelful of crabs on the train and then roll it off again when we got to Love Point. Sometimes they would pick the crabs up in the heat of the day and most of them would be dead by the time they got to Baltimore. We didn't get paid for dead crabs, I'll tell ya that. So what I'd do was break off a myrtle bush from the shore. They have a lot of little branches and I'd stick a bush in each barrel all the way to the bottom. As I'd fill the barrel with crabs, I'd shake the bush around to keep them spread out. You see, a crab will spread its claws when something startles him and by shaking that bush it caused them to spread out and give them more air.

I went to work with my granddaddy full time when I was eleven or twelve, and he taught me well. We crabbed and oystered. He had a canoe named the *Echo* that he sailed for years and then he put a four-horse-power Victor engine in her. Yep, I've been working the water a long time and I've been satisfied. Work like a mule sometimes, but I had a good wife and a fine family. I've got five boys and they all work the crabs. You can't ask for anything more. The most crabs I've ever got in one day was sixty-four baskets. That was in the fall of the year and I had to slow the boat right down to keep up with the crabs. There was one on every bait. I heard the old-timers talk about the year they got into a mess of crabs on the Chester River and every boat was catching ten or twelve barrels a day. Lordy, that was some crabs. Sometimes in the fall when it gets cool crabs will school up and burrow and that's what happened then.

During prohibition, crabs didn't bring nothing. It was dry around here, no beer or nothing hard, but when beer came back, we done all right. Ya know, boys like to eat crabs and drink beer. Back then, I'd sell to the crab house during weekdays and I'd take my crabs that I caught on Saturday to Centreville and sell them off my truck. Sometimes, I would do all right on Saturday. My good big jimmies were bringing a $1.50 a dozen and I'd get 25¢ for a dozen soups. The colored people liked the soups. They are great big jimmies but are poor (not fat with meat). Some call them white crabs. I always felt sorry for a lot of those colored people so I'd sell them fourteen for a quarter. They loved me!" chuckled Lester.

Now when I'd go on the rich side of Centreville to those lawyer's houses, they would come out with a little old pan and want three of my best crabs. Jesus, can you imagine buying just three crabs. I did just as well dealing with the poor. Sometime, when crabs weren't selling, I'd go over to Cordova and trade crabs for eggs from some of those farmers. I never was short of food. Things were rough, but they were good old days. I had six dollars to my name when I got married. I gave the preacher two dollars, bought a coal oil stove for two dollars, so me and my wife started out with two dollars.

I've caught the biggest jimmies you've ever seen in your life and sold them for twenty cents a barrel. I remember the first time I made a hundred dollars in a week. Lordy, that was the same as two thousand dollars now. You could buy something then. A loaf of bread was two or three cents.

Lester has lived his entire life in Dominion on Kent Island. At his home, a comfortable two-story clapboard house, he has a stuffed crab on the wall. "That's one of the biggest jimmies I ever caught," he said pointing to the crab. "That's one big one. Ain't he? He measures twenty-two inches from claw to claw. It's not the biggest I've ever seen, but big enough that I wanted him on my wall," chuckled Lester.

Lester then hobbled over to his bookshelf. "I want you to see this now." He pulled out a copy of *Beautiful Swimmers* by William Warner, the renowned book on the Chesapeake blue crab and a 1976 Pulitzer Prize winner. "That's me there," he said pointing to a drawing of a man working a trotline. He then flipped to a page that was the start of a chapter. It read, "Lester Lee and the Chicken Neckers."

Mr. Warner is a fine man and he has been in my house many times,. I'm proud to have been a part of this wonderful book. It sold a hundred thousand copies the first year and won a Pulitzer Prize. I've had many people tell me the best part was the chapter on me and trotlining.

You know I give those old chicken-neckers a hard time, but there's room for everyone out there and I know a lot of them. They are good people.

I'll tell you something, boy, I've lived a good life. A lot of people would have liked to have had my life. I wouldn't have done it any different.

Lester Lee died February 7, 1997 at the age of 86 in Dominion just a short distance from Crab Alley Creek where he first took up trotlining.

CHAPTER TWENTY-THREE

PATENT DIP TROTLINE

In 1987, there were three licensed patent dip crabbers working in Virginia waters. There were none in 1988. As this book was being prepared, the end of an era in the crab fishery was taking place. For crabbers like Charles "Hick" Forrest, it was sad to see the end, but as a good waterman, he adjusted to the change.

Bill Rollins of Poquoson suggested that I interview Hick for this chapter. I'd like to thank Bill because Hick turned out to be a knowledgeable and informative source. Little has been written about the patent dip trotlines, but Hick's information has helped shed some light on a form of gear that has received little recognition over the years.

A variation of the crab trotline was developed around 1910, when a Mr. Gandie of Hampton patented a new form of gear that eliminated the need for a hand dip net.

The patent dip trotline was never popular in Maryland, but was used in Virginia's lower Bay area up until the 1980s. It was particularly good in the fall of the year near the mouth of the Bay, where great numbers of large female crabs would migrate for winter.

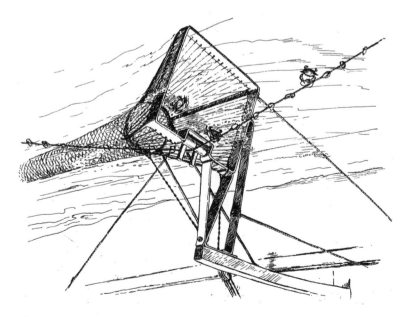

The Patent Dip trotline was developed around 1910 as an improvement to the age-old method of harvesting blue crabs with a trotline. It was not, however, totally accepted throughout the Bay region. (Courtesy of the Virginia Institute of Marine Science)

The gear was most effective in areas where there was an abundance of large crabs, mainly because of the difficulties the gear created in culling small, undersized crabs. A waterman working a regular trotline could simply knock the small crabs back into the water with his dip net, whereas the patent dip would catch everything that grabbed the bait. Consequently, watermen had to cull all these crabs by hand, and this often required a considerable amount of time. In areas where there were great numbers of small crabs, watermen often felt the patent dip created more work than it was worth.

The patent dip is a metal frame funnel structure made of iron rods with a large net and a roller (see drawing). As a crab surfaces and crosses the roller, two vertical rods welded to the frame knock it down into the metal "catch." The force of the water, caused by the motion of the boat moving forward, pushes the crab through the catch into a "patent dip net bag."

The bag is attached to the rear opening of the metal frame and has a drawstring in the bottom. When ready to harvest, watermen untied the string and dumped the crabs into barrels.

The patent dip is mounted on a boom, which is attached to a mast. While being worked, the boom and patent dip extend over the side of the workboat. When the bag is full and the waterman is ready to harvest his catch, he pulls on one end of a rope that hangs down from a block and tackle at the top of the mast. The other end of the rope reaches down to the boom and, when pulled, raises the patent dip and boom above the gunwales. There is a swivel bolt where the mast and boom meet and a guideline to swing the boom into the boat. In later years, hydraulics were used to raise the rigs up and down.

There were several styles of patent dips built around the lower Bay area. Gandie, for instance, built his rigs with a large square opening in front and a much smaller square opening in back, while Rollins Hardware Company in Poquoson had a large circular opening for the back hole. For years, Rollins sold rigs for twenty-five dollars (without net) and crabbers paid a fifty-dollar royalty fee to Gandie, until the patent expired.

• • •

Hick Forrest worked a patent dip trotline from 1939 to 1973. "I used the patent dip until 1973, when the crab pot put us out of business," said Hick.

I started working a standard trotline with my daddy in a log canoe. In 1939, I got my own boat and I've been crabbing on my own ever since. I used the patent dip long after the crab pot came along because I could depend on it better in the fall of the year. I stopped because there was no place to work. The whole Bay is filled up with crab pots and you need some room to work a trotline.

When I first started, I'd use my patent dip in the spring right on through until December. That's right, I've crabbed as late as December 5. We'd follow the crabs up the Bay in the early spring and then turn around and follow them

*Hick Forrest worked this patent dip trotline from 1939 to 1973
when he decided there was no longer enough room on the Bay for
trotlines and crab pots.*

back towards Cape Henry. I've caught as high as fifty-five barrels in a day. I could only carry about fifteen barrels in my boat, so when they were full I made a pen in the bottom of the boat and sometimes I had crabs piled up over my head. There were five and six crabs on a bait at one time and they'd come up out of the water looking like a knot. That didn't happened often, but it happened.

The line used on Hick's patent dip was eighteen hundred feet long and made of three-strand burlap rope.

When my daddy was working a regular trotline we had a snood line to tie the bait to, but later we used a soft three-strand burlap twine so we could stick the bait between the strands. The bait wasn't tied, just pulled tight between the strands.

For bait, we used tripe (cow's belly), hog maul, and sometimes croakers. For all-around bait, tripe was the best. When I first started, I got it from a slaughterhouse in Norfolk. Later, we had to drive to Suffolk. Seven or eight of us would go in together and take turns driving down to pick it up. When I first started it cost a nickel a pound for tripe and toward the last it got up to eighteen cents a pound.

In the early years, I would salt down some of my bait and sometimes I'd buy a barrel of tripe already salted. Later on, I went to fresh and frozen bait. Salted bait will last longer on a line, but fresh bait will catch crabs better. To keep my bait good and fresh I would ice it down with crushed ice before I'd leave the dock. I would bait twenty-five or thirty feet of line, drop it in a barrel and cover it with ice. Then I'd do twenty-five or thirty more feet, until it was all done and iced down good. When I would get to my crabbing spot, my bait would still be good and fresh.

Hick's trotline was rigged at each end with an anchor attached to a rope pendant leading up to a buoy, usually a empty five-gallon gas can. Another line would run from the buoy to a drag chain. The baited trotline was tied to the chain, which kept the line on the bottom and allowed it to move with the tide.

Patent dip nets could be bought at several marine supply stores around the lower Bay. According to Hick a net would last one season and was about nine feet long.

You could buy six-foot nets, but we had to either add to it with trawl netting or with another patent dip net. One store-bought net just wasn't big enough to hold all the crabs we would catch.

The best time to crab was when the tide was changing. It's sort of like hook-and-line fishing, the best time to fish is usually when the tide is about to change. Nature is a funny thing. On the York River we'd catch more crabs at night than during the day. The James River was opposite. We could be catching two barrels every time we went down the line, but the minute it got dark, they would quit. Who can figure it? The moon and tide got more to do with the water than anyone thing and the Good Lord plays a big part in all that.

I've done it all on the water, but working a patent dip trotline was about the best work I've ever done. It took a lot of time, but you've got to put the time in to make anything on the water.

"I went to crab potting because there just wasn't any room left for a trotline down here," he said, referring to the lower Bay. "Crab pots don't take the time that a trotline takes to work because you've got to stay out there and work a patent dip all day. But I liked it better."

I can see those big jimmies coming up out of the water. At times, they'd fall off before getting to the dip, but most of the time they'd hold on tight.

Don't nobody get rich crabbing but I believe I made as much working a patent dip as anything. I hated to give it up, but times change and you've got to change with them, if you're going to survive.

The information on Mr. Gandie was provided by Thomas Freeman of Poquoson who had Rollins Hardware Company build him a patent dip trotline in 1926. He paid twenty-five dollars for the rig and fifty dollars to Mr. Gandie for the right to use the concept. Once the patent dip was finished and the patent fee paid, the gear was sent to the Newport News Shipyard where it was galvanized. Mr. Freeman worked a patent dip from the 1920s until he retired in 1976.

There are no patent dip trotlines being worked on the Bay today.

 # CRAB SCRAPES

In 1989, I was sent to Smith Island (Maryland) to do a story on a fiberglass boatbuilder who operated a boat shop there on the island. After the interview was over, I was waiting around with him at the dock to catch the mail boat back to Crisfield, when I noticed a very rustic, traditional Chesapeake Bay crab scraping boat.

I asked whose boat it was and he told me it was Edward Harrison's. He also told me a little about him and what a kind and upstanding person he was. It was all I needed to hear. Two months later I went back to Smith, and Edward and I spent the day working his crab scrape.

The crab scrape was patented in 1870 by L. Copper Dize of Crisfield. Since then, the scrape has been used extensively to harvest peeler crabs and soft crabs, particularly on Smith Island, Tangier Island, and other areas in the lower Bay, where there is an abundance of eel grass growing on the bottom.

Although soft and hard-shell crabs were consumed during colonial days in Maryland and Virginia, the marketing of both remained fairly localized because of the difficulties in the preservation and transportation of the product. This changed in 1873 when the railroad arrived in Crisfield and Captain John H. Landon shipped the first load of soft crabs by rail to the firm of John Martin in Philadelphia, Pennsylvania. Soft crabs have since become an important commodity for Chesapeake Bay watermen.

Blue crabs grow by molting or shedding the hard exoskeleton, or shell. Each time a crab sheds, it comes out considerably larger. Right after shedding, the shell and meat of the crab are very soft and quite delicious when fried.

A peeler crab is a crab in one of the three stages just prior to shedding. Watermen harvest peelers and place them in holding tanks, either on shore or in the water, to wait for them to shed into soft crabs.

• • •

Smith Island is one of a chain of islands that reaches from Maryland's lower Bay down into Virginia. The island lies out across from Tangier Sound in the middle of the Chesapeake Bay about eight miles west of Crisfield.

There are no bridges connecting Smith Island to the mainland so the only way to and from is by water. The island was settled in 1657 by a group of families from

Captain Edward Harrison is one of the oldest and most well-known of Smith Island's crab scrapers. He has worked the water since he was eleven years old and, now at seventy-eight, still goes out every day during the crab season to work the shallow grassy flats around the island.

St. Clements Island in St. Mary's County, Maryland. Over the years, the people of Smith have learned the ways of the water and most make their living by harvesting the bounty of the Chesapeake.

One of the oldest and most well-known waterman on the island is Captain Edward Harrison. Captain Harrison has worked the water since he was eleven years old. He is probably most noted for the years that he and his brother, Daniel, owned and sailed the famous skipjack, the *Ruby G. Ford*. Although those years have passed, today, at seventy-eight, he still gets up early each morning during the crabbing season, from May to October, and scrapes for crabs along the grassy flats of Smith.

To catch Captain Harrison's boat, one has to get an early start, as he leaves at 4:30 in the morning from his home in Ewell. This means a visitor must catch the *Island Belle II*, proclaimed as Maryland's only mail boat, from the City Dock in Crisfield at 12:30 P.M. the day before and spend the night on the island. Ewell is one of three small island communities on Smith Island—Rhodes Point and Tylerton being the other two.

There is a traditional-style motel at Ewell, but to catch the flavor of Island life, a night at Bernice Gay's boarding house offers a step back in time to when salesmen traveled their routes by steamboat and stayed the night at a little boarding house. For thirty-five dollars, Bernice, now seventy-nine years of age, offers a clean room and a home-cooked meal in the true tradition of a Smith Island cook. Her fried soft crabs, harvested right from local waters, provide a taste of heaven on earth. Bernice has been taking in boarders for over thirty years and through all those years, she said the only things ever stolen from her home were seven bed sheets.

After supper, a visit to Captain Harrison's home was planned to set up the time frame for the early morning departure aboard his crab boat. There is no street sign to denote the narrow main road in Ewell where Captain Harrison and his wife, Ella, live. I had to ask a passerby for directions. Their home is a comfortable two-story frame house that contains many reminders of Captain Harrison's long life as a working waterman. Paintings and prints of his old skipjack, the *Ruby G. Ford,* hang on several walls and a wooden model of the vessel sits on a table. A large plaque on the wall was awarded to him in 1988 by the Chesapeake Bay Foundation when he was chosen Maryland's Conservationist of the Year; it is an award he treasures dearly.

While sitting in their living room Captain Harrison and Ella talked about their days of living and working on Smith.

"A Smith Island boy had to learn the water early and I was selling peeler crabs and soft-shell crabs when I was seven," said Captain Harrison with his feet propped up in his favorite chair. "My father got this old fellow to build me a twelve-foot skiff for five dollars and I caught a many a crab in her just poling along in the grass with a dip net.

I started working the water full time when I was eleven years old. My mother died that year and my father was in a truck accident on the mainland, so I had to go to work. There were four of us children and I worked hard to make money to help bring us all up. I waited until they were all grown and married before I took the big step and got married. Now, we've all celebrated our fiftieth wedding anniversaries and I think we all made out all right, even if there were some tight times.

The boat I loved the most was the *Ruby G. Ford.* She had a bateau hull, but was skipjack rigged. My brother and I paid six hundred dollars for her in the late thirties and the first year we worked her we dredged seed [oysters] for a nickel a bushel. That same year we got twenty and a quarter cents for a bushel of oysters to the shucking house. Now, boy, I tell ya, things were tight. Weren't they? Boy, that was something.

"Yeah, they were tight," said Ella. "When we got married, we had eleven dollars to our name, so you know I didn't marry him for the money, did I?" she said as they both laughed long and hard.

"One of the best times we ever had a-oystering was the third year we had the *Ruby Ford*," continued Captain Harrison.

We caught 1,803 bushels in Tangier Sound in one week. That was nothing, though, compared to those big schooners. I'll tell ya. I've seen the [schooner]

Mattie F. Dean catch a thousand bushels in a day. That was one great sailor—now she could solid sail."

Now, I've seen it good and I've seen it bad. All those old schooners up on the Potomac River near Colonial Beach, now that was something to behold. Oh boy, that was something. I'd give anything in the world to go back to those days again. Ain't nothing prettier in the world than a fleet of schooners catching a fair breeze up the Bay.

The captains of those boats were decent men. They would always give us the right-of-way because our boats were smaller. They treated us real good. People have treated me good all my life and I've tried to treat people good. I was always taught that it was important to be a good person. It's so important to have good friends and good credit, but the best thing in the world is a good friend.

Captain Harrison also recalls some narrow escapes when he sailed the *Ruby Ford*.

I've seen some close calls, too, when I was a-sailing. One time the skipjack *Eldora* capsized with five head of men aboard her and I took a rowboat and went over from the *Ruby Ford* and took two men off at a time. We couldn't get close to her in the big boat because it was blowing a solid gale. I got them all off, but it was a close call.

Another time John Evans of Rhodes Point and I were reefing the jib on the *Ruby Ford*. When you reef a jib, you put one foot on the foot rope and the other leg over the bowsprit. John, though, had both feet on the foot rope and he slipped and went straight down in the cold water with gum boats and all on. We sailed right over top of him and when he came up from under the stern, he threw his arm over the yawl boat. That's what saved him. Golly, I knew he was gone, but he wasn't and from then on he always had a leg over the bowsprit when he reefed the jib. I'll tell ya he did.

Yeah boy, there were some tight times back in the thirties. There weren't many good jobs back then either. We did all right, though. Ed Crockett from Tangier Island, who worked with us aboard the *Ruby Ford,* used to say we were the best around when it came to oystering under sail. Years later, he told me that if it hadn't been for the money he made a-working for us a-oystering in the winter, his two boys would have never gone away to school. One turned out a dentist and the other a principal in a high school. Ed told me that before he got the job with us, his wife was making as much money as he was taking in washing on Tangier for twenty-five cents. [Crockett had tonged for oysters before going on the Ruby Ford.] They worked hard and sent those boys to school. Yes sir, they were some fine people. Now, I've known some fine people in my lifetime and I've tried to be a good person to everyone.

The Margaret H. is a classic Chesapeake Bay deadrise crab scrape boat. Captain Harrison had her built on Smith Island in the 1960s.

Around 8:00 P.M., Ella and Captain Harrison reminded each other that 4:30 A.M. comes early and a good night's sleep is important to a crabber. Captain Harrison rises early, Monday though Saturday, to go out and work his scrapes. The time he departs each day depends on the distance away from home that he plans to work. His daily harvest of soft crabs is carried to Crisfield by boat, so he must have his catch packed and ready to go by 4:00 P.M. When he plans to go far off to work, it means getting up at 2:00 A.M. On this day in June, however, the skipper has decided to stay close to home because his Ford engine has been acting up; he will leave the Smith Island oil dock at Ewell promptly at 4:45 A.M.

A three-quarter moon is still high in the sky at 4:30 A.M. on the island. The only sound at that hour of the morning is water running from the shedding houses along the shoreline and a faint explosion of an engine cranking up off in the distance.

Captain Harrison arrived at the dock on a twenty-five-inch blue Ross bicycle. His extra-large [paperboy special] basket was filled with a can of fuel, a six-pack of Coke Classics, a brown bag lunch, and a milk container with a solid chunk of ice in it.

"Yeah boy, I see you can get up with the chickens," he said leaning his bike up against the building. "Well, let's give her a try," said Captain Harrison as he stepped out on the washboards of his boat with his arms full.

The *Margaret H.,* named after Captain Harrison's youngest daughter, is a classic crab scrapping boat with low sides, a deadrise and cross-planked hull, and a shallow draft to enable him to crab in as little as a foot and a half of water. Measuring twenty-eight feet by ten feet by one-and-a-half feet, she is the second crab scraping boat he has owned. The first, powered by sail, was built in Norfolk, while the *Margaret H.* was built on Smith Island. "I've had this one thirty years," he said, referring to his present boat.

> The first one I got cost me $330 and that was for sail, mast, boat and I even got the scrapes for that. Didn't have no power when I got my first one. We call them crab scrape boats, but on Tangier Island they call them bar cats. These boats can solid sail. I'll tell ya that. I never would have gotten rid of my first boat, but she got some bad wood in her and Captain Lawson Tyler told me, "Time I order the stuff, I can near 'bout build you a new one."
>
> He built the *Margaret H.* and he was one of the nicest fellows who ever lived. He built mine and he built my brother's too.
>
> These boats are built for scraping by hand. See how low to the water they are. The reason it's so low-sided is to make it easier to bring the scrape up over the sides. Most of the boys have gone to using hydraulics to haul up the scrape, but I guess I'll keep on doing it by hand. I do all right.

The small six-cylinder Ford engine began to grind as Captain Harrison tried to start her up. Finally, the engine started. "Boy, I've had some trouble with her. We're not going far because I'm not sure she'll get us back," he said.

Inside the boat is an assortment of gear and tools of the trade—three scrapes, an old-time wooden crab float used only when the Captain gets an overabundance of crabs, a short handle net, a very long handle dip net, a long, knobby piece of driftwood used to mark "hangs" (tree stumps, etc.) on the bottom, several old and muddy fish boxes for seats, and bushel baskets for jimmie crabs. Built into the bottom of the *Margaret H.* are two holding boxes which have small holes that run through the bottom to allow water to flow in from outside the boat. One box is for soft crabs, busters, and rank peelers. The other box is for green and medium peelers. Crabs are held in these tanks all day, while Captain Harrison works his scrapes. At the end of the day, they are removed to an onshore shedding facility there at Smith, which he and several relatives own and operate.

Although there are wooden frames for an awning on the *Margaret H.*, the canvas awning was recently ripped off in a storm. "She came on so fast and hard, she ripped the awning right off," said Captain Harrison. "I got a brand-new one but haven't had time to put her on. I tell ya, I don't keep my boat like I used to. You get old and it's all you can do to get a day's work in. When I get home, I don't feel much like cleaning up."

Captain Harrison moved his boat out into the dark channel. Along the edge of the channel, not far from where he moors the *Margaret H.*, he drops over two scrapes and drags them behind the boat. The scrapes are 3½ feet wide and the net bag has 2¼-inch mesh.

Tools of the trade include this scrape, an old-time wooden crab float, a dip net, and a long knobby piece of driftwood used to mark the location of tree stumps at the bottom of the coves and guts where Captain Harrison works.

"We're on the channel edge," he said. "Years back, we had crab houses all out here. Then the storm came and tore them all down. So, we all built nearer the land." Old pilings and remains of wharves and crab houses were all along the shore.

The sun began to rise and Captain Harrison predicted we would have a beautiful day of crabbing. As the sun broke through the darkness behind the houses, wharves, and church at Ewell, one could almost drift back a century in time and see little change in the island community. "That used to be a farm," he said, pointing over to a piece of overgrown property on the edge of the island. Most of the homes on the island are on narrow lots, but this piece of property has several acres. "They want to put condominiums on it, but the island folk are against it," he said. "They got them over on Deal [Island], and they say the people who own them won't let you walk across their yard. Crazy world, isn't it?"

Suddenly the motion of the boat stalled and Captain Harrison threw the motor out of gear and pulled on the ¾-inch rope used to tow the scrape. "We hit a stump," he said as if it happens all the time. "Used to be land and trees out here, but the Bay has taken it all away."

"Smell that," he said after freeing the scrape. "It's the menhaden factories at Reedville. My bother-in-law lives over there and when he calls I kid him about the rotten smell. I say that ain't a sweet smell but that's the smell of money to you and he laughs."

Captain Harrison put a yellow apron on and then began to pull up the first scrape. The scrape was dumped on the washboard; it was loaded with eel grass, several peelers, and one soft crab. "That's the kind I like to catch—the money kind," he said holding up a whale, which is the largest of soft crabs. Whales, jumbos, primes, hotels, and mediums are the five different sizes of soft-shell crabs that Captain Harrison sells to his Crisfield buyer.

The waterman dropped the scrape back overboard and gave the engine more gas as he pulled the other one up. "This is the way I get the mud out of her," he said, "the first scrape had too much mud." This one had a few more peelers and several soft crabs, also a pretty good-size flounder and several mud toads [oyster toads]. "I leave the toads on the washboard because in a while the gulls will be swallowing them right down," said Captain Harrison. "Once in a while I catch a nice flounder."

As he culled through the eel grass on the washboard, there were hundreds of little crabs scrambling to get back into the water. "Look at all those little crabs," he said. "Jew claw!" he exclaimed, holding up a peeler crab that had one hard claw and a small soft-shell claw on the other side. "When he sheds, the claws will both be normal. The soft claw is called a jew claw, but I don't rightly know why. Nature is something though, ain't it?"

"Look-a there," he said pointing to something breaking the water's surface. "Get my long handle net. It's a diamondback [terrapin]." The turtle had escaped capture by the time the net was in Captain Harrison's hand.

I caught three big ones yesterday—all in the scrape. I got them in a pound at the shedding house and we sell them to New York in the fall for $4.50 apiece.

Catching diamondbacks used to be a big-time thing around here. Years back, there was an old fellow who had Indian blood in him. He would sound for turtles in the winter with a pole and when he'd hit one he'd dig him up. Ya know, they burrow in the mud during cold weather. He used to catch right many.

As Captain Harrison talked, he continued to work his scrapes. "There's a little soft crab. He's not big enough to sell. I'm careful how I throw them back in the water because the gulls will swoop down and eat them every time if I give them half a chance." He yelled at the gulls and when they flew away, he tossed the little soft crab over.

"Gulls—they are something. If you don't watch them they'll come right in and drink your coffee," said Captain Harrison with a hearty laugh.

About that time, a herring gull landed on the washboard next to him, grabbed an extra-large oyster toad, and gobbled him right down. "Boy, I can't figure how they can get something that big in their mouths," he said. Throughout the day, gulls stayed perched on the awning frames waiting for an oyster toad to land on the washboards.

As he worked along the isolated marshes, he talked of the way things used to be. "Ya see over there," he said, pointing to a small island connected to Smith by marsh. "It used to be a bridge over the marsh and houses were over there. Now all the houses are gone. There used to be an old doctor who lived there. We don't have a doctor now. We have to go to Crisfield, if anything needs tending to."

"I've done some work in my day," he continued. "I don't mean to be bragging, but I guess I've handled as many crabs and oysters as just about anybody alive. I've been blessed. I was lucky to marry a good wife. She gets up every morning and fixes me a hot breakfast no matter what time it is. We don't have everything fancy, but we enjoy what we have and we're thankful for it."

"Look over there," he said pointing to another large tract of marsh grass. "There was some of the best gunning [duck hunting] in the world over there, but now the government owns it all and won't let us hunt it. By gosh, we had some good gunning around here years back."

Culling through the grass on the washboard, Captain Harrison held up a large crab. "Buckram" he said referring to a crab that was hard, but not hard enough to sell as a soft crab. "That crab shed yesterday. He's just as poor as can be. Now when he gets good and hard, he'll fatten up." He threw the crab overboard.

"By golly, an hour late," he said off the next crab he picked up. "An hour ago this crab would have been sold to Crisfield, but he's gotten a bit too hard." This one, too, went back into the water.

"Look at that bird sneaking about there for a minnow," said Captain Harrison of the great blue heron in the marsh. The bird stalked the minnow and then drove its long beak into the water pulling out a fish. "He got him. I love to watch 'em. By golly, nature is something pretty."

"Boy, it's a good crop of eel grass this year. When we first started scraping in May, the grass was that long," he said holding his hands to show about six inches. "Look how much it has grown. The grass appeared to be several feet long."

Captain Harrison was working in less than two feet of water and every once and a while he would hit bottom. "See how shallow it is here now," he said. "I told ya, she [Margaret H.] don't draw much water."

Around 10:30 A.M., the waterman changed to a straw hat. "When I put this hat on, the people on the tour boat about fall overboard to take my picture," he said with a chuckle.

The waterman seemed to tire very little as the day went on. The two holding tanks were filled with crabs before the morning was over. Captain Harrison said he would not need to use the wooden float that he pulls behind the boat when there is an excess of crabs.

At 11:00 A.M., a buyer in a runabout came out and picked up the jimmie crabs. They are sold to a buy boat that goes to Hoopers Island, Maryland. "Week before last we were getting fifty-five dollars a bushel for jimmies. They're down to thirty-five dollars now, but my brother in Baltimore said they're charging eighty dollars a bushel retail there and haven't changed the price all year. Somebody is making some money."

Just before lunch, Captain Harrison pulled up a large soft crab that had just shed. "Soft as a baby's bottom" he said holding up the crab. "I don't care how many I've handled, I always love to feel one like this."

At lunchtime the boat continued to move through the grass as the waterman sat down for a break. Captain Harrison had soft drinks aboard but he drank water most of the day. There was a milk jug frozen solid and another with warm water. He would dump the warm water into the frozen jag and then pour the ice-cold water into his cup. "Smith Island [drinking] water is the best water in the world," he said. "Sweet, sweet water. People stop here all the time in boats to get a taste of our water."

"Darn old green [horse] fly," he yelled as he swatted his arm. "Boy they can bite!"

As he pulled out a big chunk of cheese, he said,"Ya know, people on Smith Island love cheese and coffee. People away from here think it's funny, but it does taste great."

About 2:00 P.M., Captain Harrison pulled up his scrapes and headed for the shedding house just across the channel from Ewell. At the little house, a man works full-time during the crabbing season. Once Captain Harrison delivered his catch, and each peeler had been placed in the appropriate tank, he began to pack the soft crabs for the boat that would be leaving for Crisfield at 4:00 P.M. The crabs are packed in a box and covered with iced-down newspaper. When the crabs are sold to a New York market, they are packaged in black grass, which is harvested along the shore of Smith.

"We go and pick it up off the shore," said Captain Harrison. "But you've got to let it dry because if you pack it green, it will strike a heat and kill all the crabs."

"The grass is better for the New York market because the truckers who carry the crabs north are so rough on them. Grass keeps them from being beat up so bad," he said.

Besides crabs, and there were plenty of them in the shedding house, there was a tank full of diamondback terrapins. "We didn't catch any turtles today, but as you can see, we get our fair share," he said.

"Well, I guess you've learned something about scraping for crabs," said Captain Harrison. "I hope I've been some help. I learned a long time ago that people need to help one another and I always try to."

Back at the dock, a firm handshake was exchanged. Captain Harrison got on his blue Ross bicycle and pedaled home as another day of working the water was over.

Edward Harrison is deceased but crab scraping is still part of island life on Smith Island.

DREDGING FOR
BLUE CRABS

Johnny Ward and the Iva W. *are known all over the Chesapeake. I did the first of several articles on Captain Johnny in 1985. During the years since, I've traveled up and down the Bay and on at least four occasions, when I was far from home, watermen have recognized my name because of an article I did on Captain Johnny and the* Iva W., *they say.*

Captain Johnny's hard work ethic and fearless approach to the business of working the water have gained him the respect of his fellow watermen up and down the Bay. In 1987, he was recognized by the governor of Virginia as the state's waterman of the year—a well-deserved honor.

Virginia first began licensing dredge boats for the harvesting of blue crabs in the winter of 1904. The exact year watermen began dredging crabs near the mouth of Chesapeake Bay is unknown, but surely it was before the turn of the 20th century. Legend has it that a waterman working an oyster dredge out of Hampton Roads ventured a little too far over into the Bay's channel and brought up a lick, or haul, full of sooks (female hard crabs). This led eventually to Virginia's winter blue crab fishery.

Along about the end of autumn, the Bay's female crab population, after mating, begins its long migration to the lower Bay. Female crabs cannot tolerate low salinity at low temperatures, so as winter weather lowers water temperatures, the sooks move into deeper, warmer water and burrow in the bottom. The result is that a large percentage, about eighty-five percent of the winter harvest, consists of female crabs.

Of the 270 licensed dredge boats from Maryland and Virginia, most are working out of the Hampton Roads area, while others are scattered along the shores of the Bay. The senior member of the Bay's dredge fleet is Captain Johnny Ward who, at eighty-six, has been harvesting crabs in the winter for over sixty years. When I was on a recent trip with the old skipper, he talked about his life as a Chesapeake Bay crabber.

The fog drifted lightly across Davis Creek in Mathews County. The Virginia air had a cool edge to it, but it seemed more like early spring than December 13. It was 4:00 A.M., and Captain Johnny was down in the engine room of his boat greasing the Caterpillar engine, preparing for a day of crab dredging on Chesapeake Bay. Captain Johnny had performed this task many times since he first had the sixty-foot Chesapeake Bay buy boat built back in 1928.

The *Iva W.,* named after Captain Johnny's wife, lay by the dock in the fog and stillness. Then, one after another, the sounds of cranking engines broke the morning silence, as the string of crab dredging boats prepared for their journey out into the Bay.

The Iva W. *and her skipper Captain Johnny Ward, have been a part of the Virginia crab dredging fleet since Captain Johnny had her built in 1928.*

Two deck hands arrived at 4:05 A.M., and Captain Johnny, clad in blue bib overalls spattered with white paint and wearing a red hat with a Southern States logo above the brim, came up the ladder to meet the crew.

After a quick good morning, the men slipped the lines from the mooring piles. In single file, the dredge boats slowly moved out the creek toward the Chesapeake.

The two hands scurried back into the heated galley, which is warmed by the exhaust pipe from the engine. Captain Johnny turned on a small light over his compass and flipped his depth finder on as he steered the *Iva W.* out into the darkness.

Above his head was a new three-thousand-dollar radar unit, but Captain Johnny kept looking at his compass and depth finder. "Yeah, the boys talked me into putting that thing in here," he said, motioning to the radar. "But, I know nothing about them. I'm sure they're fine if you know how they work, but if you don't you might just as well pitch 'em overboard," he said with a slight chuckle.

Captain Johnny comes from a long line of Chesapeake Bay watermen. Born and raised in Crisfield, he quit school at thirteen and went to work on his father's seventy-five-foot sail-driven bugeye.

Daddy bought shucked stock oysters from around the Bay and seed from the James River. He would also haul watermelons, lumber, and whatever else he could find to haul.

Captain Johnny is the senior member of the dredging fleet. He has been dredging for crabs every year since the early 1920s.

When I started with him I was chief cook because Daddy liked my cooking. His favorite was cod fish in the morning. I'd skin the fish and soak it overnight, cook it the next morning until it would fall off the bone. I'd pick the bones out, mix the meat with mashed potatoes and onions cut up real fine. Then, I'd fry up a piece of fatback and pour the grease from it over the fish, potatoes, and onions. Boy, you got a good feed when it's all done.

When Daddy would finish eaten' the fish and potatoes, he'd always ask for the fatback. He liked it brown after the grease was all out of it.

I remember another time when I was cooking. It was the only time in my life I ever got seasick. We were sailing to Tangier Island and when we got about halfway there we ran into a squall. It was blowing a solid gale. So, Daddy got us to haul the sails down and told me to go below and fix him some food. It was rolling down in the galley and hot with that wood cookstove blazing, but I cooked him up some grub. When I took it to him, he laughed and asked if I was seasick. Lord, I was sick as a dog.

Daddy taught us a lot about working the water though. He would always tell us what a load would bring and what it would cost him. I remember he would charge forty-five dollars freight for a load of watermelons hauled from Gloucester County, Virginia to Washington, D.C., or Baltimore. One of the first things he taught us was how to sound the bottom and when that lead line hit the bottom you best let him know the water depth quick. I think he knew his boys would all be working the water one day. There was nine of us, five girls and four boys.

I was about sixteen when I bought my first boat. It was a little forty-foot frame boat with a little engine. Daddy said I'd never make any money in her because she was too small, but I ran her hard. I made a daily trip from Crisfield to the Piankatank River, up past Freeport Landing, to buy soft crabs. I'd take them back and sell them to a buyer in Crisfield. I had to get up early to make the trip every day. There wasn't any house on the boat so I'd wrap up in a piece of canvas with just my nose hanging out.

That was to keep the mosquitoes from taking me away. I'd sleep there all night until a night watchman would come around and tap on the canvas with his billy. He'd say, "Time to go Johnny."

As the CB blared overhead and the captain watched his compass, he continued to talk of those early days. "When I was eighteen years old, I bought the *Lagonia*. She was a fifty-foot log canoe. I started out buying clean-culled oysters in her during the winter and I'd buy fresh fish from pound netters and haul them to Gwynn Island in the spring and summer."

"I've had many a boat," said Captain Johnny, with a tinge of an Eastern Shore accent. "I've run just about everything there is to run. In the 1930s, I ran watermelons from North Carolina to Philadelphia in the old *Edward Parkins*." One after another, he listed the boats he had owned. "Lands, if you were to put them all in a pile, that would be one big pile of boats!" he said. The most famous of Captain Johnny's boats was the old schooner *H. H. Conway*. "I bought her and had a heavy-duty 175-horsepower Fairbanks-Morse engine installed in her. She was named after the famous skipper." Harvey Conway was the founder of the legendary Conway Fleet, which the old captain assembled from the 1880s until his death in 1931. Legend has it he started with all he owned in a twelve-pound flour sack, but was a millionaire when he died.

It was in *Lagonia* that Captain Johnny first started dredging for crabs.

> The first time I went dredging was in 1926. I couldn't make enough that first year to pay two men twelve dollars each a week. I was getting $1.50 a barrel for my crabs.
>
> I had to give it up or starve. I lacked ten dollars at the end of the week for paying off the men. I went home and asked Iva, my wife, if she had any money. She had ten dollars that she had saved, so I paid off the men and headed to Crisfield, dead broke.

Shortly after that, Captain Johnny began buying oysters from the James River and selling them in Crisfield. The first oysters he bought cost him forty cents a bushel and he sold them for eighty cents.

In the spring, he bought crabs around the Bay to sell in Crisfield. "I got ahead enough to have this boat built in 1928," he said. Deltaville boatbuilder and Captain Johnny's neighbor John Wright built the *Iva W.* for $2,350. "That took care of everything but the engine," Captain Johnny said.

As daybreak came closer, the sky lightened. "The pilothouse is just the same as when John Wright built her. I paid twenty-two dollars for this wheel, and Captain John made the spool and stand." A brass plate on the mahogany wheel read, "American Engineer Co., Philadelphia, Pa."

"I've put in many an hour on this wheel," he commented. That was obvious from the smoothly worn wooden handles. Two shiny brass handles had replaced ones that had broken off.

There was a clear tone of pride in his voice when he talked about his *Iva W.* "You see all that trim in here. That's all white oak, and when it was new it was just as bright as a silver dollar."

Before Captain Johnny had the 115-horsepower Caterpillar installed, he had a sixty-horsepower Atlas engine and used an auxiliary sail on the *Iva W.* "There was 105 yards of sail on her, and I kept it until around 1945 when I put the Caterpillar in her. The sail had rotted, so I decided not to buy another one."

Off in the distance, the lights on the other dredge boats could still be seen. Captain Johnny opened the pilothouse window so he could see better and the cool breeze chilled the house. He lit a small heater.

Behind the pilothouse, inside the house of the *Iva W.*, a picture of Jesus Christ sitting on a hillside hung on the wall. Next to it was a photo of Captain Johnny's wife inscribed "Love, Iva—1948." Across the way was a picture of an ocean liner identified as "The North German Lloyd flier *Europe*, sister ship of the *Breman*, the two fastest afloat."

Three bunks that extended from the floor to the ceiling were cluttered with an assortment of gear from life jackets to line. A chart rack loaded with charts was neatly placed overhead and a medicine cabinet hung from the wall. It contained everything from nuts and bolts to a bottle of Bufferin.

"We've been a lot of places together," he said of the *Iva W*. "I've been from Cape Charles to Crisfield in weather when the Old Bay Line steamers wouldn't come out on the Bay.

> Many a night my daddy would check down at the dock in Crisfield to see if I'd come in. He'd say, "I know Johnny didn't come up the Bay because my house was shaking from the wind."
>
> But they'd tell him at the dock, "Johnny's landed the crabs and be damned if he ain't gone back for more!"

During the crab dredging season, Captain Johnny would dredge all day and then buy from the other crabbers.

> I had fifteen boats working for me and after I'd load up with crabs I'd haul to Crisfield at night, and be back the next morning dredging again.
>
> I'd work six days a week, night and day. The engine never got a chance to cool off. I'd go home on Sunday morning and be back out on the Bay dredging Monday morning. A lot of people have asked me how I could do it, but I was young then, and that made a whole lot of difference.
>
> After a while, all I did was work crabs. I'd buy in the spring, summer, and fall, and then dredge in the winter. I've seen many a crab in my life, I have. Once, I guess it was in the early 1930s, I went into Little Creek right off from Lynnhaven Inlet, to buy crabs from some patent dip trotliners. You know, there wasn't no crab pot around then. I don't know what happened, but that night they struck a gold mine of crabs. That day, I bought 460 barrels of crabs and all the other buy boats were loaded up, too. I had to dump them loose in the hold to get them all on the boat. I'd never seen so many crabs in my life.
>
> Well that glutted the market and my buyer told me I could go back but I could only pay three dollars a barrel for them. I had been paying four dollars a barrel. The rest of the buy boat captains decided to go ahead and rig up for dredging because it was the middle of November, but I decided I'd try to make another load because I knew there were plenty of crabs there.
>
> When I got down there, I told the boys I could only pay but three dollars and they all laughed at me and said "no way." So, I told them to go ahead and find another market. Well, I knew Hampton was glutted, just like Crisfield, so I decided to wait and see.

There was a little beer joint there, near the shore, and all the crabbers were in there beering up. I went in and sat down to have a beer and it wasn't long before they came to me and asked if I'd clean them out for three dollars a barrel.

Yep, that was one time it paid to wait around. I was always one to take a chance. It didn't always pay off, but most of the time it did.

I've bought crabs for as little as fifty cents a barrel from down in Guinea Neck, but most of the time it was around $1.50 when I first started.

I've done more than just run crabs in her. I used to run watermelons in 1929 from North Carolina to Baltimore. Then, I had an old gas Regal engine in her. It would take four hundred gallons of gas for that trip. That was right bad, but fuel oil wa'n't but four and a half cents a gallon. I got ninety dollars a load to make the trip and I paid a man six dollars for labor. The next year I changed to the sixty-horsepower Atlas and she only burnt two hundred gallons a trip. So, it saved me some money.

At daybreak, Captain Johnny stepped into the wheelhouse and pulled a string that was hooked onto a bell in the galley. It was a signal for the crew to come forward and ready themselves for work.

All the windows were lowered on the pilothouse, and Captain Johnny asked one of the crewmen if he could see buoy 36 in the channel. The crew included Floyd Johnson of Newport News, who for the past twelve years has crab dredged in the winter for Captain Johnny, and Franklin Forrest of Mathews County.

"Check that dredge to make sure there's no holes in the twine," said Captain Johnny, Sure enough, there was a hole. The captain came out of the pilothouse to restring it.

When everything was ready, the dredges on the starboard and port sides were dropped overboard one at a time. "We caught our limit of twenty-five barrels day before yesterday," said Captain Johnny. "Yesterday we had sixteen barrels and six baskets of jimmies."

The price for crabs was eighteen dollars a barrel for females and eleven dollars a basket for jimmies. They were also catching some conchs, which were bringing six dollars a basket. Captain Johnny has sold crabs for as little as fifty cents a barrel and as high as sixty-six dollars a barrel.

Besides the prices, Captain Johnny has seen other changes since 1926. "When I started, I had a twenty-five horsepower Palmer in the log canoe and we could only use five-foot-wide dredges," he said. "Now we have plenty of power, and the law allows seven-foot-wide dredges."

Another change on the Bay is the competition. "There are ten times more crab dredgers on the Chesapeake than when I started," he commented. "There are over two hundred licensed dredgers from Virginia, and now they're letting Maryland crabbers come down here."

The Iva W.*'s towing post amidship holds the combined weight of the chain and dredges.*

Captain Johnny moved over to a rope on the side of the pilothouse. When he pulled down on the rope, the 175-foot chain connected to the dredges began to reel in. As the dredge moved up from the bottom, Captain Johnny slowed the throttle down and continued to pull down on the rope. A towing post amidship holds the combined weight of the chain and dredges. Hung on the top of the post are two large steel blocks through which the chain passes. After passing through the two towing blocks on the post, the chain runs below deck and around a toothed sprocket, which is driven off the main engine. Two three-foot stop chains are also attached to the towing post and by tension they keep the chains from going out farther than the skipper desires. These chains are secured by one of the hands, who hooks a two-pronged catch link into the long chain when he is signaled by Captain Johnny.

One of the crewmen picked up a two-by-four "turning stick" and, as the dredges surfaced, he used the board to straighten the dredge so the open end fell against the boat, which keeps it from coming aboard backwards. Captain Johnny then moved the rope back and forth, and the dredge went up and down in the water to wash the mud out of it. Once the dredge was on deck, the two hands shook the contents onto the deck by grabbing two large rings that are attached to the twine dredge bag.

The catch was not what the captain or crew had anticipated. There were a few crabs, a conch, and some sponges. "I've never seen anything to beat that," grumbled Captain Johnny. "It's not very good."

A turning stick, made from a two-by-four, is used to straighten the dredge as it surfaces.

Once the dredge is aboard, the crewmen shake the contents onto the deck

The dredge was released, and the chain clanked against the horizontal and vertical rollers on the side. The crewmen sorted the female crabs and placed them in a barrel. The jimmies and conchs were put in baskets, and the horseshoe crabs and sponges were tossed back.

After each lick the crew hosed and washed the work deck. The second dredge did not yield much more than the first.

At 10:00 A.M., Captain Johnny and his crew had only two barrels, and the licks seemed to get longer and longer. "When you have to take long licks like this, they don't amount to nothing." It was between ten and twenty minutes a lick.

After each lick, Captain Johnny asked the crew to check the cotton bag for holes. (A chain bag is on the bottom of the dredge and the cotton bag is above it.)

The skipper said some days they catch over a bushel to a dredge. It takes three bushels to fill a barrel. "We really need to catch a bushel a lick to do much," he said. "I've seen it when we've caught a barrel in a lick. That was some good day."

During the day, there were few breaks in the routine, except in between licks. "Today's a nice day, but some days there's ice all over the deck, and when it's cold, it ain't so nice," the captain said of the weather.

For lunch, each crewman had a sandwich and a piece of fried chicken reheated on the stove in the pilothouse. They ate in the galley. The galley walls on the *Iva W.* are of tongue-

After the dredges are emptied, crabs are sorted so that jimmies and conchs are placed in bushel baskets and sooks in barrels.

and-groove beaded paneling painted green. An old wooden-spindle "Sunday School" chair with gray paint wearing off the seat and a newer model folding chair are nearby.

Between licks, the crew would sip on a cola, take a smoke on a cigar, or get a drink of water from the old water barrel mounted on the stern against the galley wall. The barrel is a classic-style container that was typical of the type used on the old sailing vessels that were a part of Captain Johnny's youth. "I picked her up in Crisfield off one of the old boats. I've got a new-style barrel at home, but I like the way the water tastes from that old wooden one," he said.

Captain Johnny and his crew continued to work the dredges, and several licks yielded a bushel of crabs. As other boats came near, their conversations could be heard over the CB. Occasionally, Captain Johnny would ask, "What are they saying? I can't hear all that rumbling."

When the day was just about over, the *Iva W.* and her crew had harvested its worst catch in a week. There were eight barrels of sooks and six baskets of jimmies. Captain Johnny radioed one of his sons on the dredge boat, the *Thomas W.*, to come and pick up his catch and crew because he was going home to Deltaville.

Generally, he'd take his crabs back to Davis Creek to be sold, and the crew and Captain Johnny would be back dredging on Saturday. "It's just not worth the effort," he said.

Before the crew left, Captain Johnny paid them each $392 for a week's wages. The crew is paid according to the catch. The boat gets forty percent off the top each week. The expenses are paid, and what's left is divided evenly among Captain Johnny and the two crewmen. This method of pay is used on many of the dredge boats.

After the crabs were loaded onto the *Thomas W.* and his crew boarded her, Captain Johnny headed for home. Cruising up the Bay, he began talking again about his years on the *Iva W.* "I've learned a lot about life working on the water," he said. "Once I brought an old man from Crisfield to Deltaville because he was having a boat built there. His name was Jim Hurley and we ran into one bad storm. Mr. Hurley went up in the forepeak of the *Iva W.* and was tossed up and down. It near about killed him. When we got to Deltaville, I had to get some help to pull him out of the forepeak because he was banged up right bad. I'll never forget what he said to me when we got him out. He said, 'Johnny, the Good Lord looks out after boys, but when you get to be old, you have to look out after yourself.' I don't think I exactly knew what he meant by that then, but now that I'm older than he was at the time, I think I know what he meant."

"A lot of times we put in seventeen-hour days, and that's hard on an old man," he said. "But I guess it's something that just gets in your bones. It's hard to give up. I'll do it until I just can't do it no more."

With the sun down and the stars out, Captain Johnny pulled up to his dock in Deltaville on Jackson Creek. "Well, we're home one more time," he said.

In 2008, Virginia Marine Resources Commission banned dredging for crabs in state waters. Captain Johnny Ward is deceased and the Iva W. *has been converted to a "double-house" yacht.*

 # BUILDING A CRAB POT

As long as I can remember, I've known Ed Payne. As a teenager, I taught one of his children in American Red Cross swimming lessons, and I was well aware, then, that Ed's heritage was closely tied to the water.

When it came time to do this chapter, the first person I thought of to help was Ed. He had worked with me on several articles in the past and I knew he would give me a hand on this one. He didn't let me down. His knowledge of the ways of the water and his love and understanding of his forefathers have helped to make Ed a successful Chesapeake Bay waterman.

The crab pot is a relatively new method of harvesting blue crabs. Invented in the 1920s, it was not perfected until the late thirties. Prior to the introduction of the pot, the trotline was the favorite gear of most Bay watermen in the hard-shell blue crab fishery. The pot, however, was much more efficient and was to change forever the way hard crabs are harvested, not only on the Chesapeake, but throughout the United States where crabs are caught.

Ed Payne was but a child in the 1930s. He was born on Tangier Island and moved to Urbanna, Virginia, with his family after the devastating "August Storm" of 1933 flooded Tangier, leaving most of the island underwater.

Ed's grandparents had moved to Urbanna in 1928. So, when the '33 storm abruptly drove Ed and his folks from their home, Urbanna seemed an obvious spot for them to settle. His parents and grandparents were like almost everyone who migrated from the island community in that working the water was the only livelihood they knew, and Ed grew up to be a waterman.

We talked outside his house on Perkins Creek in Urbanna, where Ed was making some pots for the upcoming crab season:

> My grandfather, Henry Dize, was the first I ever saw use a crab pot. He and Grandma had left Tangier in 1928. He came to Urbanna to shuck oysters in the fall and winter and crab in the spring and summer. I recall him telling me that when he first started, the shucking house was paying him ten cents for every gallon of oysters he shucked.
>
> I also remember the first year he used a crab pot. It was 1937. I don't know how he knew about it. I guess he saw one somewhere. Everybody else

Ed Payne has been crab potting on the Bay since the 1950s. Ed makes
all of his own pots behind his home in Urbanna.

was trotlining then, but not Granddaddy. No, if he saw something a little
different, he'd give it a try.

He made his own pots and had a twenty-by-twenty-four inch frame made
of wood that he shaped each pot from.

Granddaddy didn't use staples (pig rings), like I do now, to hold the pots
together. His first ones were laced together with cotton twine and later he
started weaving three strands of wire in and out along the edges to keep 'em
from coming apart.

He was originally from Smith Island [Maryland], and he had an old sharp-
ended skiff that he could scull as fast as most men could row. I heard from some
of the old-timers on Tangier that when Granddaddy was young he would pole
and scull in that same skiff from Smith Island to Tangier to court Grandma.

He was using that skiff when he was potting on the Rappahannock. He
would get up early and scull over to Buster Ferguson's Seafood dock at Remlik

(on Lagrange Creek) and buy a box of fish for a dollar. A box had a hundred pounds in it then. After he got his bait, he'd pole out into the river where he had thirty-six pots tied to wooden stakes. Granddaddy would come to a stake, tie his boat to it, pull her up, and empty her. He'd take his time. It wasn't like we are today—going as hard as we can to catch as many as we can.

While Granddaddy was potting, each morning Grandma would run a little trotline out in the creek to help out and they would ship their catch to Baltimore. A truck would come to Urbanna each day to pick up crabs. In the early spring, they would get $7.50 a bushel for jimmies. That was good money back then. During the summertime, the price would get as low as three dollars a bushel, and then, sometimes, they didn't get enough to pay the freight. Times were tight, but we kids didn't know it. We were all happy-go-lucky and thought everything that shined was gold.

I started crab potting on my own around 1950. My first roll of [crab pot] wire cost me $8.50 and I got it from Boyd Hurley [of J. W. Hurley & Son Seafood of Urbanna]. I'll never forget it. I didn't have the money to pay for it, but he said, "Don't worry about it, just pay me in the summer when you catch some."

When I first started, I was getting ten cents apiece for jimmies and two cents a pound for sooks. I did this for about two years and then decided to go on a merchant ship. I was seventeen years old when I went on the ship from Newport News to France. It took nineteen days. Now you can sail over there in a lot less time.

I was home for Christmas in 1952, when I got word from the draft board. I'll never forget it. "Greetings," it said and I was in Korea for eighteen months. Now, that was some greetings, wasn't it?

I tried [working on] land a couple times after the service but it wa'n't for me. Working the water was where I always wanted to be and here I am. Sometimes it's been bad and sometimes it's been good, but it's what I like and what I know.

Ed has worked 150 to 200 crab pots each year since he got out of the service, and he makes all his own pots during the off-season. He generally starts potting in April or May and finishes up in November when the crabs leave for winter. Although there are numerous styles of pots built on the Bay, Ed's are fairly typical of the style used by watermen today.

He uses Keystone crab pot wire, eighteen-gauge with 1½-inch holes to make the main part of the pot. The pots are put together with standard crab pot staples or number 4 hog rings. Wire is measured in mesh size, rather than standard measurements. Meshes are counted along the selvage, or finished edge, and a mesh is the distance from the top point of the hexagon to the bottom point. In between the whole meshes are half meshes, and cuts in the wire are usually made on the half mesh of

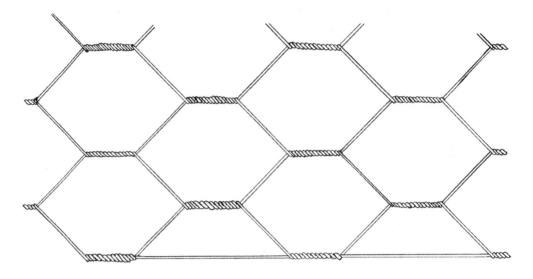

Mesh pattern. (Drawing by Ray V. Rodgers III)

the selvage (see mesh pattern drawing). For instance, when Ed cuts out a piece of wire four meshes long, he counts a full four hexagons and cuts on the half mesh after the fourth hexagon.

Ed first makes all the parts to a crab pot and then puts them together. The first step is to cut the wire for the sides, top, and bottom. He stretches the wire out on the ground and cuts two pieces, each twenty meshes long. He then takes one of the lengths, counts six meshes from the end and bends a ninety-degree angle upward on the next half mesh. Ed places a two-inch-by-two-inch board along the line where the bend is to be made to make sure it comes out straight and even. After making the bend, he goes to the other side and does the same, which should result in a U-shape with square corners (see photo 1). He then does the same to the other piece of wire.

In the next step, Ed cuts out the upstairs, which is installed inside the pot to form an upper chamber. The upstairs is made from a piece of wire ten full meshes long and is bent in the middle with an arch at the top. The rounded bend at the top is one full mesh wide. This leaves four-and-a-half meshes on each side of the roof-shaped arch (see photo 2).

The funnels and bait pockets are the last parts to be made. The funnels are the openings that allow crabs to come into the pot. Some watermen prefer pots with two funnels, while others use four. Ed uses four because he thinks they catch better than two-funnel pots.

A funnel is made from a piece of wire thirteen full meshes long and three meshes wide. With a pair of snips, Ed cuts out three meshes at a forty-five-degree angle in

Photo 1

Photo 2

Photo 3

the top corners, on each side. He does this by snipping one mesh from the edge of the first row, two off the middle, and three from the outside row of each piece (see photo 3). Once cut, there should be twelve hexagons at the bottom and ten at the top. Then Ed shapes the funnel by bending the wire around and attaching the ends (see photo 4).

The bait pocket is made from smaller mesh wire. It is eighteen-gauge, but a one-inch mesh size. The smaller wire is used to prevent eels from stealing bait from the pocket. In some areas where there are large numbers of small eels, watermen use eel pot wire for the bait pocket, Ed says. The bait pockets are made from a piece of wire cut eight full meshes long and six meshes wide. Once cut, it is bent into a cylinder shape and the sides are secured with staples. The edge at the top of the pocket are bent together with three staples, while the bottom is left open to allow Ed to put bait inside it (see photo 5).

With all the parts made, the pot must now be put together. First, Ed attaches the upstairs to one of the U-pieces, which will become the bottom and two sides. The upstairs is clamped in four corners, four meshes from the bottom. The arched upstairs is inverted (see photo 6, page 268). The cut ends on the upstairs are bent

Photo 4

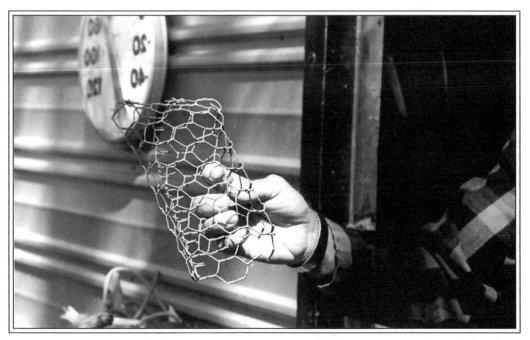

Photo 5

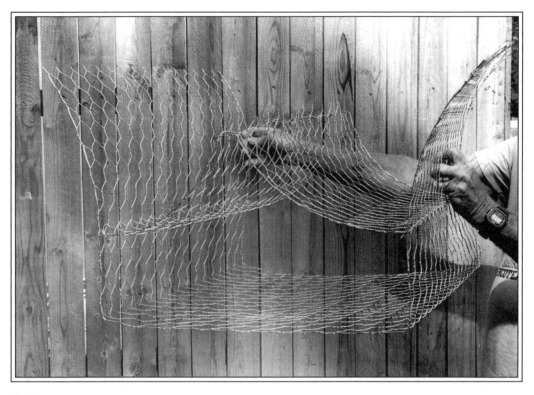

Photo 6

around the U-piece to help hold it together and so the crabber won't be scratched when he works the pot.

Next, the second piece in the shape of a U is fitted down over the piece with the upstairs to form the top and the other two sides. Once the top is fitted over the bottom, staples are used to fasten it together. One top side is left unfastened so crabs can be emptied from the pot (see photo 7).

Along the bottom center of each of the four sides, Ed makes a hole for the funnels. He first cuts across the bottom three meshes, all the time making sure the cut is centered. He then snips three meshes up, three across the top of the hole, and three back down to finish the opening. Another way of making the funnel hole is to use the circumference of the large end of the funnel as a template and simply cut it to size. When installing the funnel, the small end goes in the hole first and the large end is stapled (see photo 8).

At the very center of the bottom of the pot, one whole mesh is cut out for the bait pocket. Once the mesh is cut out, the cut ends are bent inward so the hole is large enough to slip the pocket inside. Once in place, the pocket is stapled to the bottom of the pot.

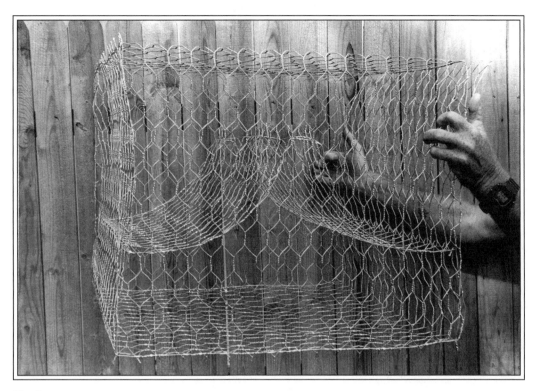

Photo 7

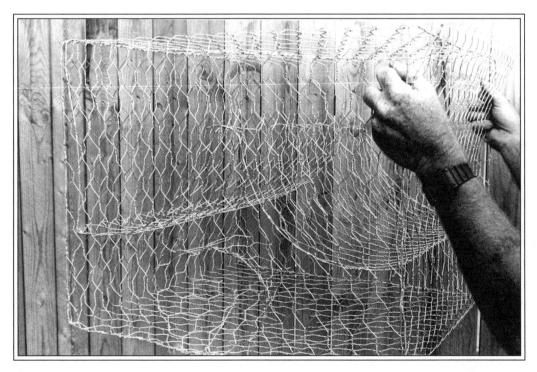

Photo 8

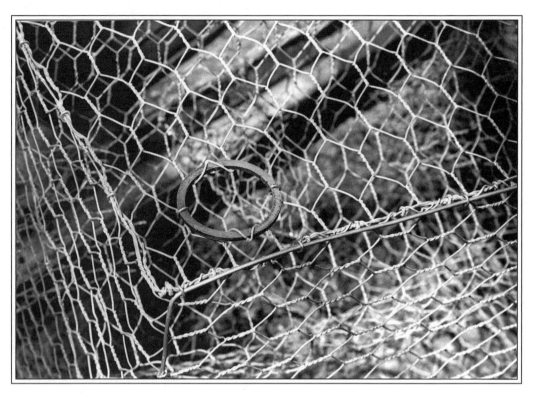

Photo 9

Some watermen use a plastic cover over the opening of the bait pocket to keep bait from falling out. Ed doesn't use a bait cover, and this is not unusual. He uses fresh bait in his pots every day and jams the bait into the pocket. Once the bait is in the pocket, he throws the pot straight down, hard, into the water. The force of the water pressing against the bottom of the pot as it goes down keeps the bait from falling out. This eliminates the need for a lid over the pocket.

Ed attaches a heavy galvanized wire around the entire top edge of the pot to give support. He also puts a frame, made from $^1/_4$-inch rebar bent to the square shape of the bottom of the pot, on the underside (see photo of Ed with a completed pot at the beginning of this chapter). Watermen use different size frames. According to Ed, the size of the rebar can range from $^1/_4$-inch to $^5/_8$-inch. The $^5/_8$-inch frames are used in areas where there is a very strong current.

One cull rig is installed near a top corner of each pot to let small, undersized crabs escape. Ed cuts out one mesh to install the rig (see photo 9). "Some put them (cull rigs) downstairs to let sea nettles run out, but I don't have that much trouble with nettles where I crab," he said.

A sacrificial anode, or zinc bar, is wired to the inside of each pot. A "zinc" through electrolytic action, slows corrosion of the pot wire caused by salt water. Ed uses $^3/_4$-pound

Photo 10

zincs because the 1½-pound zincs can cause the pot to go down through the water sideways. Yet, there are many watermen who use large-size zincs, particularly on the ocean side of the Eastern Shore where the waters are saltier.

Next, Ed makes a homemade latch from a thin strap of inner tube (¼-inch industrial rubber tubing) and a hog ring. The rubber catch is used to open and close the pot door. The rubber strip is tied to the top edge of the pot door. The hog ring is placed at the bottom edge of the inner tube and when Ed wants to close the opening, he pulls the latch down and hooks it into the side of the pot (see photo of completed pot). Many watermen are now using $^3/_{16}$-inch shock cord as latches for pot doors, he said.

Ed ties his wrap, which is used to pull the pot up and down, in the bottom right hand corner looking at the front of the pot (see photo of completed pot). "When you pull the pot up, the opening comes right to you," he said. "If you tie it somewhere else, you've got to twist the pot around to you." He uses eighteen-foot line in the summer when he's working in close to shore. During the spring and fall, Ed uses thirty feet of line to catch crabs when they go into deeper water.

The buoy used to mark the pot in the water is made from a full-size bullet cork, cut in half with a stick pushed all the way through the hole. A four-ounce lead weight is attached to the bottom of the stick to make it balanced and to make it sit up straight in the water (see photo 10).

Ed ties a short line (about three feet) to his buoy. This way he can tie either the eighteen-foot or thirty-foot line to the pot and not have to change buoys when he works different water depths. "Some watermen use long line all year long and, when in shallow water, wrap the excess around the cork," said Ed. "But that pulls the cork over in the water, and grass and barnacles grow all over it. Some say I'm just too particular, but I've found my way works best for me."

"I guess the crab pot has been as successful a piece of gear as all the rest in the crabbing business put together," said Ed. "The whole Bay is near about filled up with them. That tells you something about how good they work."

Ed Payne still makes his own crab pots in a shed behind his home on Perkins Creek.

CHAPTER TWENTY-SEVEN

BENJAMINE F. LEWIS, INVENTOR OF THE CRAB POT

B.F. Lewis was a name I had known since the 1970s, when I wrote the chapter, "The First Crab Pots," for Barcat Skipper. *When I started the research on my second book, I figured there was still someone around Harryhogan, Virginia, on the Northern Neck (about fifteen miles from the mouth of the Potomac River) who knew something of his past.*

I called Maston Krentz at Krentz Marine Railway in Harryhogan, because the yard had an old and fine reputation for building and repairing workboats. I thought someone at the yard might know something about the inventor of the crab pot. I was right. Maston and Francis Kines remembered well the old fellow who lived down the road, and they seemed to enjoy sharing with me their memories of Benjamine Lewis.

During the steamboat days on Chesapeake Bay, Lodge Landing on the Yeocomico River was a bustling steamboat landing, where steamers, such as the *Three Rivers, Northumberland, Dorchester,* and the *Anne Arundel,* made regular stops bound for Washington, D.C., or Baltimore.

Similar to most landings, Lodge had a wide pier that extended out into the river and a two-story freight building onshore. There was also a small flat-roof shed just down the beach where an elderly gentlemen had a "Punch and Judy" puppet show for the children who were waiting for the steamer. Lemonade and snowballs could be bought there, too.

This type of activity was not unusual around the Bay during the days before roads took over from the waterways as the main means of transportation. But, what made Lodge Landing exceptional was the elderly man who worked the finger puppets and sold the goodies to those who stopped by. His name was Benjamine F. Lewis—a name that probably isn't found in any of Virginia's history books—but a name that will live forever in the annals of the Chesapeake Bay fisheries.

Lewis was the designer and patentee of the crab pot, a gear that revolutionized the harvesting of blue crabs. It was on the Yeocomico River, near his home in Harryhogan, that Lewis first started experimenting with the pot.

Born in Mulberry Grove, Illinois, in 1858, Lewis came to Virginia with his family as a child. The family settled in Northumberland County at Harryhogan and, like many youngsters of those times, he grew up to work the water. He fished pound nets, oystered, crabbed with a trotline, and trapped muskrats in the winter. As the years passed, it got harder and harder for him to work a crab line, so on one hot July day, he finished laying

Benjamine F. Lewis invented the first crab pot in the 1920s. The inventor obtained two patents on the pot, one in 1928 and the second in 1938. The second patent design is almost identical to pots used today by Bay watermen. (Courtesy of Elizabeth Swicegood, granddaughter of Benjamine Lewis)

out his trotline and decided he'd never fish it again. Legend has it, he sold the line right in the water, bait, crabs, and all, and sat in the shade of a nearby willow oak tree and began thinking of a new, more efficient way of catching crabs.

He worked the rest of the summer on his wire contraption, while friends and relatives often snickered at the old boy who had given up a lifelong occupation to invent a rig that supposedly would catch a crab better than a trotline. But the snickering soon stopped when Lewis developed a wire pot that in 1928 was granted a patent by the U.S. Patent Office. He revised the pot in 1938 and received a second patent on his invention that year. The 1938 crab pot is almost identical to the pots that are used today all over the world.

Francis Kines was a youngster at Harryhogan when Lewis first started "messing around" with his idea for catching crabs. He recalls some of what went on then. "One of his first pots was made from just two pieces of flat wire that were laced together," says Kines recalling Lewis's early attempts in the 1920s.

Since the early pot had no sides, says Kines, the bait pocket in the bottom was used to separate the two sheets of wire and keep them spread apart so crabs could move around.

> There were two funnels in the top and he [Lewis] would experiment by going down to B.F. Winstead's dock there at Harryhogan. Winstead had a tomato canning factory and a herring house where Uncle Frank (as everyone around called Lewis) would sit and watch the crabs as they came and went.
>
> He noticed that once the crab grabbed the bait in the pot, it would always go to the top and, since that's where the funnels were, the crabs would usually escape. He finally ended up making a square [four-sided] pot, and placing the funnels near the bottom. Later, he installed an upstairs (upper chamber) that trapped the crabs in the top of the pot.

Maston Krentz was a teenager in the 1930s when Lewis came around to Krentz Marine Railway in search of material for his famous invention. "He was looking in our scrap pile for some strips of wood to build a two-foot square frame," says Krentz, who operated the boat yard that his father, Herman M. Krentz, started in 1911.

> He would use the wooden frames to bend the wire when he was making the pot.
>
> All he had to use was some old chicken wire that was just about worn out. When he started fishing pots, he would tie the lines to an oyster stake or a mooring pile, and scull out to fish them. Later, he got an old Sears Roebuck Waterwitch outboard motor, with two gas tanks on the sides that looked like steel bullets, to power the skiff he fished from.

When Lewis began crabbing with pots, he used brine-soaked bait in the tradition of trotlining.

Francis Kines, left, and Maston Krentz were living in Harryhogan when Lewis began experimenting with his crab pot. Krentz is holding a brass tag used by Lewis to identify crabbers who paid him his annual four dollar royalty fee on every fifty pots. The embossed tag has Lewis's patent number 2,123,471 and his name inscribed on it.

"He had worked a trotline most of his life," says Krentz, "and was used to using salted bait. [Even today, salted bait is the norm in the Maryland trotline fishery.] It was some time before anyone realized that fresh bait was the best to catch crabs in a crab pot. Early on, everyone around who was fishing pots would salt fish down in a barrel or vat for bait."

After Lewis successfully obtained his 1938 patent on the crab pot, he had the awesome task of trying to collect royalties on his invention. Once watermen learned of the success of the pot, its use spread rapidly across the Bay. Krentz says he would collect four dollars for every fifty pots.

"He would have been a millionaire in one year if he could have collected that on all the pots on the Chesapeake Bay today, wouldn't he?" asks Kines.

To keep up with the rapid growth of the pot, Lewis purchased one of the first automobiles in Harryhogan, a Model A Ford, that his son Harvey used to travel around the Bay to collect royalties on his father's invention.

"It was an impossible task," says Kines. "He wasn't able to collect a tenth of what was out there. There were so many people using them and they were so easy to make."

"If he could have set up a factory and started mass producing them," says Krentz, "then maybe he would have made a lot more money. Let me tell you though, that old man put Virginia and the Chesapeake Bay blue crab on the map. We'd probably still be out there working a trotline for a couple bushels a day if it wasn't for him."

B.F. Lewis died at the age of ninety-two in 1950 leaving behind a Bay literally filled with the wire contraptions known as crab pots. After his father's death, Harvey continued to travel around collecting royalties until 1956 when the patent rights to the famous crab pot expired.

The crab pot has continued to be the most effective gear invented to harvest Chesapeake Bay hard-shell blue crabs.

CHAPTER TWENTY-EIGHT

PEELER POUNDS

Long before I called Gilbert Johnson of Syringa, Virginia (not far from the mouth of the Rappahannock River on Virginia's middle peninsula), to ask if he would take me along to fish his peeler pounds, I had heard that he was quite a character, but more importantly that he was a good waterman who still worked the traditional style of peeler traps.

Although I had seen him just once before, the first morning we went out to fish his trap, I had a feeling from the start that he was the right person for this project. Gilbert kept me in stitches throughout the morning and graciously shared with me his knowledge of life and his skills as a working waterman.

Another form of gear used in the soft-shell crab fishery is the peeler pound or crab fyke. The origin of this gear seems to have been lost, but since its appearance so much resembles the pound net, one can only speculate that some innovative waterman used that as a model to design the peeler pound.

Peeler pounds are used by watermen to harvest peeler and soft-shell crabs. Peeler crabs are caught in the pound and transferred to shedding floats in the water or to onshore facilities. There the peelers shed their hard exoskeletons and the soft-shell crabs are harvested and sold. (Courtesy of the Virginia Institute of Marine Science)

Gilbert Johnson hauls in a pound and empties his catch into the bottom of his skiff. Johnson has been fishing pounds for over twenty years.

If this were the case, then the gear would have been developed after 1875, the year the pound net was introduced on a wide scale to Chesapeake watermen. Also, the soft-shell crab market did not begin to grow much until the late 1800s when the railroad provided an avenue for the famous "Crisfield soft-shells" to be shipped out of state. The peeler pound has since evolved into an important gear for the harvesting of peelers.

Gilbert Johnson has been "messing" with peeler pounds and soft crabs for over twenty years and he has been working the water more than sixty years. His father and grandfather were both watermen and at seventy-four years of age, he's still going strong. Each morning before the crack of dawn, Gilbert ambles down the steep hill to Morton Clark's marina on Locklies Creek off the Rappahannock where he keeps his little crab skiff.

Clark's railway is typical of the small boat yards that once cluttered the creeks and rivers of the Chesapeake years back. An assortment of workboats are moored there, ranging from modern deadrise boats to a vintage round-stern log canoe with the original Ford Model T engine still intact.

When I arrived, Gilbert was in his little skiff culling peelers and hard crabs that he had caught in his pound nearby. "You're late there fellow. I've fished two pounds

After fishing each pound, Gilbert pauses to cull his catch. He separates the peelers according to their stage of molting and places them in baskets or buckets. When he arrives at his shedding floats in Locklies Creek, he can quickly place the crabs into the proper floats.

already. Ouch! Great God! He bit me!" yelled Gilbert. "Since you're a big old peeler, I guess that's all right," said Gilbert talking to the crab about the bite.

"Looky here. He's a big boy," he said, holding him up. "I bet he won't shed, but he'll be a horse of a soft crab if he does."

Gilbert continued talking while he worked, tossing the undersized crabs back overboard and placing the jimmies and peelers in separate baskets. "I'm seventy-four years old and there ain't many people my age doing this. I thank the Good Lord every day for being able to do it.

Last year, I was walking up on the dock here with a mess of softies in my hand when I stubbed my toe and spilled my crabs all over the place. It was hot and I was tired. Well, I said a few choice words and finished by saying as old as I am I ought to be in a rocking chair.

Well, there was a fellow watching me and he asked how old I was. When I told him, he said, "Lord, Captain, half the people your age are in the cemetery and the other half are in a nursing home." We both laughed and I said, "Jesus, I guess you're right."

I enjoy what I'm doing. My children keep saying I ought to quit because they're afraid they'll find me dead one day in my boat. But if I die in my boat, I tell them to say that Pop died doing what he wanted to do. That's the way I feel about it.

"All right, twenty-six peelers, a catfish, stiff-back perch, jumping mullet, and a few little spot (fish) for my bird. Have you ever seen a stiff-back any bigger than that? I bet she weighs a pound," he said pointing to the big fish.

Gilbert's little boat is made of fiberglass and powered by a fifteen horsepower outboard engine. There's a canopy overhead to keep the sun and rain off him as he works and a stool for him to sit on while culling his crabs. Life jackets are draped over the frame to the canopy and bushel baskets are scattered about to hold his peelers until he can get them back to his shedding floats, which he keeps in the creek, a short ways from where he moors his boat.

As Gilbert heads out to his next pound, he points over to a weather beaten dock on which ice and time have taken their toll. "There she is," said Gilbert. "My bird. She's a fishing hawk [osprey]. I thought she and her husband got a divorce last year because I didn't see much of him, but they both came back this year."

The waterman pulled his boat up to the pier and tossed a little spot fish into the nest as the osprey, within arm's length, stayed perched on her nest. "Anybody else come along, she flies off. But she knows I won't hurt her.

"Oh Lordy, babies!" says Gilbert with a tone of excitement and compassion in his voice. There were two baby ospreys in the nest.

"Oh Mama, you done all right," he said to the bird with a smile from ear to ear. "I've been waiting for those eggs to hatch.

"They're a real curiosity to watch," he said going on down the creek past his crab floats and over to one of his pounds at the mouth of Locklies.

The crab pound has a hedging (or leader), a bay (or heart), and a head (or trap). The hedging is made from one-inch mesh wire, two feet tall, and extends from the shore a distance depending on the depth of water at high tide. Stakes are placed every three to four feet and the wire is tacked to the stakes.

The bay is shaped like a heart and made from three-foot-high wire. It acts as a funnel for crabs to move from the hedging into the head.

The head is a trap that is also made from one-inch mesh wire and is four feet by three and a half feet by four feet tall. Gilbert tries to place the head a distance from the shore, where at a normal flood tide the top of it is just out of the water. "Now when a good northeast blow comes along, she [the tide] will put her out of sight, but I don't gauge it by that," said Gilbert. "I don't like the normal tide to go over the pound head because I can't fish it when it's underwater." The wood frames on the head and the bottom of the hedging stakes are all coated with copper (antifouling) paint.

No bait is used in a peeler pound. Gilbert said, however, that he's had many people ask what type of bait is best.

Gilbert pulled up to the head and tied his boat to two stakes on either side of it. He lifted a cinder block that was holding the lid down and untied the wire cage. The head or trap is held in place by his weight and is also tied to two stakes in the bay.

He then unlatched the lid and pulled the head upward. Once it was up out of the water, he used the side of the boat to tilt the wire cage so the lid goes down toward the bottom of his skiff. Crabs, fish, and turtles went everywhere. Once empty, the pound head is quickly put back in the water.

"I got to take a break now. That's hard work for an old man," he said. "I used to have twenty stands around, but I'm down to six now. I just can't work like I used to.

"You see how dirty that water is?" Gilbert said pointing to a film of dirt around his crab pound. "That's why these crabs are dying. It's nothing but pollution. The scientists say it's because of lack of oxygen, but they can't seem to find out why there's no oxygen in the water."

Gilbert said he has been losing about forty-five percent of his catch. "I hate it when they start dying. They do all right in the early spring but in June, July, and August, you don't know what you are going to shed out," he said.

The waterman then sat on his little stool and started culling his catch. Green or white peelers (those about four to five days away from turning into soft-shell crabs) are placed in a basket, pink or medium (those two to three days away) are placed in another basket, and finally red or ripe or rank peelers (crabs that will shed in a day) are put in a separate one too.

Gilbert tells the difference between these crabs by examining a line on the outer section of the back fin, or swimmer fin, as it is sometimes called. If it is a peeler, the line will either be white, pink, or red, and the color determines the stage of molting.

"There's an old buster," said Gilbert. A buster is a crab that has begun to back out of its shell. He gently dropped the crab in a bucket of water.

The crabber continued talking as he worked. "Now before I can put a peeler pound in, I got to get permission from the landowner and the person who leases the oyster bottom. Most people don't mind, but there are some folks who don't like to look at them," said Gilbert. "Now, I don't exactly understand that. Looky here, here comes my buddy," he said as a well-kept deadrise workboat started to come up alongside. "Gordon Crowe! Now that's a Gordon in this world. He's a character, but a great crabber. He takes care of his stuff [gear], too, you best believe it."

Gordon came alongside and passed over some peelers. "I got twenty today Gilbert," said the waterman.

"You had thirteen yesterday, Gordon. Things are picking up."

After Gilbert paid for the crabs, Gordon went toward shore to sell his hard crabs. He works crab pots and sells what peelers he catches in his pots to Gilbert. Several other watermen sell to Gilbert, too. "I pay the boys twenty-five or thirty-five cents a crab depending on the time of the season. In the early spring, when I shed out almost one hundred percent of my catch, I can pay extra, but this time of the year [June] a lot of them die."

The next stop was Segars Island where Gilbert had another pound. "Lord, look at the sea nettles. That's something I have never been able to figure out, why the Good Lord made those devil-fetch-it things. It's my own fault though. I ran out of two-foot [high] wire when I was setting the hedging so I used three-foot instead. Don't ever use three-foot wire because you catch every stinging nettle from here to China." Most of the nettles will go over the two-foot wire, he explained.

Before hauling the pound head into the boat, Gilbert had to stand and dip the nettles out of the trap with a crab net. Once enough were out, he pulled the pound into the boat and emptied the crabs into the bottom. "That doesn't look like a bad catch of crabs," he said, letting the trap back down into the water and tying it down.

As he culled his catch, Gilbert began to talk about his past.

I started oystering with my papa when I was a boy. Papa was born in 1875. He'd be 114 years old now. We sold many a bushel of oysters for thirty-three and a third cents or a dollar for three bushels. Now Papa could catch some oysters. He could take a pair of twenty-foot tongs, shake 'em up and down, and catch a mess when everyone else couldn't touch bottom with a pair of twenty-sixes [tongs].

I wasn't very old when I started working on a farm for a dollar a day. I'd walk six miles a day to and from work. We'd put in ten hours each day, and I'd unhook the horse from the plow at 6 [P.M.] and walk home. Yes sir, those times were tight. I would always say to the children that I wish we had more coming along for them, but they say we had plenty of food, clothes, and lots of love. So, I guess things weren't so bad.

Gilbert began to rub his mouth with his hand. "You keep the last tooth in your mouth as long as you can. I got new false teeth and they tickle my gums," he said with a chuckle.

There's a sook that has not long shedded, but I can't sell her because I got to sleep tonight," he said holding up the crab. It had already turned into a paper-shell and was no longer soft enough to sell.

After working on the farm, I went to oystering in the winter and running fishing parties in the warm-weather months. I used to take parties out near Stingray Point Lighthouse. There was a stone pile out there and we'd catch a mess of sheepshead almost every time I went there. Now you don't ever see a sheepshead. I'll tell ya, it ain't the same out here.

Finishing up, Gilbert put a board over the baskets of peelers to keep the sun off them and tucked the few tiny spot he had under the seat for his fish hawk.

"The last pound is over on Clark's Island," said Gilbert as he headed the boat in the direction of the marshy island near the mouth of Locklies. Throughout the morning, Gilbert never stopped talking about crabbing and life.

I want to live as long as I can, but I don't want to be a burden on people. If I got to go in a nursing home, I'd just as well go [die].

Looks like I'm always going to funerals now. I went to one recently and the preacher came up to me and asked if I was ready [to die]. "Well,"

Gilbert says he can pack a box of soft-shells in such a manner that the finished product is as pretty as a picture.

I said, "Preacher, I look at that two ways. I hope I'm prepared for heaven but I'm not homesick."

As Gilbert guided the boat toward the island, laughing gulls and terns swooped down in hopes of grabbing a bite. "Get away boys, those spot are for my girl," he said, referring to the osprey.

The sun sparkled on the water as the waterman worked his last trap. When Gilbert had finished, he had landed about 130 peelers. He then headed on back to his floats in the creek, where he dumped the basket of green peelers in a float, the pink peelers in another one, and the red in another. Stretched over the entire float of ripe peelers was a wire top." Of all the things God made, I wish he had thought twice about sea gulls," he said. "They would eat every soft crab in the float if I didn't put this wire over it."

During the winter, Gilbert makes his own floats from white pine. They are ten feet long and forty-six inches wide and the bottom is coated with copper paint. The first month that he uses the float, it stays overboard the entire time, but for the rest of the season, Gilbert has to haul and clean each float every other week.

Although he had already fished his floats earlier, there were a few more soft crabs that had shed out since he had worked them last. Gilbert fishes his floats three times a day during the summer, but goes to them much more often in the early spring when the big peeler run comes. In addition to the big run of peelers in the spring there are some smaller runs later on. Soft crabs were bringing ten dollars for jumbos, eight dollars for primes, and six dollars for mediums. "I was getting eighteen dollars for jumbos, but that 'bear cat' cut me to ten dollars," said Gilbert about his buyer. "I'm used to that though. That's the seafood business. When there's nothing to catch, the price is out of sight and when there's plenty, you can hardly give' em away."

The floats are staked to poles that Gilbert cuts from the woods nearby. "I use just about anything for my poles, but I don't like poplar or pine wood."

Back at the dock, Gilbert put his soft crabs into a box and covered them with a cloth towel to keep the sun off, while he drives them to market.

Holding up a full box of jumbo soft crabs, he said, "They tell me I pack a pretty box of crabs. They are pretty, aren't they? It's pretty as a picture," he said with pride.

By then, it was nearly noon and Gilbert had finished another day of work.

Gilbert Johnson is deceased. The peeler pound is still a viable gear form in the blue crab fishery. However, the peeler pot, similar to a crab pot without a bait box, is today first choice of most Virginia crabbers.

CHAPTER TWENTY-NINE

HARVESTING SNAPPING TURTLES BY HOOK AND LINE

J. D. Davis is the youngest person that I selected to be in this volume. He is, however, as colorful as anyone I've ever interviewed. J.D. and I were in school together and I always admired his love of the outdoors. When I went to running traplines in 1980, we would see each other at the fur buyers and spin some yarns about all the muskrats we'd caught the morning before.

When I switched from being an outdoorsman to a reporter, J.D. was still catching rats in the winter and harvesting snappers in the spring, while working a full-time job as a maintenance supervisor at a local nursing home. I wrote several outdoor feature articles on J.D. and we had just the best old time. I learned from going along with him that it was not J.D. who could spin the best yarn about what he had caught the morning before. It was me—he can really catch 'em.

Throughout the Bay region, snapping turtles have long been sought after as a food source. One of the earliest methods used to harvest snappers was by hook and line. (Courtesy of the Virginia Institute of Marine Science)

Snapping turtles (*Chelydra serpentine*) have been harvested on the Chesapeake Bay for centuries. First Americans (Indians) caught snappers for food and used their carapace for bowls, rattles, and ornaments, while in the nineteenth century people in some localities collected the oil of the snapping turtle because it was considered a curative for bruises and strains when applied externally. For the most part though, snappers were caught because of their value as a food source.

In an 1884 United States Commission of Fish and Fisheries Report, George Brown Goode reported:

> The snapping turtle is regularly seen in the spring in markets of Washington, D.C., dressed for cooking, that is, having the under part of the shell and the entrails removed. The eggs of the snapper are comparatively small, but delicate, and are eaten in many localities. They may be found by probing in the sand with a small rod, in places indicated by the tracks of the animal.

An early method of harvesting the snapping turtle was by a pole and hook and line. Since turtle meat is still used today in soups and stews and is considered a real delicacy in some areas of the country, this method of harvesting turtles is, even today, regularly used by many turtlers on the Chesapeake.

One such turtler is J.D. Davis. Along about the end of winter, J.D. goes to a special spot where he cuts bamboo poles, ten to fifteen feet in length. "I cut about 175 poles, hoping I'll get a hundred good ones," he says. "You got to look real carefully at every pole because if there's a worm hole anywhere and you don't catch it, ol' turtle will break the pole at the point where the hole is located. At that spot, it's weak so it will break easily, ya see."

The poles are taken back to J.D.'s barn where they are stored, out of the sunlight, until he can sort through them and rig the good ones up for fishing. "If you leave them in the sun right after they're cut, the poles get real brittle. So, I keep them in my barn out of the sun. You take a pole that's been left lying outside for very long, when it gets wet it will splinter all to pieces when snapper grabs it," he says.

The pole is rigged with 250-pound-test, nylon-braided masonry line that is cut about the same length as the pole. The line is tied to the top of the pole, which is the narrower end, and a 6/0 hook is secured to the other end of the line. J.D. uses a slipknot to hold the hook and a double knot to secure the line to the pole. When asked about the best type of knot to use J.D. says, "I'll tell you like an ol' timer turtler told me. There are a hundred ways to tie a hook on the end of a line and, in most cases, one's just as good as another."

Snapping turtles feed on fish, frogs, ducks, and other waterfowl, which they drag underwater to be devoured at leisure. Another favorite food for the snapper is eel. "Fresh eel is the preferred bait for catching snapper," says J.D. "I've also caught some using frog. I've caught frogs with a gig, cut them half in two, and it makes a good bait.

J. D. Davis rigs his bamboo turtle poles with 250-pound-test, nylon-braided masonry line. He starts working his lines at the first sign of warm weather in the spring.

Some turtlers use salted eel. They catch eels in the early spring and salt them down in either barrels or tins. They put in a layer of eel and then a layer of salt, until they fill the barrel. Frozen eel is another good bait. Some won't use it, but I like it because it's easier to cut up. I also think it attracts snapper better than salted eel, because, after it hits the water and thaws out, it bleeds and this helps the snapper pick up the scent.

But, you know how that is; if you talk to another turtler he'll tell ya he likes something else. It's all what you like, but most all I've talked to think ol' eel is as good a bait as can be found.

You know how they used to catch snapper, don't ya? They'd track him down along a bank, dig up in his hole and pull him out. I don't think I'd stick my hand up in any hole and pull a snapper out by the tail

Every spring, J.D. stalks snappers and sells his catch to a buyer in New Kent County, Virginia. "I start working my lines at the first sign of warm weather in the early spring," he says. "Snapping turtles burrow in the mud to hibernate in the cold months, so when they first start shoving out the mud, I go after them."

To fish his poles, J.D. generally leaves home before dawn. He shoves a small jon boat into the back of his Chevy pickup truck and travels to the streams and ponds where he has made his sets. "It's hard to find areas that haven't been turtled recently," he says as he drives toward Cross Rip Campground in Deltaville. "The pond we're going to today should be a good one because I don't know that it has ever been turtled."

Snappers inhabit running streams, ponds, and lakes and can be caught in fresh water and in total brackish waters along creeks and coves. The pond at Cross Rip is mostly fresh water; a dam prevents it from emptying into Jackson Creek, just a short distance from Chesapeake Bay. J.D. located the pond by studying the survey maps at the county courthouse and then going to the owner to ask permission to turtle there.

On arrival, J.D. motioned toward the poles that were scattered throughout the pond. He'd set them the day before. "My golly, I think we've caught a boatload, " he exclaimed. "Look at the water moving around the poles."

The poles that he had sunk into the mud bottom were bending up and down with the weight of the turtles on the lines. J.D. grabbed the bow of his jon boat, grabbed it onto the dock by the pond, shoved it overboard, and picked up an empty barrel, a gaff hook, and an ax handle.

"What's the ax handle for?" I asked him.

"You'll see," replied J.D. with a smile on his face. "I think we're going to need it today."

The first line landed a decent-size snapper, maybe a fifteen-pounder. *Chelydra serpentine* grow to a maximum weight of about fifty to sixty pounds, which is smaller then the more southern species, *Macroclemys temmincki*, better known as the alligator snapping turtle, that have been known to grow to two hundred pounds.

J.D. yanked the turtle out of the water, grabbing its tail and cutting the nylon line with a pocketknife, leaving the hook in the snapper's powerful mouth.

J. D. landed nineteen turtles in a small pond just off Jackson creek near Deltaville. He loads the turtles into his pickup truck and carries them to a root cellar near his home for storage.

"You don't try to save the hooks?"

"You're damn right I don't! Do you want to try and take that hook out of his mouth?"

Most of the poles landed a turtle and when he was about three-quarters of the way to the end, J.D. motioned toward the ax handle. "You better pick up that handle."

"What for?"

"You'll see!"

There were about twelve turtles in the plastic barrel in the center of the boat. It all seemed harmless enough, but as the barrel filled, the turtles on top became more and more feisty.

"If you don't want them in the bottom of the boat with ya, you better give 'em a whack when they stick their heads out," explained J.D.

Whack! Whack! Whack! The ax handle was in use all the way to the last pole and onto the dock.

J.D. handled each turtle by grabbing its tail. He said he has never been bitten, but recalled the old wives' tale that a turtle will never let go if it bites you. He doesn't believe it, though. "Always have a broom straw in your hip pocket so you can shove it up his nose," he said. "He'll open right up!

"They tell me that will work, but, like I say, I don't know firsthand. You might not even be able to get the broom straw out of your pocket for pain. I've been told that the big ones have such powerful jaws they can snap a broomstick in two. You can imagine what he would do to you if he got hold of ya."

The snappers are stored in a root cellar until J. D. has enough to warrant the trip to market in New Kent County. J. D. sells his turtles alive for around fifty-five and sixty cents a pound.

J.D. had nineteen turtles, which was his best day so far this season, but not his best day ever. That came several years ago on one spring morning when he and a partner turtled a state drainage ditch and a pond in Stormont.

"We had placed twelve hooks in a state ditch there and had nine turtles," he says. "But the big catch was yet to come.

"We then went over to the pond where we'd placed twenty-two hooks. The first five turtles were so big they filled a twenty-five-gallon trash can," he says. "Before we'd finished, we had everything loaded slam-jam up."

From those twenty-two hooks, J.D. and his partner had twenty-one turtles and not a single one was under thirty-five pounds.

After loading his truck with his nineteen turtles distributed among several large trash cans, J.D. headed for home, where he stores his live turtles in a root cellar, under an outbuilding near his house. The turtles are kept there until he has enough for market and then they are hauled by truck to the buyer.

Turtles were bringing fifty-five and sixty cents a pound and J.D. says when he first started forty cents was a good price for them.

Over the years, J.D. has learned that conservation is very important. "Once I've worked a pond hard, I don't go back for at least three years," he says. "You want to leave some seed stock and it's important to me that ol' snapper will be around for many years to come."

J. D. Davis still works at the local nursing home but he no longer chases snapping turtles.

 # SCHOONER CAPTAIN

Although I've mentioned Captain Hugh Norris in a previous chapter, he is without a doubt one of the most delightful men I've ever met. When I first started visiting Captain Hugh in the early 1980s, he was still building a skiff or two in his backyard on Jackson Creek in Deltaville.

Time has taken its toll on his health, but Captain Hugh still has the same Will Rogers attitude on life. "I've never met a bad person," he has told me many times. "If you treat people right, they'll treat you right." Hugh Norris is a tribute to the many generations of men and women who have worked the waters of the Chesapeake Bay.

The age of schooners, rams, and bugeyes is a bygone era remembered by just a few now. At the turn of the twentieth century nearly eight hundred sailing vessels traveled the waters of the Chesapeake Bay from port to port, hauling lumber, coal, pig iron, fertilizer, watermelons—whatever there was to haul. Hugh Norris recalls those days, having worked as both captain and mate aboard more than a half a dozen of the old craft.

"My grandfather, James Norris, was a sea captain from Hyannis Port, Massachusetts," said Captain Hugh. "He was skipper of one of those big oceangoing sailboats and on one of his trips south, he came inside the Bay and moored at Deltaville. He came ashore in Jackson Creek, met my grandma, a fifteen-year-old, sweet little Virginia girl, and they fell in love and got married in 1842."

"My daddy was Sam Norris and my Mamma was Rachael Hurley Norris. I was one of eleven children—the only one still alive," said Hugh. "I was born in 1896 and there were nine in front of me."

Hugh's father died when he was ten, and at fourteen he went to sea. "My granddaddy was a seafaring man, so I guess that had something to do with me liking the water."

James Ailsworth, skipper of the *Joseph T. Brenan*, asked me if I wanted to go to Cape Charles to carry a load of Irish potatoes. I'd never been away from home before, so I asked my Mamma if I could go. I didn't have no daddy; he died when I was ten years old. There wa'n't nothing for me to do on land anyway except pull fodder or pick tomatoes and I didn't want that so when Mamma said it was up to me, I jumped at the chance.

Captain Hugh Norris began a career in 1910 working aboard the old sailing vessels on the Chesapeake. Before his career ended in 1928, .Captain Hugh had worked aboard a half-dozen of the old sailing craft and he loves to recall those bygone days.

Yep, that was quite a trip. We sailed from Fishing Bay to Cape Charles. The *Brenan* was a little boat, about fifty-four foot. Captain Jim most of the time sailed her by himself, but he liked company and I could help load up. The first time I ever saw electric lights was on that trip. Coming back, we went into Hampton Roads to get some building materials for a house and the place was all lit up. I thought I was in a different world. I worked for him for a while and my first pay check was fifteen dollars for a month's work."

For the next sixteen years, Captain Hugh spent most of his time sailing up and down the Bay, except for a short stint aboard the steamboat Potomac where he worked as a watchman.

There were 782 sailboats working the Bay in 1918. When I first started, we would carry four men to the big boat, but when they got engines to hoist sails and anchors, we came down to three men, and sometimes just two. I'll tell ya something too, those sails and anchors were hard to pull up by hand. I was glad to see engines come along. After a while, we had two pumps run by gasoline donkey engines to pull up the anchor and hoist sails. The early engines were Victor one-cylinder engines and you could count the explosions when we cranked her up. We bought gasoline in Baltimore for ten cents a gallon.

The food aboard the vessels was not always the best, but Captain Hugh recalls it was always tolerable.

The food was all right. It would depend on who was cooking and most all the boats had a colored cook. We didn't have any ice so there were hardly ever any perishable foods aboard unless we caught some fresh fish or something. But mostly we would have salted codfish that we would buy in a box for ten cents a pound, salt cured fat meat, ham of middling, canned sweet potatoes, molasses over bread, raisins mixed in rice, and plenty of hot coffee.

The drinking water was all right too. We had it in a fifty-gallon water barrel on deck. When it got hot in the summertime the water would almost burn your mouth and in the winter we had to keep an ice pick right by the barrel to break the skim that was there most every morning. "In Baltimore, we had to buy water and it cost twenty-five cents a barrel. Most anywhere else we could get it free. There were free-flowing wells at a lot of places and we could go and just fill her up.

During the winter months, the wood stoves were blaring most all the time.

We had two stoves on the boats, one for keeping warm and the other for cooking. Shipmate wood cookstoves and King heaters were the brands used on most of the boats. We'd buy a wagonload of wood, enough to last a trip for about twenty-five cents. We had to cut it up so there was a crosscut saw, sawhorses, and an ax on board. The King heater would use big chunks of wood, while the wood for the Shipmate wood cookstove had to be chopped real fine.

Whenever there was a decent wind, the schooners and other sailing craft sailed the Bay waters. "If the wind was anywhere near fair, we'd sail," says Hugh. "Of course, if it wasn't blowing we couldn't do much. Night or day, if there was a breeze though, we were off and sailing. At night we'd hoist a coal oil johnnie [kerosene lantern] up into the rigging so the other boats could see us."

Modern electronics on board were not available. At night a lead line was used to keep the skipper abreast of the depth of water. "On those dark nights, I'd let the lead line down and by feeling the leather marks slip through my hands, I could tell just how much water was there." Every six feet on a lead line a piece of leather is attached and by counting the number of leather strips, Hugh could determine the water depth.

"We didn't have all these fancy devices to tell us where we were or how deep the water was. Most of the skippers had a compass, a spyglass, and a shotgun to kill a duck or two," says Captain Hugh. "I was never on a vessel that run aground either. A lot of those old captains could almost tell where you were on the Bay by the smell of the mud on the lead line," Hugh winked and smiled.

When the vessels were underway, there was not much spare time on board.

When we were sailing, we didn't need entertainment. There was always something that needed attending to. But when we were in a harbor waiting to be loaded or waiting for the wind to pick up, we'd get in the yawl boat and go over to some of the other boats to visit.

Some of the boys would play cards. They didn't play for money. Didn't have much then, but we had what we needed. There was always someone who could play a mouth harp and we'd sit up on deck under the stars on a nice night and sing. Let me tell you something, some of the best singing I ever heard was on the schooners. It wa'n't no jazz stuff. They were old songs mostly. I don't remember their names, but I always enjoyed the visits and that time on board the other boats. I met some nice people and I never met a bad person.

If we weren't going anywhere, we'd sleep to about eight in the morningh. If we were loaded and ready to sail, we'd be up before sunup. I read a lot on board, mostly marine books, and living quarters were comfortable on most of the boats. Some had bunks; others had beds—iron beds, just like home. The *Corapeake* and the *Ada J. Campbell* were right big boats and they had beds. The others, though, had bunks, mostly in the forward cabin up near the forepeak."

The *Ada J. Campbell* was the largest of the schooners that Hugh worked aboard. Measuring ninety-one feet, three inches long by twenty-six-feet, five inches wide by eight feet, one inch draft, she had a three-man crew and was built in 1889 at Westerly, Rhode Island. When Hugh was a mate aboard her, Johnny Taylor of Deltaville, was her skipper, and Hugh recalls that the vessel died in Moore Creek on the Piankatank River. "Yep, Captain let her die right there," said Hugh.

Most of the vessels were hogged or cut down and ready to die by the time I came along. They were all old, beginning to rot in places, and the owners weren't making enough to fix them up, so they'd run them up in coves to let them die.

Captain Hugh sighed and then went on.

Yep, done away with them. Some were later cut into powerboats, but they weren't worth nothing. They were made for the wind and once a sailboat, always a sailboat.

The vessels Captain Hugh sailed hauled lumber, bagged fertilizer, watermelons, and coal. The fertilizer, in two-hundred-pound bags, would generally go to Salisbury, Maryland, while the coal went to the menhaden factories at Reedville.

We would run a load of watermelons from Urbanna anywhere on the Bay for $125. Coal was hauled for a dollar a ton and most boats would hold about 150 tons. Fertilizer was around $1.50 a ton and lumber was $2.00 a thousand board feet and depending on the boat we could carry about a hundred thousand board feet.

Back then, I was making about thirty to forty-five dollars a month on the boats. The highest I ever got was sixty dollars a month, unless we ran on shares and towards the end, when I was captain, I did that.

Captain Hugh and his crew would get sixty percent of the gross and the owner would receive forty percent.

Lumber was the main product that Hugh hauled over the years because many of the vessels he worked on were owned by lumbermen.

I've hauled lumber out, or in, every river on the west side of Chesapeake Bay from Dismal Swamp to Baltimore. It was hauled to the landings on wagons drawn by teams of oxen and horses. Seldom did they use mules because ol' mule don't like water much, ya know. They would drive the loaded wagons right down in the water as close to the lighters as they could get. We would get as close as we could to shore in the schooners and then they'd load up the lighters, shove out to us using long poles, and we loaded the boards onto the boat. But in Baltimore, where we'd haul the lumber, stevedores would unload and we'd have some free time, especially if there were a lot of boats waiting to get unloaded. Sometimes we would be in Baltimore for two or three days and sometimes longer.

I had a brother and sister living in Baltimore, so I had somewhere to go and spend the night anytime I was in town. There were street cars then and you could go all over Baltimore on them. In the summertime, I went to the beach there, and I could get there on the trolley car for fifteen cents. Sometimes I'd go to the amusement park and ride the racer dip [roller coaster] for a nickel. Then, I could pick up a girl anywhere, spend a quarter on her, and have a good time. I had a girl in most every port, but I never did nothing I was ashamed of though, I'll tell ya that. I never got in any trouble and never drank a bottle of whiskey or beer while I was on the vessels. Now, I've seen plenty of it. Some old captains carried it with them all the time—whiskey mostly. Most of them chewed tobacco, smoked, and some even cussed. That's where I picked up smoking, so I guess I did pick up one bad habit," he said taking a puff on a cigarette.

When I was in Baltimore, I'd often take a trip on an excursion boat and I bought most of my clothes there from a pawnshop. You could buy a suit of clothes for seven or eight dollars. They were used, but that's all we ever had. I didn't have no new clothes. I wore overalls, shirts, a sou'wester hat, oilskins, and gum boots on the boats.

The hardest boat to sail that I was ever on was the old ram *Corapeake*. You had to have a gale wind to get her to do anything. She was originally named the *Ivy Blade* and was built for Charles and Jim Blade's Lumber Company in North Carolina. She was 135 feet and had a narrow twenty-three foot, nine inch beam. The *Corapeake*, like all the rams, was built to go through the old Chesapeake and Delaware Canal, which wasn't very wide. We could go all the way to Philadelphia through the canal.

One of Captain Hugh's most memorable experiences happened aboard the *Corapeake*. As captain of the vessel around 1925, he and Mate Willie Marchant ran into a buoy and sank in the Bay.

I remember that trip good. We started at Bayport Landing near Water View on the south side of the Rappahannock River."

It was January and it had been a cold winter. We had been waiting for several days at the landing for enough loads of lumber to fill up the boat. At early dawn, we went ashore in the yawl boat to fill the water barrel from a free-flowing artesian well that was near Bayport Hotel. It was not long after we got back to the ram that the lighters came out from Parrotts Creek. We stacked the layers of lumber one on top of another with each layer crossed to keep it stable. The boards extended about two feet over the sides of the boat and were stacked around the masts. I didn't know it then, but later on I'd be some kinda glad we had a load of lumber on her.

Captain Hugh recalls that after everything was loaded and checked out, Willie went forward and cranked up the one-cylinder Victor engine used to hoist the sails and anchor. "There was a southeast wind a-blowing, and when the sails were raised, we had to tack down the Rappahannock to the Bay."

It took a while, but when the old ram finally reached the Chesapeake, the wind shifted to the northeast, driving large chunks of ice down the Bay.

We alternated at the helm, and whoever was in the house had to keep the coffee hot and the two wood stoves full of wood.

The weather kept getting worse all the time. At dusk, after the first day, the sky became overcast, and the smoke from the wood stove was blowing straight down, like it does just before a snowstorm.

The next morning the *Corapeake* was still slowly making her way toward Baltimore. "It began to snow some, and more and more ice came floating down the Bay. It got so bad that the *Corapeake* was bucking as she moved through the ice and water," said Captain Hugh.

All the next day, the old ram moved toward Baltimore, but on Saturday night the weather worsened.

I remember well that night. It was the night we sank. I was bundled up in my oilskins trying to keep warm. I could see Sevenfoot Knoll Lighthouse, which meant we were about thirteen miles from Baltimore.

When we got off from Rock Point, which is just inside the Patapsco River, the bow hit something in the dark and it scraped along her bottom until she passed over it. I was at the helm and had to jump out of the way because a buoy came from under her and hit the yawl boat that was to the davits.

Willie came running from the cabin yelling, "What did we hit?" I told him it was a buoy and that I thought we were going to sink because of the way she was leaning. I remember what he said then: "Thank the Good Lord we don't have a load of coal or fertilizer aboard, or we'd be at the bottom of the Bay." The lumber, Willie knew, would keep the Corapeake afloat.

Sure enough, we were taking on water. We quickly dropped the sails, lowered the anchor, and got the yawl boat down from the davits. I crawled up in the sails, while Willie got up on the canvas that covered the lumber, and after a while we both went fast asleep. When I awoke the next morning, the wind was throwing water up on us and ice was everywhere. The cabin and hold had filled with water, but the lumber and ice chunks jamming around the hull kept us from going to the bottom.

We got into the yawl boat and cranked up the engine and started for Baltimore. But we didn't get far when the engine cut off and wouldn't start. Boy that was a time."

Hugh was half grinning.

We drifted for a while before a tugboat out of Baltimore came out in our direction and picked us up. They took us to Baltimore and we went out the next day to get the *Corapeake* in that same tug. When we got there, she was covered in ice and we could hardly stand on deck. The anchor chain was coated in ice, but we finally got it loose and we were towed into Baltimore Harbor.

Later, the ram was brought ashore and pulled out of the water stern first to let the water inside her hold run out the hole the buoy had poked in her bow. The *Corapeake* had lost a plank when the buoy struck her. It wasn't long before the *Corapeake* was back in the water and Willie and I were back hauling,. We weren't scared at the time it all happened because we knew she wouldn't sink all the way, but when I think back on it, it could have been a close call. We were doggone lucky.

Another memorable trip for Captain Hugh occurred on a two-masted schooner named the *Emily Burton*. Hugh and his cousin Charlie Christopher, who was the skipper, were coming out of Urbanna Creek loaded down with lumber.

We had the lumber all in the hold because if we stacked it on deck the boat wouldn't go through the drawbridge on Urbanna Creek. I was at the helm and

The Maggie *was one of Captain Hugh's favorite vessels. She was built in Dorchester County, Maryland, in 1871. Captain Hugh went to work on her in 1914. (Photo by Dr. A. L. VanName Jr.)*

Charlie was in the yawl boat a-shoving us out the creek. There wa'n't no wind and we just wanted to get on the other side of the bridge to wait for a good breeze. Well, I was at the helm a-steering when I saw old Dave Lee, the bridge keeper, opening the draw. We got right up on it when I sorta lost my concentration and ran right smack into the side of the bridge.

Old Dave started cussing and a-carrying on about me hitting the side of the bridge. He was some kind of hot. So, when we got through, I got in the yawl boat and went over to shore. Captain Dave had gone into his little one-story shanty by the bridge where he lived. He had a bunch of cats and there were holes cut along the bottom of the house for them to come and go. In the winter, he tacked cardboard over the holes to keep the weather out.

I went up to the door and knocked. "What do you want?" came a voice from behind the door.

Captain Hugh, said the Maggie *was the fastest of all the boats he worked aboard. She had just been rebuilt in 1914 and was in top condition when he started on her. This photo of the* Maggie *shows the schooner under sail. by Dr. A. L. VanName, Jr.*

"I just want you to know that I'm sorry about hitting the bridge, Captain Dave," I said.

"Oh hell, you didn't do any damage. I just wanted to cuss somebody and you were closest to me," he said.

After that, I would always stop by to chat with the old fellow. I can hear him screaming now at those cats. "Get out of here cats! When I say scat, I mean scat!" he would scream. Then, those cats would haul tail through those holes he cut in the walls for them.

In the summer, he was always barefoot and would fish on the bridge with all the colored folk in town, every day of the week and even on Sunday. He knew all the best fishing spots along the bridge. I liked that old fellow.

Captain Hugh had a note of nostalgia in his voice.

Captain Hugh has a little something to say about each of the vessels he worked aboard. The *Joseph T. Brenan* was one of his favorites. "Prettiest little boat you've ever seen. She wasn't a big boat and wasn't big enough to run lumber on her. We ran potatoes and watermelons in the spring and summer and the captain would buy oysters in the winter and haul them to Crisfield. I wasn't on her but for about six months."

The *Maggie* was another of his favorites. "She was the fastest of all the boats that I worked aboard," said Captain Hugh. "She had been rebuilt in 1914 and was in good shape when I was on her. Captain Phil Ruark was her skipper and she carried a three-man crew on the boat." Built in Dorchester County, Maryland, in 1871, the *Maggie* was eighty-seven feet by twenty-three feet, nine inches by five foot, nine inches.

The *B. P. Gravenor* was a three-masted ram that was originally named the *James H. Hargrave*. "The rams were hard to sail because they were so big and clumsy," said Captain Hugh. "I only went on the *Gravenor* for one trip and that was to haul a load of coal from Norfolk to Reedville. Captain John Horner, her skipper, was from the Eastern Shore, and I didn't like sailing with captains from the shore because they liked to lay over where their families were. Since I was from the western shore, I tried to always sail with those boys from over here. When we got to Reedville, I met up with Charlie Christopher on the *Emily Burton* and took up with him. That was the first and last trip I ever took on the *B. P. Gravenor*."

The *Lucy May* was a "down-East" schooner that had come south from the Maine lumber and stone business. "She was near about dead when I went on her," said Hugh. "She had seen some hard living up in Maine. They used her to haul stone and lumber. A lot of those boats came from New England. I remember reading about her later on when she was in a storm in 1925 and lost both masts. She died over on the Yeocomico River. I guess her bones are still there."

The *Annie Belle*, a schooner built in Federalsburg, Maryland, in 1875, measured eighty-two feet, five inches by twenty-two feet by six feet, five inches. "She was a good sailor and not in too bad shape. She wasn't hogged and had been rebuilt at West Point, Virginia. I really don't know much else about her because I only sailed on her for three or four trips.

The *Goldie C* was the only bugeye that Captain Hugh worked aboard. "They were little but were good sailors," said Captain Hugh. "We hauled grain on her, mostly wheat to Baltimore. I wasn't on her long either. I liked all the vessels but don't talk to me about steamboats."

Captain Hugh spent a month on the steamboat *Potomac* as a watchman around 1920. "About a month was all I could take of that. When I told Captain Archie Long I was quittin', he said. 'I don't blame you a damn bit. I've been on it all my life with just two weeks vacation a year. It ain't no way to be a family man. I'll tell you that,' he said. Of course, I wa'n't married then. I was married in 1926 and I decided then I'd never sail no more. I didn't, too, and I haven't been to Baltimore since those days.

"My job on the steamboat was to do nothing, just stay up in the pilothouse and watch to see if we were going to hit anyone. Well, I was supposed to be on the bow, but it was bad enough just to have to sit up in the pilothouse for four hours. We were four hours on and four hours off," he said. "The only good thing I can say about it was the food was the best I'd ever eaten and all you wanted.

"I hated to see the old sailboats go, but most good things do come to an end you know," Hugh said. "It looks like we could have saved a few more of those old vessels than we did."

In 1926, Captain Hugh retired from working on the vessels and at the age of twenty-eight decided to get married. He crabbed and oystered for a living and built boats in his backyard for watermen up and down the Chesapeake. He was still tonging up a mess of oysters at the ripe old age of eighty-seven.

Captain Hugh Norris is deceased. There are very few people left today who worked aboard a sail-powered commercial vessel in the days of sail on Chesapeake Bay.

Captain Hugh worked aboard the three-masted ram, the B. P. Gravenor, *for only one trip. It was about the same time that the top photo was taken of the* Gravenor *at West Point, Virginia, in 1926. In the bottom photo the* B. P. Gravenor *is about to be loaded with lumber at Tappahannock, Virginia, near the end of her working career in 1941. (Photos by Dr. A. L. VanName Jr.)*

INDEX